DATE DUE

**Three (3) week loans are subject
to recall after one week**

CONCEPTS
OF LEISURE

CONCEPTS OF LEISURE

second edition

JAMES F. MURPHY
San Jose State University

PRENTICE-HALL, INC.
Englewood Cliffs, New Jersey 07632

Library of Congress Cataloging in Publication Data

Murphy, James Fredrick, (date)
  Concepts of leisure.

  Includes bibliographical references and index.
  1. Leisure.   I. Title.
BJ1498.M87 1981   790' .01'35   80-22349
ISBN 0-13-166512-X

Printed in the United States of America

10 9 8 7 6 5 4 3 2

Editorial/production supervision by Diane Lange
Cover design by Marc Williams
Manufacturing buyer: Harry P. Baisley

Prentice-Hall International, Inc., *London*
Prentice-Hall of Australia Pty. Limited, *Sydney*
Prentice-Hall of Canada, Ltd., *Toronto*
Prentice-Hall of India Private Limited, *New Delhi*
Prentice-Hall of Japan, Inc., *Tokyo*
Prentice-Hall of Southeast Asia Pte. Ltd., *Singapore*
Whitehall Books Limited, Wellington, *New Zealand*

TO MARY S. WILEY AND ARDITH B. FROST

Pioneers and Spiritual Leaders of Recreation Education

and

ROXANNE HOWE-MURPHY AND ERIN LYNNE MURPHY

The Most Important Persons in my Life

Contents

PART FOUR HOLISTIC PERSPECTIVES
AND THE FUTURE OF
LEISURE

Preface

Since the first edition of *Concepts of Leisure* was published in 1974 the context of leisure philosophy in general has been considerably broadened and content substantially upgraded. A number of writers of philosophical, conceptual, and/or theoretical texts have subsequently endeavored to decipher the leisure nexus and provide clearer parameters of the factors, variables, and issues surrounding the nature of leisure as a philosophy, institution, life style, and form of self-expression. Indeed, what we know of leisure at the onset of the 1980's brings us considerably closer to the possibility of being able to design and implement an effective delivery system to facilitate leisure opportunity and promote leisure as a worthwhile value system and form of personal expression in daily life. We have also become increasingly aware of the dangers of unchecked leisure expression and continued consumption of leisure products which pose serious threats to our physical environment and have the potential to exhaust our nonrenewable resources.

The first edition of *Concepts of Leisure* presented six concepts of leisure with accompanying readings providing a further understanding of various factors or underlying precepts important to grasping their unique aspects. At the time of the first volume there were essentially four college textbooks in the literature which dealt with the philosophical bases of leisure, and these had first been published from seven to nineteen years before. Three of the texts viewed leisure as stemming primarily from the Industrial Revolution and being valued as a form of discretionary time available to the individual for purposes of rest, relaxation, diversion, and personal development after the obligations of work had been fulfilled. The other text, following an exhaustive study of ancient Greece and Rome with applications of the classical concept of leisure to contemporary society, revealed a state of mind perspective which provided an alternative understanding of leisure largely applied to pre-industrial societies.

In attempting to sort out these two dimensions of leisure, I became aware that while both were useful models for describing leisure behavior, neither seemed totally useful in their application to the increasingly fast-paced change environment of North America in the early 1970's. Additionally, both of these concepts of leisure were not accurate reflections of the pluralistic value system, social policy, and life styles which were becoming more prevalent. Therefore, I proceeded to investigate alternative leisure concepts that might be suitable for understanding divergent tastes, group behavior, and life styles of people in their leisure. Although there were acknowledgments of foreign interpretations of leisure, the point of view reflected in the first edition of *Concepts of Leisure* was generally oriented to the United States.

A general model of leisure which classified it into six dimensions on a continuum ranging from constraint-obligation to spontaneity-self-determination was presented in the first edition of *Concepts of Leisure.* While this model was not based upon my own empirical research, it was designed to visually depict and classify leisure based on the works of other noted scholars, researchers, and philosophers. In this volume I will present the findings of recent similar investigations, including results of a study which applied the conceptual scheme I used in the first volume.

Leisure appears to be more of a public concern than ever before. Most industrialized societies continue to flirt with technological mastery of the economic system, allowing workers and the population in general to anticipate a social order representative of more discretionary time: more flexible work/school/retirement patterns; a greater number of choices and enlarged options; continued expansion of the leisure market and consumer products; and unparalleled opportunities for adventure and challenge from an ever-widening opportunity system. At the same time, as never before in history, highly industrialized countries face increased limits being placed on travel, consumption, and discretionary expenditures due to high inflation, unemployment, and depletion of energy systems which support and perpetuate convenience of consumption; reductions of governmental services which had greatly expanded social services to the elderly, women, minorities, disabled, and youth during the previous two decades; and divergent values regarding the form of leisure settings and the way such areas are used, particularly as represented by conservation/wilderness-oriented, non-resource-dependent users contrasted with recreation vehicle, urban-oriented, resource-dependent recreationists.

The leisure service practitioners more than ever before must become acutely aware of the options, differences, and dynamics of the community in order to effectively deliver leisure opportunities to a pluralistic clientele. By developing a sound philosophical perspective, the student engaged in leisure studies begins to develop a framework from which to evolve guidelines for personal and professional growth and practice. It is hoped that the second edition of *Concepts of Leisure* will provide a further understanding of the immensely complex nature of leisure as an area for *philosophical* inquiry; as a *conceptual* and *empirical* area leading to theoretical development; as a *life style* reflecting values, tastes, and group preferences; and as an *institution* in society which interfaces with other social institutions and services as an opportunity framework for people to realize certain needs, goals, and rewards.

This book has been prepared with the desire that readers will begin to genuinely question, debate, contemplate, and embrace leisure as a scholarly discipline and form of behavior and attitude in everyday life which deserves thoughtful inquiry and application. This may result in the deciphering of our personal anxiety, uncertainty, and confusion regarding current events, and perhaps will lead to the realization of joy through the unveiling of the infinite possibilities of human expression bound up in ignorance and skepticism about the human condition.

The author wishes to thank Ray O'Connell, editor, for his support and encouragement of the book. Additionally, the invaluable assistance of Diane Lange, who worked closely with the author in supervising the production of the book, was greatly appreciated.

J. F. M.

CONCEPTS
OF LEISURE

PART ONE

INTRODUCTION
AND OVERVIEW
OF THE PHILOSOPHICAL
BASIS OF LEISURE

1

Overview
of
Contemporary Society

Leisure, as a form of human expression, provides a basis for gaining a greater degree of understanding of oneself as a person and serves as an indicator of economic development, human satisfaction, and well-being. As an institution in North America, leisure service is undergoing dramatic change, serving to underscore the state of flux pervasive in society and the confusion as to the value, meaning, and properties of recreation and leisure. This chapter will briefly explore some of these perspectives in order to provide a background for viewing the impact of leisure in contemporary society.

In the 1970's leisure emerged as a contributor to the well-being of highly industrialized societies and as a prized value and life style determinant by more and more people. The legitimacy of leisure is represented by its significance as a personal and social value; as an element of national, state and provincial, and local government planning; as a union negotiation factor; and as a consumer product, the leading single component of the U.S. Gross National Product. These are quantitative and qualitative measures of its place in contemporary society.

There are a number of indicators which suggest that leisure is becoming an important element of the North American social structure and a force in democratizing patterns of work, retirement, education, residential growth patterns, health, and family and social group behav-

Table 1–1
Important Features of Urban Life

CATEGORY	HIGHLY FAVORABLE RATINGS			
	ALL CITIES %	SMALL %	MEDIUM %	LARGE %
UNIFORMED SERVICES				
Fire	64	67	68	58
Sanitation	59	60	66	51
Police	47	48	51	42
RECREATION				
Parks, playground	42	39	48	36
Recreational opportunities	40	31	46	42
Cultural opportunities	39	30	45	42
ENVIRONMENT				
Climate	43	51	46	31
Noise level	40	43	41	37
Air quality	31	44	32	17
TRANSPORTATION				
Highway system	38	43	38	33
Public transportation	28	33	29	20
Traffic (downtown)	15	19	14	10
Parking (downtown)	15	20	13	13
MUNICIPAL GOVERNMENT				
Mayor	22	22	24	19
Local government	21	22	22	18
City council	19	19	20	17
Councilman	19	18	22	16
JUSTICE				
Courts	19	23	22	12
Correctional facilities	14	20	14	9

ior. A Gallup poll[1] indicated that parks, playgrounds, and recreation opportunities are rated high by citizens in the United States as important features of urban life, particularly in medium (250,000–999,000) and large (1 million and over) communities. See Table 1–1.

Not only do American citizens consider recreation opportunities as an important aspect of community living but they increasingly are concerned with the quality of life and far less with the unlimited acquisition of physical goods. According to a Harris poll conducted in 1977, Americans are in the process of reevaluating materialism and technology as a major value and economic determinant and indicating a thrust toward more direct participation in community life and opportunities for individual creative expression. Some selected findings are indicated in Figure 1–1.

[1]George Gallup, "Fire, Police, Sanitation Units Rated Top Features of City Life," *San Jose Mercury News,* April 16, 1978.

1. By 73–23% respondents want to participate in community decisions affecting their lives.
2. By 72–23% respondents prefer to cooperate, rather than compete, with others.
3. By 86–9% respondents want to experience life directly rather than watching it on TV.
4. By 84–13% respondents welcome challenges to their creative abilities.
5. By 61–27% respondents think modern technology has caused as many problems as benefits to people.
6. By 71–18% respondents prefer a clean environment to one which provides many jobs.
7. By 83–7% respondents feel that the country would be better off if children were educated more to find their own inner satisfaction than to be a success and make a lot of money.
8. By 68–21% respondents felt that the economic growth falsely makes people want to acquire more possessions than to enjoy nonmaterial experiences.
9. By 79–17% respondents indicated that it is more important to teach people to live with basic essentials than to reach higher standards of living.
10. By 77–15% respondents stated they prefer spending time getting to know each other as human beings, rather than speeding up our ability to communicate through technology.
11. By 63–29% respondents said it is more important to learn to appreciate human values —as opposed to material values—than to find ways to create more jobs for producing more goods.
12. By 66–22% respondents said they wanted more emphasis on breaking up big things and getting back to more humanized living than to develop bigger and more efficient ways of doing things.

Figure 1–1
Changes in Americans
September 1977 Harris Poll*

*Louis Harris Poll, The Futurist, April 1978, p. 114.

Somewhat contradictory to the Harris poll results, however, is the realization that Americans in fact are not curbing their dependency on oil and electrical energy. Since the U.S. Arab oil embargo in 1973 gasoline consumption, perhaps the best measure of the general public's sensitivity to the energy issue, has increased by about 200,000 barrels a day (although action was taken to freeze oil imports at the end of the decade). Despite significantly higher gasoline prices, car mileage has vastly increased.[2] Additionally, soaring electric bills have not induced Americans to cut down on the use of electricity. The average electric bill for an American home stood at a little over $11.00 a month in 1969 but had reached more than $26.00 in 1977 and climbed to more than $30.00 in 1978.

Americans have developed an almost insatiable appetite for consuming leisure and those products which perpetuate a life style of convenience. Our range of options, significantly enhanced through technology, affluence, changing sex roles, longer life spans spurred by improved nutrition and medical advances, and rearranged work days/weeks/years/careers, have made it possible for more people to view

[2]Refer to "Americans Fail to Control Gluttonous Appetite for Oil," San Jose Mercury News, May 27, 1978.

their life from a perspective in which leisure or at least nonwork indicates increased possibilities for life enhancement.

GROWTH OF LEISURE

Some of the current personal and social factors having a significant effect on the growth in leisure are the following:

Increased Free Time

The amount of time available to males and females since the turn of the twentieth century has increased manyfold. The availability of more time to be used at one's own discretion, away from the obligations of remunerative work, housework, and other responsibilities has emerged as an important factor in the social organization of community and family life. With increased discretionary hours being shifted over to the individual each year, whether it be as a result of reduced work hours, more paid holidays, voluntary reduction of workweeks through job or leisure sharing, or availability of flexible work hours within each workday, workers are able to cluster the discretionary time at their disposal and gain a greater measure of personal freedom.

Individuals not working at regular paying jobs, including full-time homemakers, the unemployed, retired people, and those who are homebound, institutionalized, or otherwise disengaged from the working community, have, of course, the entirety of each week available for personal, group, and/or family activities beyond certain obligations deemed appropriate or sanctioned. These hours may be viewed as a welcome opportunity (particularly in the case of a person who is engaged in leisure sharing) or might be received with anxiety or even depression (as in the case of some disabled individuals unable to be accepted in the work force or even to gain access to community leisure facilities). The trend continues toward increased paid holidays, longer vactions, and slightly reduced workweeks throughout North America. Because of gains in free time by the individual and the possibilities for more flexible life rhythms, leisure may be viewed as a resource having more personal significance than in previous periods of industrial/technological growth when the work rhythm of life dictated the flow of community life.

Higher Level of Education

The relationship between rate of leisure participation and education has been widely documented in the literature. Particularly as evidenced in intensity and amount of outdoor leisure pursuits, individuals with a college education engage more frequently than those who possess only high school diplomas. Those enrolled in a college or university are exposed to a variety of disciplines and cultural and leisure experiences, and such opportunities increase one's interests and stimulate participation. According to Romsa and Girling,[3] education is the single most important demographic variable which influences leisure participation patterns. This is corroborated in studies in the United States by King[4]; Hendee et al.[5]; Harry, Gale, and Hendee[6]; and Hendee, Gale, and Catton.[7] According to Reinhard Wippler's analysis of sociological predictors of leisure behavior in the Netherlands, among the three measures of social stratification (educational level, income level, and level of occupational prestige) educational attainment is the most important predictor of leisure behavior.[8] Cheek and Burch,[9] in summing up the influences on nonwork behavior, indicate that while persons in higher class (income) and status (occupational prestige) have higher participation rates in nearly all leisure activities, educational attainment seems to be the best predictor.

Increasing Affluence

With the rise in personal income—although the rate of increase was considerably slowed in the 1970's by inflation, unemployment, and a recession—the expenditures for all leisure spending is approximately $200 billion.[10] Increased personal disposable income has resulted in a proportionate rise in leisure spending, leading to the further possibility of people engaging in nonwork activities. Among the major categories of leisure involvement are (1) popular sports, both participant and spectator activities; (2) outdoor recreation, including boating, hunting, fishing, and camping; (3) travel and tourism, including amusement

[3]Gerald H. Romsa and Sydney Girling, "The Identification of Outdoor Recreation Market Segments on the Basis of Frequency of Participation," *Journal of Leisure Research* 8: 247–255, 1976.

[4]David King, "Some Socioeconomic Comparisons of Huron and Manistee National Forest Family Campers with Market Populations," Papers of the *Michigan Academy of Science, Arts and Letters* 50:49–65, 1965.

[5]John Hendee et al., "Wilderness Users in the Pacific Northwest—Their Characteristics, Values and Management Preferences" (Portland: U.S. Forest Service Research Paper PNW-61, 1968).

[6]Joseph Harry, Richard Gale, and John Hendee, "Conservation: An Upper-Middle-Class Social Movement," *Journal of Leisure Research* 1:246–254, 1969.

[7]John Hendee, Richard Gale, and William Catton, "A Typology of Outdoor Recreation Activity Preferences," *Journal of Environmental Education* 3: 28–34, 1971.

[8]Reinhard Wippler. *Social Determinants of Leisure Behavior.* English Summary. (Assen: Van Gorcum, 1968).

[9]Neil H. Cheek and William R. Burch. *The Social Organization of Leisure in Human Society* (New York: Harper and Row, Publishers, 1976), p. 71.

[10]Richard Kraus. *Recreation and Leisure in Modern Society,* 2nd ed. (Santa Monica, Calif.: Goodyear Publishing Co., 1978), p. 101.

Table 1–2
Adult Participation in Selected Leisure Activities
During One Year, Percent and Rank Order*

ACTIVITY CATEGORY	%	RANK
Visiting friends/relatives	93	1
Boating/swimming/picnicking/driving for pleasure	76	2
Going to religion-related activity	73	3
Going to movies	63	4
Going to neighborhood park	59	5
Going to fair/exhibit	54	6
Going to park outside city	52	7
Watching sporting event	49	8
Going to club meeting	47	9
Going to nightclub/bar	46	10
Playing active sport	40	11
Going to zoo	38	12
Going to class/lecture	36	13
Fishing/hiking/camping/hunting	34	14
Going to theater/concert	27	15
Going to museum	26	16

*Neil H. Cheek, Jr. and William R. Burch, Jr. The Social Organization of Leisure in Human Society (New York: Harper and Row, Publishers, 1976), p. 28.

complexes; (4) other forms of commercial entertainment and cultural activity; (5) various forms of leisure centered around real estate, including new residential communities and shopping centers; (6) gambling; (7) television; (8) technologically based activities (e.g. electronic games, artificial ice rinks and snowmobiles); and (9) a variety of other miscellaneous hobbies.[11] According to Cheek and Burch[12] there appears to be a relatively stable empirical pattern of participation in leisure activities among the U.S. adult population in terms of rank ordering for time frames of weekly, monthly, and annual participation. The rank ordering of selected leisure activities of adult participants during one year is indicated in Table 1–2.

Changed Attitudes Toward Pleasure

It has been noted by a number of writers that contemporary American society is being viewed less as a largely economic, functional one and more as a social system increasingly characterized by pleasure-seeking. This recent occurrence in American life may be partially attributed to the liberalization of church doctrines and decline in popularity of the Christian belief in original sin. In addition has been

[11]Refer to Kraus, *Recreation and Leisure*, pp. 101–117 for a more complete discussion of leisure participation.

[12]Cheek and Burch, *Social Organization*, p. 25.

the emergence of what has been characterized as a growth society in which more individuals desire self-fulfillment and joy and have more opportunity to choose how they wish to spend their time, with fewer constraints being exerted by the work place, discriminatory laws, and archaic sex-role stereotypes.

Population Mobility

The availability of the automobile, airplanes, streamlined transit systems, trains, buses, and a myriad of recreation vehicles and off-the-road motor vehicles combined with improved and efficient highway systems and inexpensive commercial means of travel provide North Americans a tremendous opportunity for touring. Tourism has emerged as a major industry, "tied to the development of major amusement complexes and to charter flights and tours arranged through industry, membership organizations, and even public recreation and park departments."[13] Certainly the influx of bicycling, hiking, camping, canoeing, cross-country skiing, and hiking through improved trail systems, expanded marked routes for nonmotorized travelers, and improved accessibility of various kinds of travel systems has also contributed to the increased mobility of people.

While leisure-related travel opportunities have greatly enhanced mobility, the evolving of a "leisure-centeredness" has resulted in more people seeking to reside in the suburbs to take advantage of the amenities and unhurried pace. This trend toward suburbanization and even ruralization (and the type of life prevalent prior to the Industrial Revolution and the development of an urban society) suggests that people do not need to reside close to their work place and are not dependent on urban transportation. Additionally, suburbanization suggests that nonurban living is more congruent with informal, neighborhood relationships and with a degree of home-centered activity reflected in gardening, backyard play, and ease of child-rearing, as well as increasing economic independence from the central city.

Advancements in Modern Technology

The development of modern technology has resulted in increased employee productivity, meaning the worker has the prospect of more free time. Technology has provided many so-called "labor-saving devices" to the economic marketplace, removing much of the toil from everyday life. Additionally, as noted by Kraus:

[13]Kraus, *Recreation and Leisure*, p. 6.

Technology has made traditional pastimes more accessible through such innovations as artificial ice-skating rinks, snowmaking machines, and ski lifts, and has made entirely new forms of play available to us, including skin diving and scuba diving, electronic games and most pervasive of all —home television entertainment.[14]

Technology in the twentieth century has created a number of unprecedented opportunities for the masses to pursue free time, opportunities unknown in previous eras. An interesting point in the development of leisure as a prized value is its relationship to the emergence of new technological conditions and the democratization of economically free time.

Thus the creation of time itself as a value is given substance by the selling of goods and services that require time to use: cars, vacation tours, camping equipment, and the like. Thus *the value of work* (a rationale for commitment to production) is balanced by *the value of leisure,* both now promoted by comparable marketing techniques.[15]

The Expansion of Human Services and Social Welfare

The generation of a host of programs for the economically and culturally deprived, for those suffering from physical or mental disabilities, for the elderly, for "problem" youth, as well as various other federal, state, and local programs for alcoholics, drug addicts, and others, have expanded the leisure opportunities to individuals who have a variety of human needs and for whom these opportunities are not normally available. Although many communities in a number of states have been cutting back a certain amount of human services, the general trend by local government has been to assume responsibility for identifying all community social needs, and for planning, coordinating, and evaluating programs to alleviate social problems within its boundaries. The League of California Cities suggested that each local government unit "should ensure the delivery of all essential social services either by serving as an advocate or catalyst to ensure the most effective delivery of service by the appropriate public and/or private agencies or by delivering such services themselves."[16]

Inclusion of Minority, Disabled, and Nonaligned Groups

Expanded opportunities for many previously excluded groups in Canada and the United States to participate in everyday life has resulted

---

[14]*Ibid.,* p. 6.

[15]Max Kaplan, Letter to Honorable James R. Mills (D), California Legislature, Senate Select Committee on Investment Priorities and Objectives, Leisure Sharing, November 1, 1977.

[16]James F. Murphy and Dennis R. Howard. *Delivery of Community Leisure Services: An Holistic Approach* (Philadelphia: Lea & Febiger, 1977), p. 211.

in an increased expectation and desire among minority groups of all kinds—racial, ethnic, economic, sex-related, age-related, and disability-related—to seek a more meaningful role and more active involvement in every aspect of life. As a result of legislation, of increased awareness of previously nonaligned minority groups, of more assertive demands by people on the fringe of society, and of demands for freedom of access and inclusion in all areas of human endeavor, the leisure needs and interests of formerly excluded individuals are being articulated and expressed more readily and publicly.

The issues of women's liberation, civil rights for the disabled, gay rights, and equal rights for everyone are more than clichés used to gather a group and protest a local ordinance or federal law. These words represent demands for recognition of the need for creative, expressive, growth-oriented opportunities previously squelched by discriminatory laws, prejudiced attitudes, guilt, and a work ethic serving to limit possibilities of human potential for nonmainstreamed individuals.

Leisure provides untold opportunities for human growth in a society more and more disposed toward acceptance of pleasure; there are increased opportunities for creative self-expression of previously downtrodden and discriminated groups; advanced technology has made it easier to engage in leisure behavior and move about at one's own discretion; furthermore, there is available more free time and more flexible hours, weeks, and years in which to blend work/leisure/education in one's life span.

LIMITS ON THE GROWTH OF LEISURE

Certainly societal conditions have increased the potential of leisure as a form of human expression but there are also several factors which have served to negate these positive developments and possibly even alter their meaning. Godbey suggests four such factors:

1. *Limitless Materialism.* Many people in our society today have an inability to satiate their material desires. . . . The acquisition, maintenance and use of the vast number of material goods which we increasingly want takes time and increases the amount of work we are compelled to undertake in order to sustain our life style.

2. *Increased Societal Complexity and Change.* Coping with the increased complexity and accelerated rate of change within our society has blunted our leisure potential. . . . Decisions have become more complicated and time-consuming. The average citizen is being forced to absorb more and more information, often of a complex technical nature, at an increasingly accelerated rate. [This condition has resulted in pathological behavior in many highly technological societies and is due to "sensory overload"—a condition brought about by constant mental strain from the increased tempo of life.]

3. *The Increasing Demands of Labor.* While the amount of time spent at work has doubtlessly increased since the turn of the century, evidence is contradictory concerning whether there has been any further decrease in the amount of work activities since World War II. There has been an increase of 70 percent in the number of people engaged in service occupations and a decrease in persons producing goods. There has been a concomitant increase in persons working overtime, longer hours, job sharing, and the percentage of adult women employed in the labor force, reaching close to 50 percent.

4. *The Carryover of "Work Values" into Leisure.* Many of the goals, methods and styles of our work institutions are increasingly spilling over into our leisure institutions. In much of our "leisure" activity, no less than in our "work" activity, we place a high value on advanced planning and goal setting, competition, incremental improvement through the mastery of special knowledge and technique, the efficient utilization of time and winning. . . . This seriousness of approach has led to the decline of many forms of pleasure.[17]

Additionally there are several other challenges facing the Recreation and Park Movement which have emerged from the physical, economic, social, political, and moral changes which have transformed the consciousness, daily work and leisure routine, and life style of all our lives. The changes in society have had an impact on the delivery of community leisure services. The chapters that follow will discuss these in relationship to some of the varied leisure concepts and philosophical perspectives of work, recreation, leisure, and play and will outline important considerations regarding each.

SUMMARY

Recreation and leisure is an important feature in urban contemporary North American society—more so than concerns for the environment, transportation, municipal government, and justice in the United States. The growth of leisure has been spurred by increases in free time, higher level of educational attainment, increasing affluence, more favorable attitudes toward pleasure, population mobility, advancements in technology, expansion of human and social services, and expanded opportunities of minority, disabled, and nonaligned groups. While these developments have expanded leisure opportunity, certain societal conditions have deterred leisure expression. These include limitless material consumption, societal complexity and accelerated rates of change, increasing job demands of workers, and spillover effect of work values in leisure.

---

[17]Geoffrey Godbey. *Recreation, Park and Leisure Services* (Philadelphia: W. B. Saunders Co., 1978), pp. 11–12.

2

Philosophical Dimensions of Leisure

This chapter will describe philosophy, the philosopher's tasks, major philosophical approaches, and their relationship to leisure. Relating philosophy to leisure will be explored and discussion of the interplay between theory development and leisure philosophy will provide a basis for an understanding of the presentation of various concepts of leisure.

The relationships among our major societal institutions, including work, religion, the family, education, and leisure, have changed considerably during the past eighty years. At the turn of the twentieth century leisure was not recognized as a separate, distinguishable institution in North America. The family assumed the major responsibility for giving children their basic play orientation, equipment, and environment. While the family remains the center of the child's play experience, the broader society has assumed more responsibility for allocating facilities, equipment, and instruction and for enhancing leisure opportunities for community members.

The recreation and leisure service field has been guided largely by principles and practices emanating from the American Recreation and Park Movement during its formative years. The sociopolitical environment has changed significantly since that time, particularly with the advent of television, communications satellites, and computers. The accelerated rate of sociotechnological change has left many North

Americans numb. Guidelines which provided understanding and direction have become obsolete, even disintegrating in our post-industrial society.

BUILDING A PHILOSOPHY OF LEISURE

The leisure service practitioner, recreation educator, student, and ordinary lay citizen *must* have meaningful guidelines to direct their lives and the lives of others. These guidelines must be founded on a sound philosophical premise. Earle F. Zeigler notes that the philosopher attempts to appraise existing knowledge, beliefs, and human relations. "Subsequently he evolves a systematic and coherent plan that may give the ordinary person an understanding of life. It may help to give him a focus so that he can determine that which is important and significant. Thus it can help him decide what he should do in the years ahead."[1]

The recreation and leisure service field, an integral part of the human service profession, has largely failed to provide the prospective educator and practitioner the opportunity to develop a meaningful, comprehensive interpretation of leisure, because of the lack of significant guidelines and a rather narrow concept of leisure. The knowledge, values, and beliefs which guided the Recreation and Park Movement in the United States in 1900 were characteristic of a still largely agricultural, segregated, rural, blue-collar nation operating on a scarce economy and oriented toward work. The early development of organized recreation operations in Canada had a similar orientation as that in the United States. The rewards of industrial technology for the masses would not be realized for several decades. Our highly affluent society has need for recreation and leisure personnel to reassess the values which guide the field. While there certainly are increased opportunities for people to experience concentrated amounts of leisure, many people are very much concerned about a fragile economy and heavy demands on resources. Others wonder whether the shortages in fuel and other forms of energy which propel people to distant recreation areas and quench our thirst for a life style of consumption and convenience will not result in an ultimate deterioration of the environment and quality of life.

Fundamental questions about our perceptions of the world, human relations, free will, good and evil, and so on must be answered within a philosophical framework to lend meaning to our existence. Meaning-

[1]Earle F. Zeigler. *Philosophical Foundations for Physical, Health, and Recreation Education* (Englewood Cliffs, N.J.: Prentice-Hall, Inc., 1964), p. 11.

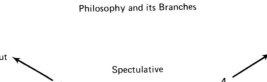

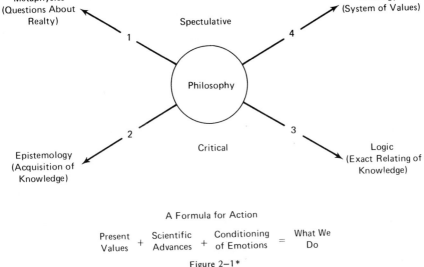

Metaphysics
(Questions About
Realty)

Spectulative

Axiology
(System of Values)

Philosophy

Epistemology
(Acquisition of
Knowledge)

Critical

Logic
(Exact Relating of
Knowledge)

A Formula for Action

$$\frac{\text{Present}}{\text{Values}} + \frac{\text{Scientific}}{\text{Advances}} + \frac{\text{Conditioning}}{\text{of Emotions}} = \frac{\text{What We}}{\text{Do}}$$

Figure 2–1*

*Earle F. Zeigler, Physical Education and Sport Philosophy (Englewood Cliffs, N.J.: Prentice-Hall, Inc., p. 34), 1977.

ful leisure opportunities become operable when people comprehend the value of exercising self-expression and satisfying individually determined needs within a given milieu. It is important that we answer questions related to leisure and that we examine our philosophical positions on education, technology, the economy, political structure, religion, the family, and so on. "What we decide as professionals, and laymen will accept, will exert considerable influence on the place of . . . recreation in our educational systems and other institutions as well and, subsequently, in our communities at large for our mature citizens."[2]

Zeigler's diagram explaining philosophy and its branches (see Figure 2–1) provides a descriptive relationship of the end result of philosophizing—axiology—a system of values. This system of values then serves the aims of humanity, the field of recreation and leisure services, and, of course, the individual. By recreators coming to realize a set of personal values, they will pursue the human services profession and the Recreation and Park Movement with a reasonable degree of understanding and proficiency.

Zeigler describes the philosopher's task:

[2]*Ibid.,* p. 11.

... we see philosophers as scholars dedicated to, and perhaps ultimately responsible for, the outlook and values of the various societies and cultures in which they live. Still further, philosophers attempt to evaluate what we know and believe about the universe and our own sphere of human affairs. Subsequently they may evolve a systematic and coherent plan by which a human being may live. Following this, they may attempt to justify their position in various ways against other competing philosophical approaches. In the process they may analyze these other positions carefully; they may make comparisons; and they may show what they believe to be their deficiencies. It is conceivable that they may gradually, or even suddenly change their own position because of cumulative scientific evidence which appears to refute what was previously held to be true. Finally, they may even abandon the traditional or "scientific" approaches to philosophizing completely, if they become convinced that up to now it has not been possible to be clear about exactly what we are saying or even exactly what the question is that we are asking.[3]

Philosophers may pursue their work from a number of different standpoints—*speculatively, normatively,* or *analytically.* They may speculate about various aspects of life from what we know and believe about the universe and human affairs. They may approach such questions normatively, that is, in terms of a standard of behavior that is deemed appropriate within a social system. This standard of behavior may provide the basis upon which the philosopher evolves a systematic and coherent plan for daily living or, in a specific sense, for administering a leisure service agency. Finally, they may seek to analyze other philosophical approaches critically and make comparisons which might result in a clarification of concepts and ultimately in new information about the various perspectives in question.

There are differences in the tasks of the philosopher and the scientist. It is briefly explained by Zeigler.

Rather than aiming at a solution of a limited number of factors and variables through rigid experimental control, the philosophic method attempts instead to include every factor or variable that is either directly or remotely relevant to the problem. In this way an effort is made to arrive at a synthesis which is not only consistent with the best current data but also with the best experience drawn from the past.[4]

MAJOR PHILOSOPHIES

Philosophy, which emerged in Greece over 2,500 years ago, originally meant knowledge or wisdom. The first method used by philosophers was speculation, an approach which is still in wide use today and

[3]Earle F. Zeigler. *Physical Education and Sport Philosophy* (Englewood Cliffs, N.J.: Prentice-Hall Inc., 1977), pp. 13–14.

[4]*Ibid.,* p. 14.

which is an integral part of the scientific method. The following are brief descriptions of major philosophical approaches.

Idealism

Idealism, which can be traced to Plato, essentially states that homo sapiens is a real, existent being with a soul; that in each person is a spirit or mind which is basically real; that the essence of the entire universe is mind or spirit.

Idealism and Leisure. Idealists believe the individual is a purposive being who is striving to achieve those values which are embedded in reality itself. Zeigler comments: "To the extent that idealists can realize the external values through the choice of the right kinds of play and recreation without flouting the moral order of the world, they will be progressive enough to disregard a dualistic theory of work and play—a theory that has plagued us in North America down to the present day."[5]

Realism

A philosophy emanating from Aristotle, realism emphasizes that Homo sapiens lives in a world which is real; that things actually happen exactly the way people experience them; that Homo sapiens does not change any knowledge that may enter into our consciousness; that things are just the same as they were before such experiences occurred; and that reality "out there" is independent of the human being's mind.

Realism and Leisure. Realists accept the world at face value and believe our experiencing of it does not alter it one bit. They sharply differentiate work and leisure. They see play serving a useful purpose at recess or as an *extra*curricular activity after school, but believe that it should *not* be a part of the regular curriculum. They would agree that the use of leisure is significant to the development of our culture, but it is not an essential force in the monumental area of everyday life. By and large they see leisure pursuits as an opportunity to get relief from work, as experiences having a re-creative purpose. Leisure can serve in this sense as a safety valve (emitting of surplus energy) for the reduction of life's psychic tensions.

Pragmatism

With its roots going back to Heraclitus, pragmatism, which was utilized by Francis Bacon, John Locke, and John Dewey, adopts a view of the world which is *consistently* changing; an idea is not true until

[5] *Ibid.,* p. 200.

it is tested through experience. Meaning of conceptions or ideas are to be recognized in their practical beings. The function of thought is that of a guide to action. Truth is tested by practical consequences of belief.

Pragmatism and Leisure. Pragmatists or experimentalists don't support the fractionalization of aspects of leisure into component parts. Pragmatists believe that education for leisure is basic to the curriculum of the school; play should foster moral growth; and overorganized sports competition is not true recreation, since the welfare of the individual is relegated to having only secondary value. Additionally, pragmatists make it clear that it is a mistake to confuse the psychological distinction between work and play with the traditional economic distinction.

Existentialism

This view of Homo sapiens, an introspective humanism, states that individual human beings are dependent on themselves for shaping the course and quality of their own life. It is a philosophy which states that the existence of the individual precedes his or her essence. Specifically, it stresses the individual's responsibility for making him or herself what he or she is.

Existentialism and Leisure. Leisure holds an important place in existentialist thought.

> Personal liberation is highly desirable and this is most certainly a function of play. In sporting [and recreation] activities individuals can be free as they select their own values and achieve self-expression. Children can create their own world of play and thereby realize their true identities. . . . Existentialists at play want no prescribed formations, no coach calling the plays and destroying the players' "authenticity," and no crowd exhorting them to win at any cost.[6]

Humanism

Humanism is the philosophical doctrine that Homo sapiens is the supreme value in the universe and that human beings should therefore be primarily concerned with human interests rather than with the assumed interests of the deity. Humanism rejects supernaturalistic notions of creation, heaven and hell, inherent sin, etc., and strives to unite people on the basis of a code of social morality rather than on the basis of creed or denomination. The humanistic movement is recognized as a "third force" in psychology, serving as an alternative to the Freudian (psychoanalytic) and behavioristic psychological models. A

[6] *Ibid.*, p. 200.

humanistic perspective involves facilitation of human potential as well as a concern for eliminating barriers which hinder or restrict self-development.

Humanism and Leisure. "Humanism involves recognizing human dignity and power in some of its important dimensions, accepting responsibility for their cultivation and for making them effective in the whole sense of life. . . . Its universal tendency is to stress human self-understanding and self-determination."[7] In this sense, leisure provides each person an opportunity to realize his or her full potential. Leisure expression can occur in any situation; through the encouragement of dignity and self-determination for each person, individuals will have the opportunity to achieve joy, mastery, uniqueness, self-realization, and shared experience. Leisure serves as a well-spring for personal liberation and in this way can enable individuals to be personally autonomous, not only in their intellectual beliefs, but in their esthetic experience, their romantic or sexual preferences, their moral tastes and values, and ultimately in their fullest development as a human being.

RELATING PHILOSOPHY TO THEORY

Philosophy is an attempt to evaluate what we know and believe about the world and our sphere of human affairs; the result may be the evolving of a systematic and coherent plan by which we come to order our lives. Scientific *theory* is a set of interrelated, testable propositions; every science is in the process of developing theory. At one level, theory is the effort simply to describe accurately a set of interrelated phenomena—perhaps the wilderness camping behavior of white, middle-income homeowners compared with recreation vehicle camping of a similar socioeconomic group. At the other extreme there is an attempt to map out the entire social universe. While there are no current theories of leisure which could attest to such a "grand" theory, one may be developed some day which, in combination with all other social phenomena, will explain the behavior of all humans.

It should be realized that theory and action and philosophy and action are not mutually exclusive. An action inevitably stimulates speculation. This results in the formulation of an hypothesis which sooner or later must be tested if it is to survive in a reputable system of knowledge. In Figure 2–2, Theory Development and Philosophy of Leisure, it can be recognized that a philosophy of leisure will inevitably result in the development of concepts and theories, and vice versa.

[7]Horace L. Friess, "Humanist Responsibilities," in *The Humanist Alternative,* ed. Paul Kurtz (Buffalo, N.Y.: Prometheus Press, 1973), p. 42.

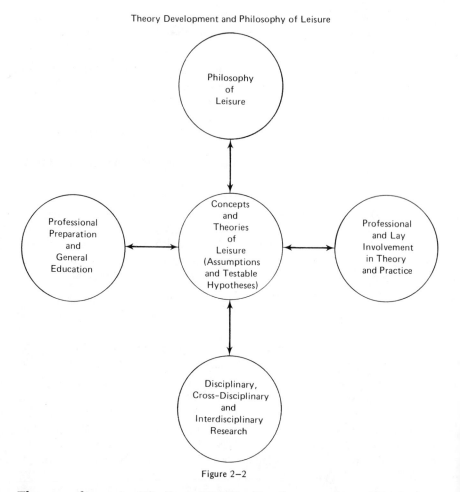

Figure 2-2

The prevailing scientific thought will often then result in the exercise of various aspects of tested knowledge. This in turn results in the development of professional preparation and occasionally general or liberal education efforts to form a logical and coherent educational orientation for individuals studying the discipline for either personal or vocational use.

Research continues to lead to increasingly reliable methods for testing hypotheses and propositions, the evaluation and measurement of variables arising from new empirical relationships, and validation of abstract thought through testing procedures. Research may be stimulated by public concern about problems demanding action, accidental observations of a person thinking about the general relationships which the particular incident makes vivid, or it might be the result of rigorous inductive investigation in an attempt to evolve new possibilities. It should be realized that the application of research can serve as an end product as well as an initial stimulus to theory building.

THEORY BUILDING

As is shown in Figure 2–3, theory building occurs at several levels. There is an ongoing search for more refined, more precise definition of terms or clearer concepts. At the first level, *observation* leads to the development of conceptual groupings and associated labeling. The second level involves special *observational procedures* which are developed to measure the relative presence of a given class of behaviors. It is at this point that the interplay between theory and data gathering becomes pronounced. Measurement permits the assigning of numerals, of identification, and of data comparison. The next stage results in the *testing of hypotheses about relationships among conceptual groupings* in leisure, for example, and between a given conceptual grouping and nonleisure variable (e.g., intensity of satisfaction, physical dimension like time, distance traveled, and so on). Hypotheses which are tested yield *empirical relationships.* Each empirical relationship permits a low level of prediction (and often control) under those conditions for which the empirical relationship is constant.

The *first level* of theory composition constructed explains one set of empirical relationships and results in other theories to explain other sets of relationships. The next level, of *middle-range* theory, seeks a consolidation of related insights at a more abstract level. The highest

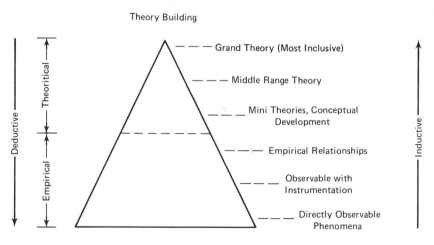

Theory Building

Figure 2–3

level of theory development permits the deduction of many miniature theories and their related empirical consequences, points the way toward a resolution of apparent contradictions among the miniature theories, and provides a bridge to the discovery of new empirical relationships. Such *grand* theory attempts to explain *all* of any given type of phenomenon. In general, the intention of theory in contemporary science is to summarize existing knowledge, to provide an explanation for observed events and relationships, and to predict the occurrence of as yet unobserved events and relationships on the basis of explanatory principles embodied in the theory.

CONCEPTUALIZING LEISURE

Most "theories" of leisure are developed only at the conceptual level; that is, they represent philosophical ideas which have not met the test of widespread application through testing and validation of data. The term *leisure* is used as an all-inclusive term to describe the meaning, conditions, functions, and opportunity complex in which recreation/play behavior occurs. It is no easy task to delineate the nature of leisure expression. It is a most difficult aspect of human behavior to comprehend. And of course, like any field of endeavor or aspect of human life, the propositions that comprise a theory to explain the ordering of human existence are constantly subject to further questioning, empirical testing, and revision.

Because of the multidisciplined and interdisciplinary nature of leisure, a broad approach is required to identify, define, and order it. Because of the variation in leisure orientations, arising principally from the disciplinary focus of the scientist, philosopher or practitioner, it is necessary to develop a model of leisure concepts which incorporate these different approaches.

Each conceptual view of leisure has various weaknesses and strengths. There have been many attempts by philosophers and social scientists to articulate a particular model of leisure, and most have value for the practitioner and student. The following descriptive paradigm is oriented around a categorization of leisure according to *time, function, spatial/environmental,* and an integrative-synthesizing perspective, *holism.* Such a descriptive model was used by Immorlica in her study of selected adults who were asked which of the commonly accepted leisure concepts most closely related to their life style.[8] Figure 2–4 provides an illustration of this leisure model.

[8]Annette G. Immorlica, "An Exploratory Research Study of Leisure Orientations of Selected Adults," Master's Thesis, Department of Recreation and Leisure Studies, San Jose State University, December 1977.

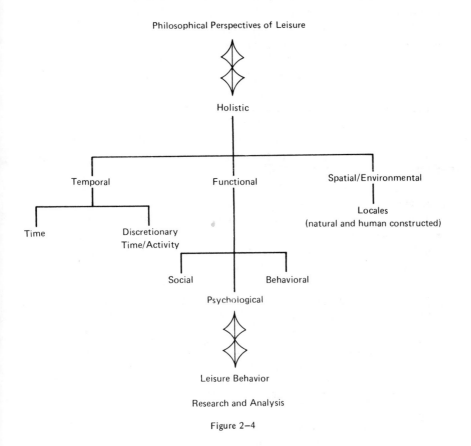

Figure 2–4

LEISURE'S ROOTS

Leisure as a concept emerged in ancient Greece with the "cultivation of self" interpretation developed by Aristotle (348 B.C.–322 B.C.) during the decline of the Greek empire. According to Gray, this classical interpretation held that leisure "is an activity which involves pursuit of truth and self-understanding. It is an act of aesthetic, psychological, religious and philosophical contemplation."[9] This concept of leisure as the contemplative life views leisure as a life style free of work and commitments. Additionally, the classical concept is derived from the ancient term *schole,* meaning leisure, implying freedom or the absence of the necessity of being occupied.

[9]David E. Gray, "This Alien Thing Called Leisure," Paper presented at Oregon State University, Corvallis, Oregon, July 8, 1971.

Leisure was certainly made possible by the existence of slavery in Athens and the aristocratic quality of the ancient democracy gave the leisure class a tradition of taste and elegance which was maintained by the nobility. However, this sense of style was spread to a wider circle of citizens and was enriched by writers and artists who gave new meaning to traditional forms and broadened the horizons of a few select families. "By it [slavery] the common people of Athens had a degree of leisure which is almost unknown in a modern proletariat. . . .Athens differed from many slave-owning societies in its large proportion of free men to slaves, which has been calculated as about two to one."[10]

This apparently was far different from the scale of slavery in imperial Rome or any Asian Empire, or even classical Sparta. This was partly due to Athens being too poor to buy or maintain slaves in large numbers. Slaves were usually not employed on the land but in mines and quarries and in ships, and slave women were often nurses in well-to-do homes. However, it remains that the way of life in Athens precipitated the opportunity for leisure for the privileged and was conditional upon the availability of slave labor.

> We cannot doubt that the distinction of the Athenian democracy owed much to slavery, since it provided the free citizen with leisure to spend his time on other matters than finding his livelihood. The majority of citizens still had to work hard, but at least they had times when they could leave their work and attend to public affairs or the graces of leisure. . . . The citizens composed the greater part of the population and almost the whole indigenous part of it. And this was indeed democratic in the extent of its powers and its responsibilites.[11]

The classical interpretation of leisure was popularized by Aristotle. Aristotle believed leisure to be *essential* so that citizens could carry on the business of government, law, debate, culture, and contemplation. Of course, slaves were required to carry on the "work" of the state. According to Richard Kraus, this "meant that leisure was given to a comparatively few patricians and made possible by the strenuous labors of many."[12]

The term leisure is derived from the Latin word *licere* or "to be permitted to abstain from occupation or service," with direct reference to the Athenian ideal of absolving select citizens from daily physical toil (*ponos*) and freeing them to engage in intellectual, cultural, civic, and artistic endeavors.

---

[10]C. M. Bowra. *The Greek Experience* (New York: Mentor Books, 1957), p. 86.

[11]*Ibid.,* p. 86.

[12]Richard Kraus. *Recreation and Leisure in Modern Society,* 1st ed. (New York: Appleton-Century-Crofts, 1971), p. 295.

Additionally, the Greek influence of leisure may be traced to the word *schole,* which was closely related to leisure and education and is the derivation of the English word *school. Schole* referred to a place where one was permitted to engage in scholarly pursuits. The implication of leisure in this sense refers to a disregard for material concern and is strongly linked to individual freedom and self-determination and an immunity from occupational requirements.[13]

Schole is the opposite of *aschola,* the Greek word for mental toil. The parallel in ancient Roman society was the word *otium,* or leisure, (equal to *schole*) and its opposite, *negotium,* the word for work. As with the Greeks, any work that had to do with the production of food and clothing was held in low esteem. Anderson writes of the Greco-Roman perspective of leisure.

> Whether *schole* for the Greeks or *otium* for the Romans, it was for them a serious business of life. They managed their livelihoods and engaged in politics and political discussion. They learned music and played it and enjoyed the physical arts of war and sport. They were skilled in intellectual conversation, and that consumed much time. But they rarely had an interest in talking about handwork and ordinary labor or even cared to understand its meaning. In their way of life there was no hurry. The scholar or the religious man was quite within the meaning of the notion of leisure if he did nothing but sit and contemplate.[14]

Thus the classical view saw leisure as the basis of culture. Then the Industrial Revolution, as Sebastian De Grazia notes, changed the concept of time, including free time, the gateway to leisure. "Time became industrialized." Large-scale industry necessitated coordinating the movement of men and materials to the regularity of machines. Leisure was seen not as a condition of life, a state of being in which a person could orient him or herself to individual time and natural rhythms independent of any artifical or mechanical time reference. Instead, in contemporary Western society, life is oriented principally to the clock, and time has been equated with money; like monetary rewards, time is a valuable commodity to be saved, spent, earned, and counted. De-Grazia states:

> From the moment of our birth, everything we see and hear is touched by the clock. We learn that time is valuable, scarce. It ticks off in a straight line—runs steadily like an assembly line—used up evenly, minute after minute, hour after hour, day after day, inexorable, impersonal, universal

[13]James F. Murphy. *Recreation and Leisure Service: A Humanistic Perspective* (Dubuque, Iowa: William C Brown Co., 1975), p. 5.

[14]Nels Anderson. *Dimensions of Work: The Sociology of a Work Culture* (New York: David McKay Co., 1964), p. 91.

time. In our obsession with pacing our lives by the mechanical clock, we have all but lost the rhythmical, recurring sense of time.

The tide ebbs and flows while in infinite variation the days come and go, the moon waxes and wanes, the seasons take their turn—seed time, the harvest, the falling leaf and thawing ice, the cry of the newborn lamb. Everything in its own time lives, dies, and is born. Day after day, we bind ourselves to the clock. Machines by now have manipulated everyone into living by the dictates of the clock. An ignorant visitor from a clockless land might wonder why we reject the tyranny of men while submitting to the tyranny of time.[15]

If we are to achieve a state of leisure in the classical tradition, De Grazia suggests, we must strive to (1) reply less on commodities and purchases, (2) slow down our pace of life in a more "leisurely," less hurried setting, and (3) achieve better tastes. Robert Theobald recommends that Americans begin discussing and understanding what is needed to function in our post-industrial, leisure-centered society. One condition essential to our understanding the consequences of a leisure society is the acceptance of diversity—"diversity in time patterns, diversity in space patterns, diversity in whether people wish to be involved in the technological age or prefer to live in families."[16]

In ancient Athens work was understood as the absence of leisure, rather than leisure being understood as the absence of work. "From this perspective, one works only that he may be freed from the necessity of being occupied. It would be a flagrant contradiction to this view to suggest that the problem of leisure is to find occupation for every moment."[17] In the classical sense, a leisure activity is done for its own sake and for no other purpose. But leisure understood in this sense involves a certain state of being, blessedness, or attitude.

LEISURE AS TIME

The predominant concept of viewing leisure as time is *discretionary time,* which holds that leisure *is that portion of time which remains when work and the basic requirements for existence have been satisfied.* The concept of leisure as discretionary or nonobligatory time parallels the economic concept of discretionary money. Time falls into three classes: time for existence, sleeping, eating (meeting biological requirements); time for subsistence (working at one's job); and leisure

[15]Excerpt from the film "Of Time, Work and Leisure," presented at the National Recreation Congress, St. Louis, Missouri, 1963.

[16]Robert Theobald, "Leisure—Its Meaning and Implications," Paper presented in panel discussion at the National Recreation Congress, St. Louis, 1963.

[17]Thomas F. Green. *Work, Leisure, and the American Schools* (New York: Random House, 1968), p. 69.

(time remaining after the basic necessities of life and work requirements have been accomplished).

The concept of leisure as time free from work-related responsibilities is held by many North Americans. Our dominant view of how time should be spent is that of the industrial worker: hours are to be devoured in order to receive sustenance. Participation in the daily routine has become the goal of life itself. Americans have inherited from the time of the Industrial Revolution in the nineteenth century a sociopsychological attitude which equates individual self-worth and productivity with working. Don Fabun states that this definition of work as a normal outlet for an individual's energies was fostered in the sixth century.

This idea may have had its first concrete expression in the Sixth Century when St. Benedict at his monastery at Monte Cassino pasted rules for the monks. "Idleness is the enemy of the soul," begins Rule XLVIII. "And therefore, at fixed times, the brothers ought to be occupied in manual labor, and, again at fixed times, in sacred reading."

For the first time not work as such, but work for a stipulated time, became integral to Western thought. In later years we were to confuse the two, so that "putting in the time" became more important than the work. But what was new here at the beginning with the monks of Monte Cassino, was that work was good for the soul. This was the myth that has become a monster in our times; it drives even the rich to maintain the illusion that they are working, and those who do not work into an incessant apologia for being alive. The "work" monster gained substance from the idea that the progress of a society or a culture is something like the natural progress of man; as he grows older and works harder, he accumulates more wisdom and more material things.

It is probably no accident that the idea of social progress and the sanctity of work as a means to achieve it grew into a now virtually unexamined ethic at the same time that the Industrial Revolution began to need more "workers." This kind of work was not like the work that had gone on before; it was specially oriented in space (in the factory or foundry) and structured in time (the necessity for the worker to be in a certain place, at certain times, performing certain prescribed activities).[18]

The glorification of work through industrialism led to the separation of work and leisure and an emphasis on economically productive functions as the most significant aspects of life, with the eventual relegation of leisure to the status of "spare time." Anderson views leisure as time free from work and other obligations however it may be used while recreation concerns particular ways of using free time.[19] As a result, it is possible to diagram the relationship of leisure as free time to work (an activity of earning a living). See Figure 2–5.

[18]Don Fabun. *The Dynamics of Change* (Englewood Cliffs, N.J.: Prentice-Hall, Inc., 1967), pp. 13–14.

[19]Anderson, *Dimensions of Work*, p. 93.

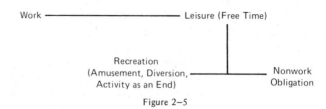

Relationship of Leisure as Free Time to Work

Work ——————————————— Leisure (Free Time)

Recreation
(Amusement, Diversion, —————————— Nonwork
Activity as an End)   Obligation

Figure 2–5

Anderson believes that this separation of work and leisure is not an evil, but the consequence of an evaluation in which work inevitably has been "stripped to the running gears," the better to serve a world filling with people. Also it meant less work rather than more work achievement, and less full concentration on it, with greater opportunities for leisure.[20] Accordingly, leisure is viewed as an end in itself while work is defined as economic activity for a purpose.

One must recognize that the view of leisure as free time or time/activity is based on leisure activity being determined by and set apart from work. This frequently accepted concept of leisure serves as a premise upon which the formal organization of recreation and leisure service agencies function; however, this approach may actually be misleading and erroneous in design. This view of leisure as free time (that is, what is left over after all the essential requirements of existence and subsistence have been fulfilled), is peculiarly limited to industrial societies. The nature of work is somewhat different in modern societies from what it is in primitive agrarian and pre-industrial societies. This single-factor theory—based on the premise that one's occupation stems from the organization of work—has become largely accepted as the main factor determining all other aspects of everyday life, including leisure. Cheek and Burch comment on their view of the limits of this view for understanding leisure, even in contemporary societies:

> The confusion is exacerbated by assessing discretionary time as a property of individuals, rather than appreciating ... that leisure is a property of social groups and is not conditional upon any particular mode of economic production present in a society.[21]

Additionally, Cheek, Field, and Burdge have noted that several methodological errors exist in traditional user preference surveys, including the monumental Outdoor Recreation Resources Review Commission report (1962), which for years has served as the premise in

[20] *Ibid.,* p. 98.

[21] Neil H. Cheek, Jr., and William R. Burch, Jr. *The Social Organization of Leisure in Society* (New York: Harper and Row, Publishers, 1976), p. 240.

estimating and predicting user demand for outdoor recreation places: "...in explaining differential participation among participants, social aggregate variables fail to explain the differences that arise in frequency of participation."[22]

Therefore, the discretionary time concept as a predictor of leisure behavior has limitations and is statistically not significant in explaining or predicting leisure behavior. This is so principally because it is tied to economic rationale and social aggregate variables while it ignores the concept of the social group and the available opportunity of potential users, and it fails to recognize that some recreation activities are interchangeable.[23]

LEISURE AS FUNCTION

In addition to having temporal characteristics, leisure is viewed as serving various functions. In this sense, leisure has at least three perspectives: behavior, psychological, and social.

Behavioral Context of Leisure

In a behavioral context, leisure can be viewed as *nonwork behavior in which people engage during their free time.* Such leisure experience includes all the potential nonwork opportunities available and "stresses that leisure is voluntary activity carried on in free time, in sharp contrast with work, which is required, is utilitarian, and is rewarded in economic terms."[24] Leisure behavior, however, must be recognized as an expression of the individual's total self; cognitive, affective, and motor domains are potentially engaged. E. William Niepoth[25] suggests that the perceptions of the individual engaging in leisure are the basis for that individual's response. Behavior is inferred; to understand its meaning, we must know what its context is.

Niepoth suggests that leisure services are those activities which, through the creation and/or manipulation of human and physical environments, provide opportunities for the expression of a wide variety of recreation behavior. Behavior is goal-directed. The leisure experience, then, is a direct result of goal-seeking. The degree of success or failure of an individual's engaging in leisure behavior will influence

[22]Neil H. Cheek, Jr., Donald R. Field, and Rabel J. Burdge. *Leisure and Recreation Places* (Ann Arbor, Mich.: Ann Arbor Science Publishers, 1976), p. 66.

[23]*Ibid.,* pp. 151–152.

[24]Kraus, *Recreation and Leisure,* p. 256.

[25]James F. Murphy, John G. Williams, E. William Niepoth, and Paul D. Brown. *Leisure Service Delivery System: A Modern Perspective* (Philadelphia: Lea & Febiger, 1973), pp. 80–92.

his or her decision to continue, modify, or terminate participation. Leisure service delivery, viewed from a behavioral perspective, must seemingly be based on a commitment to provide opportunities which encourage and facilitate people's engaging in leisure behavior, both individually and collectively.

Behavioral Functions of Leisure Activity

According to Joffre Dumazedier,[26] leisure fulfills three functions: relaxation, entertainment and personal development. Relaxation "provides the individual recovery from fatigue," entertainment "spells deliverance from boredom," and personal development "serves to liberate the individual from the daily automatism of thought and action." To Dumazedier, "Leisure is activity—apart from the obligations of work, family, and society—to which the individual turns at will, for either relaxation, diversion, or broadening his individual and his spontaneous social participation, the free exercise of his creative capacity."[27]

To permit ourselves to satisfy the desire for leisure, we have developed an elaborate rationalization of leisure as a respite from work, something that provides rest and relaxation and that is recuperative in nature. The view of leisure as activity gained significance with the Industrial Revolution, according to Bennett Berger. Time that was separate from work—off-the-job living—came to be vulnerable to the "ministrations of the Devil ... unless it were used productively to restore or refresh the organism for its primary purpose, work, or for unambiguously 'wholesome' purposes such as prayer, Bible reading ..."[28] and so on.

Psychological Function of Leisure

The psychology of leisure represents a subjective approach to the study of human behavior, primarily as it relates to the individual, either alone or in a group. The psychological perspective of leisure is described by Neulinger:

> To leisure means to be engaged in an activity performed for its own sake, to do something which gives one pleasure and satisfaction, which involves one to the very core of one's being. To leisure means to be oneself, to express one's talents, one's capacities, one's potentials."[29]

[26]Joffre Dumazedier. *Toward a Society of Leisure* (New York: The Free Press, 1967), p. 14.

[27]*Ibid.*, pp. 16–17.

[28]Bennett Berger, "The Sociology of Leisure: Some Suggestions," *Industrial Relations* 1 (February 1962), p. 25.

[29]John Neulinger. *The Psychology of Leisure* (Springfield, Ill.: Charles C Thomas, 1974), p. xi.

Neulinger suggests that leisure is a discrete category of human behavior not seen in opposition to work.

> The important point ... is that leisure is not to be seen in opposition to work. It is not necessary that we downgrade work in order to raise the value of leisure. Leisure is not *not-work;* leisure is not time left over *after work.* Leisure is a state of mind, it is a way of being, of being at peace with oneself and what one is doing. It is doing what one wants to do and what one chooses to do.[30]

The psychological perspective of leisure places the emphasis of leisure participation on personal fulfillment and self-development rather than on the number of activities engaged in or frequency of participation. Therefore, the psychological perspective would tend to analyze leisure activities according to the needs they satisfy. London, Crandall, and Fitzgibbons emphasize the use of needs rather than using groups of leisure activities as the basis of participation.

> Knowledge of what needs individuals wish to satisfy when they engage in various types of activities may be sufficient for designing leisure delivery systems that will be of value to, and will be used by, most individuals. The particular set of leisure activities and attributes examined will depend upon the situation.... Mean differences in ratings of needs that people desire to fulfill by their participation in different leisure activities may provide sufficient data for some purposes. Such information would go beyond the rates of participation data typically collected in order to understand why individuals engage in particular activities. For example, knowledge about the needs of both users and non-users of leisure qualities can be used to modify leisure services to maximize need fulfillment, and as a consequence, participation.[31]

In fact, it is argued that selection and participation in leisure activities can contribute significantly to the life satisfaction of the individual. In a study conducted by Tinsley, Barrett, and Kass[32] it was strongly suggested that 42 of 45 needs satisfied by five commonly selected leisure activities investigated (watching television; attending plays, concerts, and lectures; reading books and magazines; bicycling; and drinking and socializing) were leisure-activity-specific needs (that is, needs that can be satisfied much more through participation in some leisure activities than in others); there was much less support for the notion that some needs were leisure-activity-general (needs that can be

[30]*Ibid.,* p. xv.

[31]Manuel London, Rick Crandall, and Dale Fitzgibbons, "The Psychological Structure of Leisure: Activities, Needs, People," *Journal of Leisure Research* 9:262, 1977.

[32]Howard E. A. Tinsley, Thomas C. Barrett, and Richard A. Kass, "Leisure Activities and Need Satisfaction," *Journal of Leisure Research* 9:110–120, 1977.

satisfied to approximately the same degree by all leisure activities). Needs for sex, catharsis, independence, understanding, getting along with others, and affiliation appear most leisure-activity-specific. Therefore, the psychology of leisure purports to follow the theories of Allport,[33] Maslow,[34] and Murray,[35] who stated that behavior is a function of needs. Leisure behavior according to this perspective is a function of the needs of the individual. "Leisure activity choice, therefore, becomes an aspect of the personality."[36]

The Social Function of Leisure

The social basis of leisure behavior is an emerging perspective which has gained considerable impact in recent years. It stems largely from the research of sociologists who argue that the most significant determinant of what one does in leisure is membership in a social group (leisure is a means for establishing and sustaining intragroup solidarity) and that the leisure place helps shape and control leisure behavior.[37] Taste, according to Cheek and Burch, becomes a primary shaper of the social group, and life style tastes (preference exercised in response to felt normative pressures) arise from small social groups, which are based on kinship and friendship. Individuals tend to belong to a number of social circles consisting of people who share common interests. Taste may provide social boundaries and binds social circles. However, social circles are permeable, that is, they can also cut across geographic, ethnic, and social class differences where individuals hold a common interest.[38]

Leisure and Socioeconomic Characteristics

A substantial body of leisure research has focused on the identification of socioeconomic-demographic factors (age, gender, education, occupation, income, social class, race, and so on) associated with leisure participation, and on whether the identified factors are useful for predicting leisure behavior. These studies have either found or imply that socioeconomic differences exist between the derived groups of leisure participants; therefore, socioeconomic variables are worthwhile predictors of participation by activity clusters.[39] These assessments have pro-

---

[33]G. W. Allport. *Becoming: Basic Considerations for a Psychology of Personality* (New Haven: Yale University Press, 1955).

[34]A. H. Maslow. *Motivation and Personality* (New York: Harper and Row, Publishers, 1954).

[35]H. A. Murray et al. *Explorations in Personality* (New York: Oxford University Press, 1938).

[36]Tinsley, Barrett, and Kass, "Leisure Activities," p. 111.

[37]Cheek, Field, and Burdge, *Leisure and Recreation Places*, p. 153.

[38]Cheek and Burch, *The Social Organization.*, pp. 124–149.

[39]Gerald H. Romsa and Sydney Girling, "The Identification of Outdoor Recreation Market Segments on the Basis of Frequency of Participation," *Journal of Leisure Research* 8:247–255, 1976.

duced apparently objective evidence pointing to increased demand for virtually all facilities that have been objects of the inquiries. However, there is a need to exercise caution and even skepticism toward some of these presuppositions. On the basis of their research, Romsa and Girling[40] suggest that standard socioeconomic-demographic variables are not reliable criteria with which to differentiate groups of recreationists. Of course, a number of studies do exist which have investigated various socioeconomic-demographic relationships and some point toward the uniqueness of certain population groups of leisure users.

While a number of these studies have made a contribution to the study of leisure and the organization and delivery of leisure services, the possibility exists that the socioeconomic-demographic indicators commonly used in leisure research are not reliable criteria for identifying groups of recreationists. "Unreliable criteria could lead to inaccurate interpretation of research results which in turn could result in inappropriate recreation policy decisions and/or hinder the progress of recreation research."[41]

ENVIRONMENTAL PERSPECTIVES OF LEISURE

The environment provides a basis for understanding the influence of physical settings upon social groups. Social groups view the environment from a symbolic, ritualistic, or functional point of view.

The physical environment is seen as an independent variable affecting leisure behavior. Leisure locales, places where people engage in nonwork behavior, contribute to the way in which people participate and react in such settings. It is suggested that leisure locales, such as amusement parks, scout camps, zoos, shopping centers, museums, theaters, and school playgrounds, provide unique experiences for people, and that they provide the substance for reaffirming one's identity.

Because people perceive leisure settings in a variety of ways, leisure resource planners, managers, and service providers must learn more about the differences in goals and aspirations of recreationists. The physical environment provides a framework for supporting behavior which results in leisure expression.

HOLISM AND LEISURE

The holistic view of leisure serves as an integrative, very broadly defined concept of leisure. Holistic is derived from the Greek *holos* or

---

[40] *Ibid.,* p. 254.
[41] *Ibid.,* p. 254.

entire and provides a philosophical approach for emphasizing the organic or functional relation between parts and wholes.

This concept of leisure, as discussed by Hendricks and Burdge, seeks to fuse

> ... work and nonwork spheres and establish the relationship and relevance of leisure in terms of other human behavior. Leisure is not seen simply as activity but rather includes time and attitudes toward time and nonwork activities.... Leisure in the holistic orientation is seen as a complex of multiple relationships involving certain choices which indicate both societal and individual aspirations as well as life styles.[42]

The holistic concept of leisure is seen as a potentially synthesizing theoretical perspective in which elements of leisure are to be expressed in all aspects of human behavior—in work, play, education, religion, and other social spheres. There is much debate as to whether the unique character of leisure, particularly as influenced by the social organization of work, can effectively be analyzed and operationalized because such a conceptual approach has not lent itself to either empirical testing or accurate prediction.

There are a growing number of writers and researchers who now argue that there is need for a more holistic approach in research and analysis of leisure activity and behavior.[43] One method undertaken by several researchers is the multiple satisfactions concept, the concept that leisure activities are interchangeable in satisfying participants' motives, needs, and preferences. This concept of substitutability emanated from the conceptual typologies of leisure based on underlying meanings and consequences of activities to participants. Following this empirical work that indicated that leisure activities do cluster along some logical theoretical lines,[44] a more holistic premise emerged in the literature. In a study of the "Leisure Activities of Metropolitan Coaltown Residents," Hendee and Burdge applied the concept of substitutability to 69 leisure activities and yielded five clusters based on the similarity of participation patterns and activity rates of respondents. These activity clusters were labeled as: (1) "cultural" hobbies, (2) organized competition, (3) domestic maintenance, (4) social leisure, and (5)

[42]Joe Hendricks and Rabel J. Burdge, "The Nature of Leisure Research: A Reflection and Comment," *Journal of Leisure Research* 4:216, 1972.

[43]Cheek, Field, and Burdge, *Leisure and Recreation Places*, p. 154.

[44]Refer to J. C. Hendee, R. P. Gale, and W. R. Catton, Jr., "A Typology of Outdoor Recreation Activity Preferences," *Journal of Environmental Education* 3:28, 1971; W. T. Moss and S. C. Lamphear, "Substitutability of Recreational Activities in Meeting Stated Needs and Drives of the Visitor," *Journal of Environmental Education* 1:129, 1970; and D. R. Yoesting and D. L. Burkhead, "Significance of Childhood Recreation Experience on Adult Leisure Behavior: An Exploratory Analysis, *Journal of Leisure Research* 5:25, 1973.

outdoor activities.[45] Since participation in these leisure activity clusters is highly intercorrelated, activities in the same cluster may provide similar satisfaction. This means that for many people these activities may be substitutable with little loss of satisfaction.

Such a holistic analytical perspective suggests that specific groups select similar activities and this premise simultaneously takes into account the leisure setting, leisure activity, and social group. Through use of such a holistic philosophical and research-oriented approach, new ways of viewing leisure as a complex, multifaceted aspect of human behavior may result in more careful detailed theoretical analysis as contrasted with overly simplistic, singular, and segmented approaches to leisure inquiry. Leisure assumes a more vibrant, active, dynamic posture within society from such an integrative approach, and this perspective may suggest new possibilities for confronting various factors contributing to human misery and suffering, identity problems, health and fitness, environmental and energy problems, divorce, boredom, worker dissatisfaction, and physical, social, and psychological restrictions.

SUMMARY

Philosophy provides the individual with an approach or method of viewing daily events, fundamental beliefs, and values, and serves as a foundation for various institutions and professions, including recreation and leisure service. Philosophy's branches includes metaphysics, epistemology, logic, and axiology. Several major philosophical premises were presented: idealism, realism, pragmatism, existentialism, and humanism. Each provides those engaged in philosophical speculation and analysis a way of critiquing and comparing leisure concepts.

Theory building is an important concern of every science. It is a process ranging from direct observation of phenomena, observation of phenomena with instrumentation, testing of empirical relationships, and development of theories which explain a limited set of relationships at a more abstract level, to propositions which account for all of any given type of phenomenon.

A typology of leisure related to a philosophical perspective was presented. This holistic paradigm provides a way of viewing leisure from a temporal viewpoint, as time or discretionary time; as activity fulfilling behavioral, social, and psychological functions; and as behavior related to a spatial/environmental framework.

---

[45]Cheek, Field, and Burdge, *Leisure and Recreation Places,* p. 153.

PART TWO

INDUSTRIAL
AND TEMPORAL
PERSPECTIVES
OF LEISURE

3

Work-Leisure Relationships

This chapter will discuss basic terms associated with work, provide an understanding of the evolution of work in industrialized Western culture, and offer a treatment of work-leisure concepts. The historical meanings of work are discussed and relationships are drawn to the contemporary "problem" of leisure. The nature of work satisfaction provides a premise for understanding current views regarding the reduction and reorganization of the workweek, job enrichment and innovations in the work place, and a cyclic lifetime integration of work, education, and leisure.

What kind of social structure can give all people opportunities for fulfillment in work and leisure? Can various individual needs be reconciled with the needs of society itself? The quality of the work and leisure lives of the mass of people in North American society has become a "problem," because the two spheres are generally seen as irreconcilable.

Work has varied meanings but, as with the leisure nexus, one must delineate the different interpretations in order to develop an understanding of work-leisure relationships. Work must be further contrasted from labor in order to comprehend its full meaning. According to Green, labor is related to production for consumption and work is related to production for use.[1]

---

[1] Thomas F. Green. *Work, Leisure, and the American Schools* (New York: Random House, 1968), p. 23.

Kelly provides additional insight into the work-leisure discussion. He defines employment, occupation, work, nonwork, and leisure, suggesting that both work and leisure may be seen as satisfying, expressive, and unifying terms, rather than alienating for self and community.

Employment: A job with specific responsibilities and rewards.

Occupation: A type of employment.

Work: Productive activity which yields a result of economic or social value.

Nonwork: Activity that is outside the employment schedule and obligations and includes leisure, required activity, such as maintenance and residual time.

Leisure: Activity chosen primarily for anticipated experiences, intrinsic and relational.[2]

According to Kelly, the critical difference between work and leisure is that work contributes to the survival and well-being of society; this, he states, validates work as being *productive.* Leisure, on the other hand, is *nonproductive* in the sense that its results are primarily personal. "It is free expression of the self and of satisfying relationships *for their own sake.* In leisure even the act of producing something finds its meaning in the act rather than in the product."[3]

Kelly states that while both can be satisfying and fulfilling, this fact does not make them identical. In addition it can be argued that Kelly's description of work as contributing to the survival and well-being of society may be only half-truth. Increasingly it appears that "work" oriented toward survival needs of society reflects only 5 to 8 percent of the work force's duties, while fully 92 to 95 percent are engaged in consumption-oriented responsibilities. This may suggest that the leisure domain may be pressured to assume more of work's former societal role. What may be occurring is "not the eradication of necessity and futility, but a transformation of the sphere in which they occur. Modern man is ecologically related to his 'social and economic system' in the same way as the gatherer of food is ecologically related to the 'systems of nature'. What has been changed is the conception of 'the world,' the conception of nature."[4]

[2]John R. Kelly. *Leisure* (Englewood Cliffs, N.J.: Prentice-Hall, Inc., 1980), In press.
[3]*Ibid.*
[4]Green, *Work, Leisure,* p. 19.

Additionally, this "problem of leisure" exists only insofar as we contemplate it as the disappearance of work or the lessening of the amount of clock time commitment to work over the course of a calendar year. This problem, based on our immediate past history of a fledgling survival society of the eighteenth and nineteenth centures which stumbled into the twentieth century of assembly-line, mass industrial work, does not allow us to even conceive of leisure. Green states:

> ... we lack the intellectual capital even to think about leisure as a conception that is meaningful in its own right. We think of it instead as leisure *time,* as time away from work.[5]

Work as conceived in industrialized Western culture, typified in North America, provides Homo sapiens not only with financial reward but also with self-respect. However, there is a growing awareness that the tradition of work (and thereby the modern tradition of leisure) as the moral and religious core of life is no longer so widely accepted. This has caused a corresponding erosion of the view of leisure as discretionary time, time away from increased efficiency and productivity.

The autonomous craftsperson, responsible for the total creation and performance of a product, has virtually disappeared from the North American industrial scene (except for scattered enclaves of craftspeople who work on various hand-made goods to sell at flea markets, on street corners, or in small collectives). The highly specialized assembly-line nature of modern industrial work has left the individual with little opportunity to use judgment or take initiative. However, the trend away from work as a source of emotional and social satisfaction does not mean that such satisfaction is no longer important for the worker. For many workers the job continues to fill what would otherwise be a void in life. In a society where most men and nearly a majority of women work, jobs continue to furnish important identity recognition, to smooth the individual's routine of waking and sleeping, with time on and time off the job.

Significantly, the changed attitude toward work has resulted in what Bennett Berger describes as the "problem of leisure."[6] Work has steadily lost its influence and power to command people's identification and loyalties; as they attempt to find alternate sources of moral experience, society loses an important source of normative integration. Berger suggests that the transfer to the leisure institution of functions formerly performed by the institution of work results in enormous in-

---

[5]*Ibid.,* p. 59.

[6]Bennett Berger, "The Sociology of Leisure: Some Suggestions," *Industrial Relations* 1 (February 1962).

crease in the attention devoted to the problem of leisure. The strain on the individual of this shift in potential sources of fulfillment is seen as significant because of the dramatic shift in the economy toward abundance, supported by discretionary money.

Automation has done much to free the mind and liberate human beings from repetitive, monotonous, and often hazardous kinds of labor in poor environments beneath the ground, in polluted atmospheres, and in unattractive settings, but so far it has not enhanced personal gratification. The social constraints and moral sanctions which limit our behavior have not been altered substantially to guide behavior which has little relationship to work. Accordingly, many Americans and Canadians are searching for ways to behave off the job.

LEISURE AS DISCRETIONARY TIME

The social patterns associated with the technological changes that began in the nineteenth century were assimilated into the popular culture through twentieth-century innovations. Industry has effectively incorporated many of the concepts of the Protestant Ethic into work and even conditioned the worker in his or her off-work hours. The glorification of work in the Protestant Ethic has produced for many people a residual feeling of guilt toward the enjoyment of leisure. Those who assumed the separation of work ethic and leisure ethic generally face a dilemma: they need a major value reorientation if they are to realize the potential benefits of increased leisure. It seems rather clear that to pose work and leisure as antithetical concepts tends to obscure the more fundamental value of personal fulfillment in all of life's endeavors.

Many people feel that the industrial and technological thrust in North America has had a detrimental influence on the fostering of leisure. To permit ourselves to take advantage of the leisure made possible by our economic system, we have developed an elaborate rationalization that holds leisure to be time earned as a respite from work—time for rest and relaxation. It is to be basically *recuperative* in nature. The depreciation of leisure as justifiable only as release from work time relegates off-the-job living to second-rate status and only compounds the leisure problem.

Work: The Dominant Rhythm of Life

The discretionary-time conception of leisure is rooted within traditional North American culture. Work is the dominant rhythm of society and leisure is valued as reward for people who are gainfully

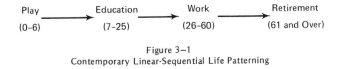

Figure 3–1
Contemporary Linear-Sequential Life Patterning

employed. One cannot claim virtuous leisure if he or she has not earned it; therefore, the central focus is a steady pattern of productive work. All other aspects of social life, including family relationship, existence requirements, engagement in community and civic activity, and political, educational, and religious participation, *gain significance in their relation to the work requirements of the culture.*

The traditional work rhythm of a scarce economy required people to work long hours and to be frugal with time and money, merely to survive. The definition of leisure as recuperation, relaxation, and reward for hard work is changing with decreased emphasis on the old rhythm of life in which one enjoyed work and was permitted limited relaxed nonwork activity. Margaret Mead stated that we need to revise the discretionary concept of leisure.

> This must be a revision which will make the members of a society—where delight in high proficiency should now replace dogged willingness to work long hours for very limited rewards—able to integrate the shorter hours of work and the new engrossing home rituals into some kind of a whole in which these outmoded sequences, heritage of an age of scarcity, can be overcome.[7]

The linear-sequential pattern of living in traditional American culture is illustrated in Figure 3–1. It is oriented around the mechanistic work rhythm, which forces the postponement of exhilarating moments and experiences until after work, next season, or retirement; this concept is being eroded by a freer, more permissive psychological time reference. A more personally natural, rhythmical, recurring pattern of human development, involving play, education, work, and disengagement (also known as retirement) would conceivably allow contemporary technological human beings to synthesize their experiences. Instead of suffering the sequential and inevitable terminal states of human development, human beings might be able to allow instincts and awareness of the ecological framework of the society to determine when one played, worked, pursued education, or relaxed. Later in this chapter alternative work-education-leisure models will be discussed.

[7]Margaret Mead, "The Pattern of Leisure in Contemporary American Culture," *The Annals,* 313 (September, 1957), p. 15.

WORK-LEISURE THEORIES AND CONCEPTS

There are several "theories" which have been developed, some empirical and others philosophical conjecture, which attempt to explain leisure behavior in relation to work behavior. Wilensky[8] offers two approaches:

> *Spillover Theory:* Work may be said to "spill over" in leisure to the extent that leisure is the continuation of work experience and attitudes.

> *Compensatory Theory:* Leisure is compensatory if it seeks to make up for dissatisfaction experienced in work.

Leisure is a compensation for the deadening rhythm of factory life. In other words, Wilensky claims that a person, particularly a blue-collar worker, engaged in repetitive, low-skilled, machine-paced work, will seek directly opposite activity in his or her leisure. On the other hand, an auto worker, for example, bored with the stultifying effects of assembly-line labor, develops a spillover routine in which alienation from work becomes alienation from life. The mental stultification produced by work permeates one's leisure.

Burch[9] examined Wilensky's two concepts and added a third perspective, the *personal community* hypothesis. His perspective suggests that the social circles of one's workmates, family, and friends has a marked impact on attitudes toward social issues and psychological drives. These transactions with the socialization in one's social circles will shape the nature of one's leisure activity.

Stanley Parker[10] defines leisure in relation to a person's "life space" —the total of activities or ways of spending time that people have. He states that the two worlds of time and activity are *dimensions* of work *and* leisure and not the domains of work and leisure. His model is illustrated in Figure 3–2 in a two-dimensional time and activity scheme.

The two dimensions of time are segmented into *work* and *nonwork,* while activity ranges from *constraint* (obligatory activity) to *freedom.* While leisure is found at the freedom end of the constraint-freedom scale, it is not restricted to nonworking time, according to Parker's paradigm. Parker comments:

[8]Harold Wilensky, "Work, Careers and Social Integration," *International Social Science Journal* 12:4, (1960).

[9]William Burch, Jr., "The Social Circles of Leisure: Competing Explanations," *Journal of Leisure Research* 1:125–148, 1969.

[10]Stanley Parker. *The Future of Work and Leisure* (New York: Praeger Publishers, 1971).

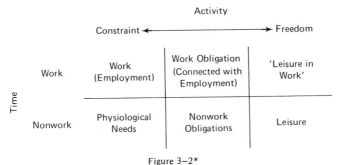

Figure 3–2*
*Stanley Parker, The Future of Work and Leisure, p. 28.

"Work" and "leisure in work" may consist of the same activity; the difference is that the latter is chosen for its own sake. Thus mountaineering is work for the guide but leisure in work for the amateur climber. . . . In addition to such bases of leisure in the desert of working time, there remains the point that leisure means *choice,* and so time chosen to be spent as work activity—though not involving the constraint of employment—can be leisure just as much as more usual leisure activities.[11]

Parker goes on to analyze the types of work-leisure relationships, depicted in Figure 3–3.

General Description	Individual Level	Societal Level
Identity	Extension	Fusion
Contrast	Opposition	Polarity
Separateness	Neutrality	Containment

Figure 3–3
Types of Work-Leisure Relationships*
*Stanley Parker, The Future of Work and Leisure, p. 101.

According to Parker, *identity* describes any situation in which work and leisure feature similar structures. *Contrast* is a definition of content of one sphere as the absence or opposite of the other. *Separateness* means that there is a situation of minimal contact or influence between the spheres. In defining the *individual* level of the work-leisure relationship and primary function of leisure, Parker offers the following interpretation and combines other meaning with Wilensky and Dumazedier's discussion of work-leisure meanings:

[11]*Ibid.,* pp. 28–29.

Extension: (Wilensky's spillover leisure and Dumazedier's function of personal development): A pattern of similarity of at least some work and leisure activities and the lack of demarcation between work and leisure. Characterized by social workers, successful businesspersons, doctors, teachers, and craft workers with *high* autonomy in their work and a feeling of being stretched by their work.

Opposition: (Wilensky's compensatory leisure and Dumazedier's modified function of recuperation/relaxation): A pattern of identical dissimilarity of work and leisure and strong demarcation between the two spheres. Characterized by people with demanding physical jobs (like miners and oil rig workers) and by unskilled manual assembly-line workers who hate their work so much that any reminder of it in their off-duty time is unpleasant.

Neutrality: A pattern partly defined by a "usually different" content of work and leisure and an "average" demarcation of spheres. It denotes detachment from work rather than either passive or negative attachment. Neither fulfilling nor oppressive, these professional workers tend to be as passive and uninvolved in their leisure as they are in their work. Such workers as typists and toll bridge and highway employees have *low* autonomy and a feeling of being bored with their activity.

In viewing the *societal* level of Parker's work-leisure relationship, the following definitions are provided:

Fusion: An integration of work-leisure spheres.

Polarity: A separation of work-leisure spheres.

Containment: An overlapping sphere, in which work-leisure segments are comparatively unaffected by each other.

Parker[12] summarizes his analysis by drawing upon philosophies of holism and segmentation to compare with the general individual and societal types of work-leisure relationships.

Holism represents a person who sees that the parts of his or her life are integrated, each one affecting and being affected by the others. Such a person is likely to have an *extension* pattern of work and leisure and participate in a social circle in which the spheres of work and leisure are fused (identity).

Segmentalism represents a person who sees the parts of his or her life as *separate* segments in which either contrast or separateness work-leisure types of relationships are likely to exist.

[12]*Ibid.,* pp. 109–110.

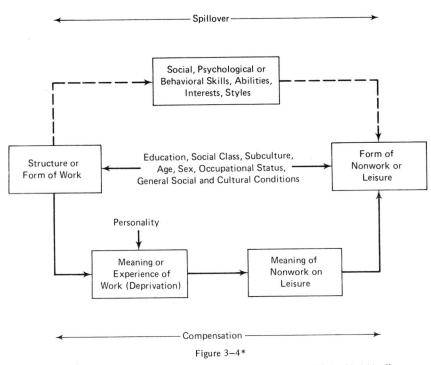

Figure 3–4*

*Kando and Summers, "The Relationship between Work and Leisure and Other Variables,"
p. 318.

Kando and Summers[13] emphasize the need to integrate the study of forms of work and leisure and their underlying significance. In other words, *similar* forms of work or nonwork may have different meanings for various individuals participating in them, or conversely, *different* forms may have similar underlying meanings. This dilemma leads to further confusion when we allow the form of work or nonwork behavior to stand for its underlying meaning because we do not recognize the impact of variables correlated with work, such as occupation, class, ethnicity, subculture, and age in addition to cultural and social conditions. These variables can all mask meanings. Kando and Summer's paradigm, The Relationship Between Work and Leisure and Other Variables, depicted in Figure 3–4, indicates how the structure of work (independent variable) affects leisure patterns (the dependent variable). This paradigm attempts to explain the complex set of relationships within which work influences nonwork.

[13]Thomas M. Kando and Worth C. Summers, "The Impact of Work and Leisure," *Pacific Sociological Review* 14:310–327, 1971.

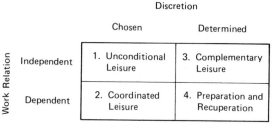

Discretion

		Chosen	Determined
Work Relation	Independent	1. Unconditional Leisure	3. Complementary Leisure
	Dependent	2. Coordinated Leisure	4. Preparation and Recuperation

Figure 3–5*

*John R. Kelly, "Work and Leisure: A Simplified Paradigm," p. 55.

(1)Work leads to the development of certain psychological, social, and behavioral skills and life styles which may spill over into nonwork and shape the leisure form; and (2) work, when it leads to a certain subjective exposure, may result in efforts to compensate for this in nonwork activity.[14]

This structure of two paths by which work affects nonwork suggests that the former—the spillover path—is one whereby form (of work) affects form (of nonwork), and the second—the compensatory path—is one whereby meaning (of work) affects meaning and secondarily form (of nonwork). Therefore, this model of work-leisure relationship indicates the importance of distinguishing between form (structure) and meaning (subjective experience). Some possible theoretical dimensions of *structure of the work situation* include complexity, supervision, training, social contacts, and technology; for *underlying meaning or significance,* alienation, boredom, intrinsic-extrinsic, self-esteem, interests, self-actualization; and for *form or pattern* of nonwork or leisure, sports, TV viewing, political activity, active-passive, ordered-disordered, highbrow-lowbrow.

Kelly[15] provides a simplified conceptual scheme for the work-leisure relationship by using the two dimensions of *freedom-discretion* and *work relation.* As is depicted in Figure 3–5, it is an attempt to explain these two dimensions using a four-called scheme. The two basic dimensions which serve as inclusive terms are defined by Kelly:

Discretion: Leisure may be either freely chosen or determined by work constraints or the pervasive norms of society. Freely chosen activity would be defined as being optional.

[14]*Ibid.,* p. 317.

[15]John R. Kelly, "Work and Leisure: A Simplified Paradigm," *Journal of Leisure Research* 4:50–62, 1972.

Work Relation: Leisure may be either independent of work or dependent in the meaning that work gives to it. The work relation includes not only the economic reward for tasks performed, but also the preparation, appearance, community relationships, residence, and demeanor required or rewarded by the work position.[16]

Kelly's leisure concepts therefore are reflected in each cell as:

Leisure 1: This is *pure* or unconditional leisure, as in the Greek ideal —*for its own sake.* This Aristotelian, classical ideal views leisure as not being work-related in content or purpose and not being an escape from work.

Leisure 2: *Coordinated* leisure, as in the spillover perspective articulated by Wilensky, is reflected in associated skills of craftsmanship, enjoyment of relationships, and high satisfaction in work, particularly as evidenced among white-collar workers.

Leisure 3: *Complementary* leisure is activity that is determined by structural or social factors (socioeconomic class and demographic variables) in form and content but is independent of the work relation. Complementary leisure is not freely chosen and is determined to a significant degree by role expectations or by the need to compensate for work conditions. In this perspective, social determinants of class, status, occupation, education, and family are related to leisure behavior. Additionally this type of leisure is identified as being *compensatory*—representative largely of blue-collar workers who see nonwork as a relief from the conditions of the job or as having no relation to the job at all.

Leisure 4: This is *recuperative or preparatory* nonwork activity that is socially determined and related to work in form and content. Such activity is identified as being either preparation for further work or recuperation from previous work responsibility. Here there is a lack of *choice:* recuperation is made necessary by past work, or preparation is required for future work. Kelly states that this form of nonwork activity is *not* leisure since preparation and recuperation are determined by the work relation and are required rather than discretionary. Not all nonwork activity is leisure, in Kelly's definition, and the primary dimension is discretion over the use of time. Cell 4 indicates that recuperation and preparation nonwork activity are not leisure. "However, leisure may be unconditional

---

[16] *Ibid.,* p. 55.

Perceived Freedom

Freedom				Constraint	
Motivation			Motivation		
Intrinsic	Intrinsic and Extrinsic	Extrinsic	Intrinsic	Intrinsic and Extrinsic	Extrinsic
(1)	(2)	(3)	(4)	(5)	(6)
Pure Leisure	Leisure– Work	Leisure– Job	Pure Work	Work– Leisure	Work– Job

← ——————————————— State of Mind ——————————————— →

Figure 3–6
A Paradigm of Leisure: A Psychological Definition*

*John Neulinger, "The Need for and the Implications of a Psychological Conception of Leisure," The Ontario Psychologist 8:15, June, 1976.

or conditioned by its own coordination with work or the influence of the roles or constraints of work. Leisure may be freely chosen or a complement to work requirements."[17]

Neulinger[18] offers a Paradigm of Leisure (Figure 3–6) which is primarily concerned with those factors that make a distinction between leisure and nonleisure possible. Neulinger's conceptual scheme includes *perceived freedom* as the primary determining characteristic, similar to Parker's model (constraint/freedom) and Kelly's paradigm (chosen/determined). However, unlike Parker's (work/nonwork) and Kelly's (work-independent/work-dependent) work-leisure models, Neulinger's scheme does not include work as the independent variable since he does not perceive work as being in opposition to leisure and therefore it cannot be part of the determining frame of leisure configuration.

The paradigm indicates that the prime distinction between leisure and nonleisure is made along the dimension of *perceived freedom*. There are three categories of motivation: *intrinsic, intrinsic and extrinsic,* and *extrinsic,* which are divided into six cells: 1 through 3 being *leisure,* and 4 through 6 *nonleisure.* Neulinger's paradigm represents a psychological orientation with behavior attributed to self rather than external forces, characteristic of sociological perspectives developed by Kelly and by Kando and Summers, for example. It is explained thus:[19]

[17]*Ibid.,* p. 61.

[18]John Neulinger, "The Need for and the Implications of a Psychological Conception of Leisure," *The Ontario Psychologist* 8:15 June, 1976.

[19]*Ibid.,* pp. 16–17.

Cell 1: This represents the purest form of leisure: an activity freely engaged in and done for its own sake—leisure in the classical sense. This *pure leisure* requires freedom in the sense of absence of external control, but implies the condition of being able to enjoy satisfaction denied from intrinsic reward without having to pay attention to potential extrinsic ones. A person's needs have been satisfied to such a degree that they no longer represent a conscious issue.

Cell 2: This type of leisure represents a wide range of activities, all of which are freely chosen and are extrinsically and intrinsically rewarding. In *leisure-work,* a person can quit whenever he or she wants to. Activities characteristic of this type of leisure are doing antique furniture refinishing, chores around the house, or carpentry work.

Cell 3: *Leisure-job* is a type of leisure since one engages in it without coercion but the satisfaction does not come from the activity itself, but from its consequence. Examples of this form of recreation include playing cards for money, playing a game to overcome fatigue, or engaging in athletics (such as jogging or tennis) to be in good health. The activity, while reflecting an experience of perceived freedom, is only extrinsically rewarding, thus resembling a job.

Cell 4: This behavior is denoted as nonleisure since it is undertaken under constraint. It is labeled *pure work* because it is intrinsically rewarding only. Examples include doing homework in which one is very interested or being involved in compulsory responsibilities that one enjoys (such as mowing the lawn).

Cell 5: This category represents *work-leisure,* behavior engaged in under constraint but having both intrinsic and extrinsic rewards. The work experience is satisfying in and of itself and the very sense of satisfaction is likely to render less the perception of constraint.

Cell 6: Behavior in the (*work-job*) category represents the opposition of leisure: an activity engaged in by necessity and under constraint and with no reward in and of itself, but only through a payoff resulting from it. Neulinger comments that this form of nonleisure is a job one *has* to have in order to earn a living, one that is of no interest other than for its monetary rewards.

Neulinger's model distinguishes between work and job, suggesting that work does have aspects of both leisure and nonleisure. The difference (perceived freedom) and the similarity (intrinsic motivation) of leisure-work and work-leisure are apparent and both are contrasted with the job. Second, the model clarifies the role the individual plays in creating the conditions of leisure. "It is evident that, to a large degree, a person's perception of freedom is a function of his position in society.

It is the result of factors over which he, as an individual, has relatively little control."[20] However, since motivation is a personal response, the individual has the potential for change in this respect, for personal growth and for overcoming limitations.

TWO VIEWS OF INTERPRETING HUMAN NATURE

It should be recognized that there are essentially two popular approaches to interpreting human behavior (notwithstanding the major philosophical approaches reviewed in Chapter 2). One is the *structural-functional* perspective, serving as a sociological tactic, and the other is a *social action* approach, primarily a psychological view of human nature. The structural-functional model emphasizes the importance of institutional and societal forces in shaping and constraining human behavior. The social action approach to behavior emphasizes the importance of subjective factors, and Homo sapiens is seen as acting on and influencing a given situation rather than just reacting passively to events. Haworth and Smith elaborate:

> The perceptions and meanings which the actor (individual) ascribes to a situation are considered to play a significant part in influencing choice and action options. Norms and values are located in man as well as in the situation. Thus in this case also, man is not seen as just a passive recipient of the external world but as constantly interpreting and shaping its meanings for himself through a universe of symbols. Hence, social interactions are affected by background expectancies, and individuals interact in terms of shared meanings or meanings they attribute to each other's actions.[21]

The social action approach views the nature of reality in light of subjective experience, with greater weight being given the importance of general cognitive factors in determining the outcome of the interplay between Homo sapeins and the environment. The structural-functional school has been criticized by Glasser as the primary reason that leisure is treated as a residual instead of as an integral part of life. In this regard the technological bases of Western society is steadily forcing people to abandon any hope of fulfillment through working hours and to seek it during leisure time. In this transition from a craft-based society disciplined by religion to one based on technology in which religion is weak and moral goals are indistinct, there is a tendency for sociologists and

---

[20]*Ibid.,* p. 22.

[21]J. T. Haworth and M. A. Smith. *Work and Leisure: An Interdisciplinary Study in Theory, Education and Planning* (Princeton, N.J.: Princeton Book Co., 1976), pp. 3–4.

many leisure scholars to investigate and interpret leisure purely as a demand for facilities. This treatment typically does not involve the examination of the nature and extent and the merits of the desires that produce the demand. Glasser comments:

> This demand for facilities is to be met in the same non-normative manner as any other in our rational society, by counting heads, by the marketing approach, a view that regards the leisure phenomenon in the same way as the demand for sewage disposal, for water supplies, for roads to drive upon, for tranquilizer pills or beer, cinemas or contraceptives. This view of leisure sees only the time to be filled, not why the demand presents itself in certain forms, whether all these forms are valid according to some accepted standard of moral value, or whether they may be evidence of deeper needs that are not being satisfied by the conditions and policies of modern society.[22]

Such a supply and demand approach to work and leisure interpreted by structural-functional theorists has a simplistic view of human nature—one which holds that the answer to the needs of the human condition is to organize an unlimited supply of distraction and forgetfulness. As a result we must fill every moment of free time. We remove symptoms of discontent by means of organized leisure distraction. Glasser suggests that in high-consumption societies we use tranquilizers to eliminate the conditions that produce pain and friction with the environment. In this vein, the supply-and-demand philosophical view treats leisure as merely a different kind of tranquilizer.[23] He suggests that it is more theoretically sound and more representative of the complex nature of the human condition in studying human behavior to use a social action hypothetical form of the individual who conceives goals, and who attempts to realize them in his or her way of life. A social action perspective of human behavior suggests that an individual's own goal setting and behavior will condition one's attempts at fulfillment in one's freely disposable time. The compulsion of the individual, governing all of his or her actions and attitudes, is to pursue a desired identity. "People have a basic need to attain an identity that is as close as possible to that which society and the inherited culture sets up as a standard of emulation."[24] *Leisure is thus seen as an integral part of the pursuit of a desirable identity.*

> People demonstrate by their choice, in clothes, furniture, speech, manners, leisure activities, friends, as far as possible work, their individual interpretation of the ideal identity they are pursuing. The goals of leisure and life are inseparable, as are the means of achieving them. Leisure is

[22]R. Glasser, "Leisure Policy, Identity and Work," in Haworth and Smith, *Work and Leisure,* p. 36.

[23]*Ibid.,* pp. 37–38.

[24]*Ibid.,* p. 42.

not a residual, to be viewed on criteria different from those we must employ in choosing the abilities, directions, behavior we adopt in life as a whole.[25]

TOWARD THE WORK SOCIETY

According to Aristotle, work had a purpose outside itself (work was a means) while leisure was viewed as an end in itself. In ancient Greece and Rome work was explicitly connected with a slave class and leisure with the free class (the elite aristocracy). In a primitive social order, work and leisure are fused, as are all institutions. In the pre-industrial, feudal social order, the beginning of a work-leisure differentiation appeared: while the masses worked, the elites, who were free from labor, engaged in intellectual pursuits. With the movement toward an industrial order, the work-leisure distinction became fairly complete, with separate work-leisure roles, clothes, settings, expenditures, and the like. As American and Canadian societies have become increasingly characteristic of a post-industrial social order, a refusion process appears to be emerging: the work-leisure dichotomy is decreasing, and a neoprimitive synthesis of daily routine is breaking down the strict separation of work-leisure behavior. See Table 3–1 for a historical summary of the evolution of community life, work, and free time.

In primitive and pre-industrial societies "man" was defined chiefly as a creature of leisure, *Homo ludens,* but with the appearance of bourgeois society in the industrialized culture, "man" became defined as a working being, *Homo faber,* a tool-making animal. Johan Huzinga[26] explores the play element in culture and concludes that the need to play is instinctive and that play is engaged in simply for fun; it reaches beyond all moral, biological, and esthetic consideration. *Homo faber,* in contrast, is concerned with the Protestant Work Ethic, "the ethic of serving God by extreme restraint, by giving up pleasure, by constant work and the accumulation of means for spreading the material basis for work."[27] However, both conceptualizations, of "man" explicitly as a fun-seeking creature or as a tool-maker, diminish "man's" characterization as Homo sapiens, a multidimensional being.

HISTORICAL MEANINGS OF WORK

The emergence of work as a distinct concept is a relatively modern phenomenon, and the more specific reference to employment is an even more recent development. As noted earlier in this chapter, Green com-

[25]*Ibid.,* pp. 49–50.

[26]Johan Huzinga. *Homo Ludens: A Study of the Play Element in Culture* (Boston: Beacon Press, 1955).

[27]Jonce Josifovski, "Work and Leisure," *Society and Leisure* 2: 11, 1970.

ments on the distinction between work and labor that existed in early civilizations. Roughly, labor meant providing for the necessities of life —a concept symbolic of Homo sapien's subservience to the physical laws of nature. Principally, this activity was performed by slaves or a class of laborers. Work was seen in a different perspective: it was a type of creative, intellectual expression engaged in by free citizens and the elite class. However, as frequently noted by historians, the idea that there could be a meaningful way of life separate from the voluntary pursuit of intellectual and creative ideas deemed relevant and significant *did not occur* among such people in antiquity nor was work a *barrier* to the advance of the culture.

Parker comments on the lack of a sharply drawn line between labor and leisure in early civilizations, under preliterate conditions:

> In so far as there is no separate "leisure class," the separation of productive activities into work and labor is also less obvious in more civilized societies. Primitive people tend to approach a great many of their daily activities as if they were play. The orientation of life is towards long periods of work interspersed with occasional periods of intense expenditure of energy.[28]

As such, in preliterate societies (depicted essentially as "folk" societies in Table 3–1) there are no clearly defined periods of leisure per se, but economic activities, like hunting and market-going, have their recreational aspects. Similarly, telling stories, singing, and so forth at work have a comparable relationship, but the idea of setting aside a period of time for enjoyment is unfamiliar in most preliterate societies.

The evolvement of the concept of work has changed since the existence of early civilization and appears principally to have been altered by the occurrence of four factors: (1) the shift from dominance of nonscientific and ritualized natural laws to prevalence of societal orientation governed by science and technology; (2) a shift from a nomadic food-gathering, agrarian orientation to a highly mechanized, specialized, and technologically dependent economy, characterized by consumption; (3) shift from highly moral and religious influence on daily routine and afterlife to emergence of highly personal, self-regulatory and autonomous basis of existence and control over one's destiny; and (4) "the degree to which work and leisure are experienced in fact and in ideology as separate parts of life seems to be related to the degree to which society is stratified, work being the lot of the masses and leisure of the *elite.*"[29]

[28]Parker, *Future of Work,* p. 39.
[29]*Ibid.,* p. 41.

Table 3-1
Transformation of Culture: Toward a Society of Leisure.

	FOLK SOCIETY	FEUDAL SOCIETY	INDUSTRIAL SOCIETY	POST-INDUSTRIAL SOCIETY
Community Life	Small, isolated, non-literate, homogeneous communities with a strong sense of group solidarity. No distinction of class. Social structure is rigid. Mobility is slow and infrequent. Organic, human relationships.	Relatively large peasant population and small elite. More stratified and more heterogeneous. Small core of literate persons, priestly class. Some government apparatus. Integration of all phases of daily life for aristocracy.	Large community size and relatively dense population. Heterogeneity of people and cultures. Anonymity, transitory and impersonal relationships. Social mobility. Fluid class system, mass literacy. Predominance of secondary contracts.	Shared community decision-making based on pluralistic, cooperative relationships.
Work Life	Energies wholly oriented toward the quest for food. Little or no specialization of labor. No food surplus. People produce their own artifacts.	More occupationally differentiated than folk communities. Trade, commerce, and craft specializations well developed.	Occupational specialization, division of labor. Economy of scarcity dominated by manual labor, assembly-line work.	Economy of abundance, economic independence. Still large work force dominated by science and technology. Growing number of craftsmen and artisans characterized by individualistic, nonmachine and stylistic qualities.
Free Time	Behavior is traditional, spontaneous, spiritual, personal. Sacred prevails over secular. Leisure is part of living, condition interwoven into the main fabric of life.	Leisure available to an elite upper class, integrated into the rituals, celebrations, weddings, and day-to-day routines of the masses.	Mass leisure. Leisure a specific block of time, earned from work. Socially acceptable leisure behavior predominates.	Individualized and liberated leisure based on inherent right and specified by particular individual needs. Many personal options, diverse styles of life. Fusion of work-leisure relationships.

Essentially there have been four dominant philosophies of work:

1. The absence of a sharp demarcation between work and leisure in most preliterate (folk) and rural societies characterized by two aspects: "the more leisurely character of work, but the greater importance of nonwork obligations as compared with the type of leisure most often experienced in modern industrial societies."[30]

2. The ancient Greek view in which work was seen as an important function of the free citizens to engage in the pursuit of intellectual and creative endeavors, and in which labor (providing for the physical needs of society) was relegated as unworthy of the "leisure class."

3. The view of various forms of Protestantism which have exerciced the most influence on modern industrial work. Work is seen primarily as an activity which derives meaning from religious sanctions. Work justifications are not intrinsic to the activity and experience, but are religious rewards.

4. The Renaissance view of work, which sees it as intrinsically meaningful, centered on technical craftsmanship—the manual and mental operations—of the work process itself. It identifies the reasons for work in the work itself and not in any ulterior realm or consequences.

THE PROBLEM OF WORK AND LEISURE

The problem of leisure and the problem of work are seen as a dual dilemma. On the other hand, the quantity of free time is increasing (refer to Chapter 4, which shows, for example, how "free time" has increased and work time remained largely the same). On the other, continued routinization of work, application of automation in industry, reduction of physically arduous work requirements, and job compartmentalization have led to increased boredom among workers. Worker dissatisfaction is increasing in some forms of work; given more time off the job, workers tend to choose more income, a second job, and overtime instead of leisure. However, the time may be approaching when continued development of automation and technological progress will ultimately mean that more people will choose leisure because the choice will not be dictated by economic necessity.[31] There still exists in contemporary society people who cringe at the notion of being able to have a job and experience pleasure as well, because, according to the Protestant Work Ethic, one should endure pain and suffering through labor

---

[30]*Ibid.,* p. 41.
[31]*Ibid.,* p. 11.

for a more heavenly reward. The future relationship of work and leisure, Stanley Parker suggests, should be complementary rather than one sphere of life having more value than another.

> .... experts in the various social sciences agree that both work and leisure are necessary to a healthy life and healthy society.... Maximum human development in both work and leisure spheres requires that they be complementary rather than that one be regarded as "good" and the other "bad."[32]

Parker cites some evidence that people who are minimally involved in their work are similarly uninvolved in their leisure, and that frustration in one area accompanies frustration in another. The antiquated work ethic has been rejected by youth and others outside the mainstream who do not find the ideals and proposed means of a capitalist nation to be as free, self-fulfilling, and satisfying as promised. Even workers in more traditional blue-collar occupations are now fed up with the unfulfilled promises of a free enterprise system which has continually been fraught with inflation, denying workers the fruits of their labor: a decent income, oppportunity to spend it on essentials and on avocational interests, and a chance to continue to engage in their work without the fear of a declining market, largely a result of increased governmental crackdowns and regulations responding to the need to curb further exploitation of limited resources. Fulfillment in both work and leisure seemingly will require a coordinated program to realize human potentialities.

The task of the worker is absurd when viewed out of context. A task has meaning only when it is related to the production of an object. Separating the task of the industrial worker from the point of completion or fulfillment has meant that much of the craftsmanship and meaning have been eliminated from work. Mass leisure pursuits, particularly various forms of mass entertainment and spectator events, also have weaned individual skill requirements, achievement, and spontaneity from experiences. In both instances, participation in modern technological society has become not a part of life, but a *means* to life, in which both working and playing are seen as things of merely extrinsic value, useful only if they permit the individual to escape the frustration and alienation of other spheres of life.

According to Leo Perlis,[33] we are faced not only with more free time off the job, but with a duller time on the job, and both problems require our attention.

---

[32]*Ibid.,* p. 12.

[33]Leo Perlis, "Implications for Labor Unionism," in *Technology, Human Values and Leisure,* ed. Max Kaplan and Philip Bosserman (Nashville: Abingdon Press, 1971), pp. 99–100.

Assembly-line or push-button work in modern times is no great joy in itself. There is no diversity. There is no craftsmanship. There is no opportunity for achievement. There is no chance for excellence. There is only the time clock every day and the paycheck every week. There was a time when a man fulfilled himself in large party by the job he did. There are many men who still derive a sense of fulfillment from their occupation, although the complete man concept has rapidly been gaining ground so that the job no longer means as much as it once did.

WORK SATISFACTION

There appears to be a growing correlation between work dissatisfaction and the amount of available opportunity for workers to become a part of the entire work process, to be able to exercise more creative control over the tasks involved, to receive recognition, and to have available channels for professional growth and advancement. Employee satisfaction seems to be linked with inexorable change in the rhythm of industrial life which intersects with community life as expressed in more freedom of personal movement in all of one's daily life spheres: family, education, work, and leisure.

Studies over the past thirty years seem to demonstrate that what workers want most is to become masters of their immediate environment and to feel that their work and they themselves are important.[34] These studies have shown that an increasing number of workers want more autonomy in handling their tasks, greater opportunity for increasing their skills, rewards that are directly connected to the intrinsic aspects of work, and greater participation in the design of work and the formulation of their tasks.

The desire for more meaning by workers in their jobs as represented by intrinsic rewards is shown in a study by the Survey Research Center, University of Michigan; 1,533 respondents, a representative sample of American workers at all occupational levels, were asked to rank some of the 25 aspects of work in order of importance to them. The eight most important items were tabulated as follows.

1. Interesting work
2. Enough help and equipment to get the job done
3. Enough information to get the job done
4. Enough authority to get the job done
5. Good pay

[34]Robert L. Kahn, "The Meaning of Work: Interpretation and Proposals for Measurement," in *The Human Meaning of Social Change*, ed. A. A. Campbell and P. E. Converse (New York: Basic Books, 1972).

6. Opportunity to develop special abilities
7. Job security
8. Seeing the results of one's work

There is confusion over the question of worker satisfaction. One must discern: what type of work is the employee engaged in and, given his or her choice, would the person change jobs. Typically, many studies have reported that the professional, upper managerial, and education-related employees are most satisfied with their work while unskilled laborers, assembly-line workers, and all clerical people are most dissatisfied with their work (refer to Table 3–2).

Even so, various Gallup polls have shown that upwards to 60 percent of auto and assembly-line workers find their work "interesting." However, a significant report by a special task force on work in America stated that:

> Since a substantial portion of blue-collar workers (1) report being satisfied with their jobs *but also indicate they wish to change them* and (2) report they would continue working even if they didn't have to *but only to fill time,* then this can only mean that these workers accept the necessity of work but expect little satisfaction from their specific jobs.[35]

In other words, perhaps what such workers are indicating is that they are not dissatisfied with work as it relates to pay and security but their work may not be intrinsically rewarding or correlated with their newly accustomed liberated life style which has given them a greater range of opportunities for personal expression. Another measure of work satisfaction has been a response to the question: "What type of work would you try to get into if you could start again?" The percentage distribution of those who said they would choose the same work is shown in Table 3–3.

Most significantly, of a cross-section of white-collar workers, only 43 percent said they would voluntarily choose the work they were doing and only 24 percent of a cross-section of blue-collar workers would choose the same kind of work if given another chance.

Satisfaction appears to be most characteristic of high-status workers and of crafts people, groups that have autonomy, opportunity to work on a "whole" problem, and participation in decision-making. Unfortunately, employment opportunities in the 1970's were concentrated in middle and lower levels of the occupational structure. The principle of "scientific management" as espoused by Frederick Taylor in *The Principles of Scientific Management* (Harper, 1911) helped to propagate a view of work which remained largely successful for many years.

[35]James O'Toole. *Work in America* (Cambridge, Mass.: The MIT Press, 1973), p. 14.

Table 3–2
Hypothesized Occupational Differences in Job Satisfaction*

OCCUPATION	MOST SATISFIED	VERY SATISFIED	SATISFIED	AMBIVALENT	SLIGHTLY SATISFIED	SOMEWHAT DISSATISFIED
Professional-Technical	Professor Librarian School teacher (female)	Public adviser Other people-oriented Nurse Artist	Scientist Accountant	Engineer School teacher (male)	Technician	
Management	Salaried (upper management)	Salaried (other)	Self-employed (large firm)		Self-employed (other)	
Sales			High-status	Sales clerk (female)		Sales clerk (male)
Clerical			Secretary Bookkeeper	Miscellaneous clerical		Repetitive clerical
Skilled			Foreman			
Semiskilled				Craftsman	Skilled	
Unskilled				Higher	Middle	Laborer
Service		Protective	Armed	Household Other (female)		Other (male)
Farmer		Owner (large)		Owner (small)		Laborer

*Robert L. Kahn, "The Work Module: A Proposal for the Humanization of Work," in Work and the Quality of Life, ed. James O'Toole (Cambridge, Mass.: The MIT Press, 1974), p. 209.

Table 3–3

Percentage of Workers Saying They Would
Choose Similar Work Again*

OCCUPATION	PERCENT	OCCUPATION	PERCENT
PROFESSIONAL AND WHITE-COLLAR		SKILLED TRADES AND BLUE -COLLAR	
Urban university professors	93	Skilled printers	52
Mathematicians	91	Paper workers	42
Physicists	89	Skilled auto workers	41
Biologists	89	Skilled steelworkers	41
Chemists	86	Textile workers	31
Firm lawyers	85	Blue-collar workers	24
School superintendents	85	Unskilled steelworkers	21
Lawyers	83	Unskilled auto workers	16
Journalists (Washington correspondents)	82		
Church university professors	77		
Solo lawyers	75		
White-collar workers (nonprofessionals)	43		

*Robert L. Kahn, "The Work Module: A Proposal for the Humanization of Work," in Work and the Quality of Life, ed. James O'Toole (Cambridge Mass.: The MIT Press, 1974), p. 204.

Briefly, he articulated a view of efficiency in which work tasks were simplified, fragmented, compartmentalized, and placed under the scrutiny of continuous supervision. This approach to management, combined with diminishing opportunities for people to be independent and autonomous like the small business person, had become representative of fewer than 9 percent of work classifications by the late 1970's.

A number of individuals, such as Argyris,[36] McGregor,[37] Maslow,[38] and Sheppard and Herrick,[39] have suggested that there is an inevitable conflict between contemporary humans and organizational needs, especially as evidenced in mass production industry. According to such views:

1. Workers are seeking social acceptance, independence, and personal growth. They are desirous of ascending Maslow's hierarchy of needs scale from physical, through safety, social, and egoistic, to self-actualization needs. These "universal" needs, which ascend from basic survival needs to higher ones, contributing to a fuller expression of the "whole" person, are deemed desired by workers on the job.

[36]Chris Argyris. *Human Behavior in Organizations* (New York: Harper and Row, Publishers, 1954).

[37]Douglas McGregor. *The Human Side of Enterprise* (New York: McGraw-Hill Book Company, 1960).

[38]A. H. Maslow. *The Farther Reaches of Human Nature* (New York: Viking Press, Inc., 1961).

[39]Harold L. Sheppard and Neal Q. Herrick. *Where Have All the Robots Gone? Worker Dissatisfaction in the 70's* (New York: The Free Press, 1972).

2. Typically, organizations fail to recognize these needs and follow what McGregor has referred to as "Theory X" assumptions, that is, that workers dislike work, are lazy, and wish to avoid responsibility. As a result, organizations force workers to behave in an immature and dependent fashion.

3. As a consequence, workers have become alienated from their jobs. The blue- and occasionally white-collar "trap" results in workers' rebuffing the old work ethic (through union activity, sabotage, output restriction, absenteeism, etc.),[40] or they withdraw and produce no more than a minimum amount of work. Typically, management's response is tighter controls through closer supervision, resulting in still further employee resentment and anger.

4. The only way to eliminate this vicious cycle is for management to adopt "Theory Y" assumptions about human nature, that is, that people enjoy work and can exercise self-control and that they are imaginative and creative. Management should therefore develop policies that promote intrinsic job satisfaction and individual development.

While some of the preceding discussion of blue-collar worker reactions to the contemporary work place is apparently related to shifts in the economic cycle, a significant change in values seems to be occurring, inflation and tax revolt not withstanding. An important question must be asked: "How important is work in human life?" It is apparently quite important, particularly as it provides a meaning to life for many people, and especially males. However, work problems spill over into off-the-job settings too. Studs Terkel's exhaustive volume *Working* tells, for example, of the frustrated assembly-line workers who often displaced their job-generated aggression on family, neighbors, and strangers. And perhaps most important, there is a changing shift in values as was characteristic among workers during the 1940's and 1950's when having *steady work* was the single most important factor in their jobs. Similarly a study by Herzberg[41] revealed that among job factors influencing satisfaction, interesting work ranked fifth in importance behind job security, opportunities for advancement, company and management policies, and wages. By sharp contrast in a 1969 survey by Herrick,[42] interesting work came first and job security was rated seventh, and six of the eight most desired aspects of work were related to job content.

While there have been increased efforts on the part of management to "humanize" the work environment, to provide greater employee

---

[40]"Is the Work Ethic Going Out of Style?" *Time* October 30, 1972, pp. 96–97.

[41]Frederick Herzberg et al. *Job Attitudes: A Review of Research and Opinion* (Pittsburgh: Psychological Service of Pittsburgh, 1957).

[42]Neal Q. Herrick, "Who's Unhappy with Work and Why?" *Manpower* 4, No. 1 (January 1972), 5.

involvement in the whole process, and to respond to the workers' off-the-job needs, some critics suggest these steps may be nothing more than a ploy to induce workers to increase output. This may be so, but a variety of organizational changes have occurred in recent years, seemingly representing a response to the changing rhythm of life—one which is becoming more reflective of a balance among work-leisure-education spheres.

The primary goal of organizations is organizational effectiveness, or increased and better output through positive human factors. Most managements realize that they must create an environment "in which employees can work effectively to accomplish the goals of the enterprise and at the same time obtain substantial satisfaction of their needs."[43] Managerial styles and attitudes are changing concerning the nature of human beings. New concepts of management have emerged —participative management, job redesign, job enrichment, positive motivation, supportive leadership—all of which recognize the human needs of autonomy, achievement, self-expression.[44] These new concepts appear to contribute toward a worker's self-direction, self-control, and worker choice.

These new concepts reflect increased freedom of choice through the work cycle by a large segment of our society. Three main categories became evident: variable work time, such as the rearranged workweek and flextime; variable employment patterns, such as job sharing, leisure sharing, and part-time work; and variable benefits, such as insurance and corporate child day care. Alternatives to the traditional work environment and worker choice will contribute to the view that the employee is a rational, responsible person.

VIEWS REGARDING THE REDUCTION AND REORGANIZATION OF THE WORKWEEK

Essentially there are three principal developments that have occurred in recent years with respect to the reduction of the workweek: (1) there is a movement toward decreasing the importance of work by decreasing the number of hours worked and at the same time increasing the emphasis on the importance of leisure; (2) there is a movement toward making the workweek more meaningful by encouraging worker involvement in company policy, attempting to improve the working conditions, and enriching work itself; and (3) there is an at-

[43]Dale S. Beach. *Personnel, the Management of People at Work* (New York: Macmillan Publishing Co., 1975), p. 29.
[44]*Ibid.,* p. 44.

tempt to overcome the obstacles of rising unemployment by reducing the workweek while elevating the value of leisure with a long-term goal of redistributing work, education, and leisure throughout one's life in order to develop a more cyclic lifetime pattern.

1. Experiments with Reduced Workweeks

The experiments with four-day workweeks, while generally increasing, have not had a significant impact on shortening the workweek. In essence the question emerges: "What is the meaning of the four-day week? A retreat from work or assent to leisure?" It might be neither. However, as previously noted, the gross reduction of work hours is appearing to have an effect on the personal life rhythms of some workers who are getting accustomed to having one more day of concentrated free time. This has resulted in a lessening of the almost religious sanctity of work and in a new measurement standard for judging the worth of work—the leisure sphere serving to provide the worth of work—the leisure sphere serving to provide the standard by which work is judged. The question now is *whether one's work blends with the rest of one's life rhythm, as opposed to the traditional yardstick of requiring everyone to adjust to the work rhythm of life* regardless of the demands of family, education, or other concerns.

The movement from the customary five-day, 40-hour workweek to a four-day, 32- to 36-hour workweek gained momentum during the late 1960's and 1970's. J. D. Hodgson, former Secretary of Labor, commented on the gains in leisure as a result of a reformation of our working life, attributable to (1) the five Monday holidays which provide new opportunities for the American worker to indulge in leisure-time pursuits; (2) earlier retirement, creating additional blocks of leisure for the worker; (3) the sabbatical, which has become more extensive; and (4) shifts (reductions) in work life since the turn of the century, resulting in time free of the necessity of earning a living.[45] Additionally, Hodgson noted that the shift in the ratio of working hours to leisure hours has had the following effects on the average American workers: (1) it has made them more conscious of the opportunities of their leisure hours; (2) with more money in their pocket, they have become culture conscious; and (3) it has also increased the demand for professional recreation workers.[46]

The future arrangement of work and leisure may be very different from today's pattern. Phillip Bosserman[47] characterizes industrial soci-

---

[45]J. D. Hodgson, "Leisure and the American Worker," *Leisure Today* 1(1972).

[46]*Ibid.*

[47]Phillip Bosserman, "Implications for Youth," in *Technology, Human Values and Leisure,* ed. Kaplan and Bosserman, pp. 117–163.

ety as one of uniformity, standardization, and homogeneity, and the leisure (post-industrial) society as one of diversity, life styles, income, and discretionary time. Because individuals seek to be identified by their life style and cultural taste rather than by their occupations, an important shift in values and central life interest emerges in a post-industrial economy. With a renaissance of interest in the inner or affective side of life, the work order will have to promote human fulfillment as its primary conscious goal and foster an environment in which flexibility and options are available to the worker. Bosserman suggests several options which might be available to the worker, whose length of stay in any one job will decrease.[48]

Daily half days, 5 days a week
half nights, 5 nights a week
2 days and 2 nights each week
3 days a week at 12 hours each day
4 days a week at 10 hours each day
Or any other combination, depending on the job and the employee.

Weekly 3 weeks each month
6 weeks on and 3 weeks off at 40 hours each week
Or any other combination, again depending on the nature of the work and the personal needs of the employee. Actualization is the goal.

Monthly 6 months on and 6 months off
3 months on and 3 months off
2 months on and 2 months off
8 months on and 8 months off
Any combination would be feasible, again considering the job.

Yearly 2 years on and 1/2 year off
5 years on and 1 year off
Again, any combination is conceivable.

"It is the task of society . . . not to impose a pattern of social relationships on the individual but to offer him a set of alternatives."[49]

Other efforts used by industry, business and human services to experiment with reduced or altered workweeks include the following:

Job Sharing. Essentially this concept means two people divide one job between them, thus providing full-time coverage, with each being responsible for half the work. They share salary and benefits. They may each work a shorter workweek, rotate or stagger shifts, or use any other method by which work hours are reduced. Examples of occupations include microbiologist, research assistant, attorney, or teacher.

[48]*Ibid.*, pp. 162–163.
[49]Parker, *Future of Work*, p. 117.

Job Pairing. This approach is one in which two people share one full-time job with equal responsibility for the total job, each working only half-time but together providing full-time coverage. Examples include curator, account specialist, parole officer, or property assessment technician.

Split-Level Work. This concept refers to work which requires two distinct levels of training or ability. Two employees, each working half time at different skill and pay levels, provide full-time coverage for a single job. Examples include training officer, job service assistant, or medical technologist/research analyst.

Leisure Sharing. This concept, coined by Senator James Mills of California, is a new work strategy enabling workers to trade income for more free time. Commonly, this term has been referred to as work or job sharing. The idea would allow workers the option of selecting more free time and exchanging their vacant work slot with someone who has *too much* leisure according to Senator Mills.[50] In effect, such a redistribution system of work hours would allow for more flexible work and leisure hours and help to reduce unemployment. Mills selected the term "leisure sharing" instead of "work sharing" for two primary reasons. First, work sharing is a narrow application of a broader concept. Second, he is attempting to overcome the outmoded Puritan Ethic and give support to those who choose to work less (or not at all). It is through such a modification that one can be viewed as making a positive contribution to social well-being without the stigma of not being actively involved in the work force steadily throughout one's adult years. According to this plan, if every one of the 70 million full-time workers in the United States took off an extra hour each year, and the production represented by the cumulative amount of time lost could be recovered by making additional jobs, the economy would gain 1.6 million new full-time jobs.

2. Job Enrichment and Innovations in the Work Place

One approach to improving the *context* of the work place has been innovative efforts to improve the *content* of the job itself—through the redesign of work. The aspects of job content that workers complain most about are fractionalization, repetition, and lack of control; there is a desire for more variety and autonomy. Various solutions have been proposed. The examples listed here were incorporated by a General Foods manufacturing plant:

Autonomous Work Groups. Self-management work teams of from eight to twelve members were formed and given collective responsibil-

---

[50]James R. Mills, "New Supply of Jobs," *Townhall Journal,* June 28, 1977, pp. 224–226.

ity for larger segments of the productive process. These work teams were large enough to handle a full set of tasks and small enough to allow face-to-face meetings for decision-making and coordination.

Integrated Support Functions. Activities typically performed by support units such as custodial and personnel units were built into the operating team's responsibilities. The team accepted full responsibility for seeing to it that they maintained quality standards.

Challenging Job Assignments. The plant endeavored to design every set of tasks to include functions requiring higher human abilities and responsibilities. Where possible, they also tried to eliminate dull or routine jobs.

Job Mobility and Reward for Learning. By developing a single job classification for all operators, with pay increases geared to mastering an increasing proportion of jobs, first within the team and then in the plant, General Foods rewarded team members for learning more and more aspects of the total manufacturing system. Since there were no limits on the number of personnel who could qualify for higher pay levels, employees were encouraged to teach each other.

Facilitative Leadership. In lieu of "supervisors" whose responsibilities are to plan, direct, and control the work of subordinates, a "team leader" position was developed with the responsibility to facilitate team development and decision-making. Ultimately it was envisioned that in time the team leader position might not be required.

Managerial Decision Information for Operators. The new plant design called for operators to be provided with economic information and managerial decision rules enabling production decisions ordinarily made higher up in the organization to be made at the operator or front-line level.

Self-Government for the Plant Community. The new plant design provided for rules for plant management to evolve from collective experience. This procedure enabled everyone to participate in the governance of the plant.

Congruent Physical and Social Context. An important concern which served as a divisive factor in creating a pecking order was minimized by reducing differential status symbols that characterize traditional work organizations. For example, a common decor was maintained throughout offices, cafeteria, locker room, and so forth and the parking lot was open to everyone. The overall technology and architecture was designed to facilitate rather than discourage the congregating of team members during working hours.[51]

---

[51]O'Toole, *Work in America*, pp. 96–98.

3. Toward a Lifetime Redistribution of Work, Education, and Leisure

As indicated earlier, the industrial rhythm of life has been dominant in Western culture. According to this *linear life plan,* most persons in our society enter the world and engage in mostly play activities prior to going to school, then start their formal education in youth, work during the adult and middle years, and eventually retire between age 60 and 65. While this pattern has emerged as a product of the industrial economical structure, the tremendous growth of economic productivity, individual autonomy precipitated mobility and increased personal discretionary income have resulted in tremendous increases in nonwork time as a proportion of one's total lifetime. The New York Metropolitan Life Insurance Company computed the years of total lifetimes spent in major life activities during different stages of societal development; Figure 3–7 provides a dramatic illustration of this growth in non-work time. These estimates indicate that about 33 percent of the primitive era person's total lifetime was spent on work, 28.6 percent of an agricultural person's lifetime, and about 13.5 percent of an industrial era person's life.[52]

The largest increase of nonwork time has come in the form of a reduced workweek. As noted by Hedges and Moore[53] the average U.S. workweek has declined from approximately 60 hours to 39 hours over the last century. However, during much of the last three decades the workweek has remained substantially the same and much of the increased nonwork time has come in the form of longer vacations and more holidays.[54]

Similarly, a study by Robinson[55] revealed that changes in the use of time between 1965 and 1975 showed a stability in the workweek but a sharp decline in hours devoted to family care. As can be noted from Table 3–4, "Changes in the Use of Time, 1965–1975," the amount of free time increased by four hours, beyond the requirements for sleep, work, family care, and personal care. This shift in the amount of time available for personal discretion indicates perhaps a gradual shift in values of members of society. Kelly notes that this real shift in values may be reflected in the increase in free time of four hours a week.

Many persons do not treat their leisure as residual. The residual approach assumes that once everything else is completed, there is time left over for

---

[52]John McHale, "World Facts and Trends," *Futures,* September 1971, p. 260.

[53]Janice Hedges and Geoffrey Moore, "Trends in Labor and Leisure," *Monthly Labor Review,* February 1971.

[54]John D. Owen, "Workweeks and Leisure: An Analysis of Trends, 1948–1978," *Monthly Labor Review,* August 1976.

[55]John P. Robinson. *How Americans Use Time.* (New York: Praeger Publishers, 1977).

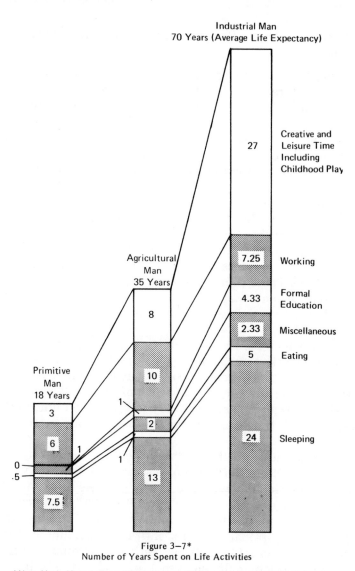

Industrial Man
70 Years (Average Life Expectancy)

27 Creative and
    Leisure Time
    Including
    Childhood Play

7.25 Working

4.33 Formal
      Education

2.33 Miscellaneous

5 Eating

24 Sleeping

Agricultural
Man
35 Years

8

10

2

13

Primitive
Man
18 Years

3

6

1

1

0

.5

7.5

1

1

Figure 3–7*
Number of Years Spent on Life Activities

*New York Metropolitan Life Insurance Company. Cited from McHale,
John, "World Facts and Trends," Futures, September 1971, p. 260.

leisure. The marked increase in such time for leisure suggests that more
and more persons are giving priority to that aspect of their lives and
compressing the "duties" related to family and household maintenance.[56]

These data suggest the possibility that we may have reached or
perhaps passed a point of "diminishing returns" for the linear life plan.

[56]Kelly, Leisure, Chapter 8.

Table 3-4
Changes in Use of Time: 1965-1975

	1965 URBAN SAMPLE	1975 URBAN SAMPLE
Sleep	53.3	54.7
Work for pay	33.0	32.5
Family care	25.4	20.5
Personal care	21.5	21.5
Free time	34.8	38.8
Total hours/week	168.0	168.0

John P. Robinson. How Americans Use Time *(New York: Praeger Publishers, 1977).*

Additionally, it has been suggested that there may be likely alternatives to the linear lifetime patterns, including a "cyclic life plan." This pattern's main idea is that current time spent on education and retirement be redistributed to the center of life in the form of extended periods of leisure or education.

In their treatise of the lifetime distribution of education, work and leisure, Fred Best and Barry Stern analyzed the significant variables influencing the emergence of a cyclic lifetime trend. The following is a summary of these factors.[57]

Demographics. The distribution of age cohorts, longevity, and health are important considerations. Briefly, the distribution of age groups in American society is a major determinant of lifelong distribution of education, work, and leisure. Because of the post-World War II "baby boom," resulting in an inordinately high proportion of persons now in the 16 to 30 age group, competition for jobs has been severe. Additionally, as these highly educated persons compete with experienced workers above them in the career ladder, more pressure for earlier compulsory retirement, for more jobs, and for sharing of existing jobs will persist. Also, with the relative stability of the U.S. lifespan of about 70 plus years, greater numbers of people may be unwilling to postpone extended leisure until retirement. However, with improved health in old age, there is less likelihood that older workers may want to opt for earlier retirement. Healthy older workers may want to work more, not less; and because work in the future will probably be less demanding, older workers will be able to work more.

Sex Roles and Family Structure. It is indicated that growing family discreteness, declining dependence ratios, natural constraints on female workers, and increasing flexibility of sex roles may foster a more cyclic distribution of lifetime activities. It is possible, for exam-

---

[57] Fred Best and Barry Stern, "Lifetime Distribution of Education, Work and Leisure: Research, Speculations and Policy Implications of Changing Life Patterns" (Washington, D.C.: Institute for Educational Leadership, George Washington University, 1976), pp. 26–50.

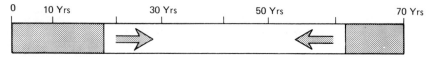

Linear Life Plan: Extended periods of nonwork during youth for education and during old age for retirement. Most work activities performed in consecutive years during midlife. Most increases in nonwork taken in reduced workweeks and expansion of time for education and retirement in youth and old age.

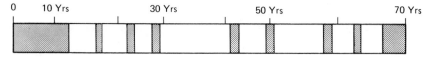

Cyclic Life Plan: Significant portions of nonwork time now spent on education during youth and retirement in old age redistributed to the middle years of life to allow extended periods of leisure or education in midlife. Most increases in nonwork time taken as extended periods away from work during midlife.

Figure 3–8*
Alternative Future Lifetime Patterns

*Fred Best and Barry Stern, "Lifetime Distribution of Education, Work and Leisure," p. 10.

ple, to expect the more traditional male "bread winners" to have less pressure in earning the principal family income, partly because of the rise in number of women workers and particularly working wives (the number of women in the work force increased from approximately 31 percent in 1947 to about 50 percent by 1980), and to choose in favor of having more free time or at least a better distribution of leisure within the family unit. Also the decrease in family size will likely result in a decrease in household chores (as shown by Robinson, in Table 3–4), enabling parental members of family units to have more free time and income both during and after child-rearing years for nonwork activities. Meadows, in *The Limits to Growth,*[58] indicates that the decline in number of children may lead to a commensurate increased expenditure of time and money per household child. The women's liberation movement has helped to foster more equity among husbands and wives as they have become increasingly flexible in exchanging work, household, and child-rearing responsibilities.[59] This increasing sex

[58]Donella Meadows. *The Limits to Growth* (New York: Signet Books, 1972), pp. 119–124.

[59]Daniel Yankelovich. *The New Morality* (Garden City, N.Y.: Doubleday and Co., 1974), pp. 95-102 and Majda Cordell, John McHale, and Guy Streatfield, "Women and World Change," and Alexander Szalai, "Women's Time: Women in the Light of Contemporary Time Budget Research," *Futures,* October 1975, pp. 364–399.

role flexibility, particularly as it is experienced within the family unit, may well lead to major increases in life pattern options. The rise in divorces is increasing the number of one-parent families (particularly in poorer households) and causing greater financial and time constraints for the sole parent, although many divorced persons do remarry.

Developmental Stages of Adulthood. There is an increase in literature relating to the developmental stages of adults as a continuation of the stages experienced in childhood. Briefly, adults appear to experience successive phases of stabilization and consolidation followed by change and growth as they pursue new goals and confront changing crises in different ages. In terms of lifetime patterns, the cyclic life plan has potential strengths to support the periodic realignment of values and life styles which are characteristic of adult development. The cyclic patterns correspond more to the needs and rhythms of adulthood than linear patterns. An important point is that the existing linear life plan is robbing society of much creativity and productivity which, according to current evidence, occur naturally among adults during midlife stages.[60] In other words, where our various organizations and institutions are representative of people stunted by particular developmental crises, a recognition of the productive potentials of midlife self-renewal through granting of sabbatical leave in business, industry, government, and academia, for example, would enable more people to revise or enrich personal and professional plans as part of a cyclical life orientation.

Methods of Education. Reform in educational settings appears to be moving toward more support of cyclic than linear life patterns. The old traditional system of preparation of students following a straight succession of lectures, reading assignments, and paper and pencil tests within the classroom is being challenged by more diverse educational approaches which recognize that different individuals learn best under varying methods and time frames. Some of these examples include: student-initiated courses, field work, academic credit for work and other life experiences, nongrading courses, decentralized campuses, vouchers and "learning contracts," lifelong learning curricula for working people and the elderly, and equivalency programs. Such nontraditional types of learning foster flexibility in scheduling education, and therefore enable more opportunities for departure from current linear plan patterns. Such approaches enable people to work, go to school, and engage in leisure in a manner which supports a rhythm of life revolv-

[60]Judith Bardwick, "The Dynamics of Successful People," *New Research on Women* (Ann Arbor, Mich.: University of Michigan, 1974).

ing around more personal life choices than strictly a work or education pattern.

Education and Social Opportunity. The failing link between educational attainment and occupational advancement is resulting in social tension which may lead to more cyclic life patterns. The "overeducated" individuals with highly developed skills and extensive educational certification are not as much in demand in the labor market. The widespread desire for personal achievment within the context of equal opportunity has extended the years of schooling as a path toward social mobility. But because the levels of overeducation are expected to increase, resulting in job dissatisfaction, political discontent, and counterproductive effects on occupational aspirations, it seems clear that new channels for social opportunity and personal achievement must be developed.

Increasingly North American society is being represented in the work force by individuals with human capacities for achievement which surpass the opportunities for achievement. Work used to be valued as a psychological area for display of work and identity. In the future it appears to be necessary to either expand the opportunities, redistribute opportunities for personal fulfillment and productive effort, or confront stagnation. It may become necessary, therefore, to share jobs and even the quality of the work, or provide people several psychological avenues in the leisure spheres for creative expression, for example, for which there is public sanction and moral reinforcement.

Social Change and Life Functions. The rate of technological change (for example, the time periods for the discovery, development, and commercialization of major technologies such as the automobile or radio has declined sharply) has a crucial impact upon lifetime patterns by influencing the frequency and intensity of major junctures and adjustments within individual lives. With the rate of technological change occurring at such a fast pace it seems obvious that people need to develop adaptive and coping abilities within their individual paths and to have the opportunity to exercise educational, family, work and/or leisure options when confronted by change. Given the state of national resource depletion, rising unemployment, increased inflation, critical international relations, and other forces, people will increasingly need to be able to make adjustments which will encourage growth and development.

Values Toward Time and Income. There appears to be a number of indications that the Canadian and American worker may prefer time-income tradeoff and work scheduling reforms which foster cyclic life patterns. In a study by Best[61] five major conclusions were reached regarding the worker tradeoff preference between income and free time. It was generally determined that preference may be shifting toward more free time:

> First, the income level of the average American worker allows enough discretion for the exchanging of money for more free time. Second, income remains a higher priority than free time. Third, the gap of preference between income and free time is declining. Fourth, future gains in free time are preferred in the form of extended time away from work such as vacations. Fifth, and most important, the way potential free time is scheduled is an important determinant of whether or not workers are willing to give up existing or potential income for free time.[62]

Another study conducted by Best[63] with a limited sample of workers from Alameda County, California, gives further indication of overall lifetime scheduling preferences. Workers from a nonrandom sample of 151 workers from manual and nonmanual occupations suggest a high preference for cyclic life patterns as shown in Table 3–5, "Personal Preferences and Opinions Toward Alternative Lifetime Patterns." The workers selected from among three broad options for scheduling education, work, and leisure throughout life. These were: (1) the "linear life plan" (a traditional life pattern of straight progression from school to work to retirement); (2) a moderate cyclic plan (with most school occurring in youth, with several rotations between work and free time throughout the remainder of life); and (3) a fully developed cyclic plan (basic schooling in early youth with continuous rotation between education, work, and free time throughout the remainder of life). It can be seen from the summary data that the moderate cyclic plan was selected by the greatest number of respondents (37.7 percent), the fully developed cyclic plan being the second choice (29.8 percent) and the linear plan being selected last (21.2 percent). Additionally, workers were asked to indicate what type of life plan they thought other workers would prefer. The results revealed that 37.1 percent of the respondents thought others would prefer the linear life plan, 37.7 percent thought their choice would be the moderate plan, and only 15.2 percent thought others would prefer the fully cyclic plan. Finally, the sample of employees were asked which life plan would be best for the overall well-being of society. Most chose either one of the two cyclic plans. The

[61]Fred Best, "Changing Values Toward Material Wealth and Leisure," Policy Research Paper prepared for the Office of the U.S. Assistant Secretary for Education, Washington, D.C. (Contract No. POO–75–0221), January 1976.

[62]Best and Stern, "Lifetime Distribution," p. 44.

[63]Refer to Best and Stern, p. 45.

Table 3-5

Personal Preferences and Opinions Toward Alternative Lifetime Patterns

LIFE PATTERNS CHOICES	PERSONAL 1ST CHOICE[1]	VIEW OF OTHERS' PREFERENCES[2]	BEST FOR SOCIETAL WELL BEING[3]
A. *Straight Progression from School to Work to Retirement:* A life pattern in which all schooling and pre-work training is accomplished in youth or early adulthood, where one works full time with limited annual vacations during middle adult years, and enters full time retirement sometime after age 60. Thus school education is restricted to youth, work to middle adulthood, and free time to old age.	21.2%	37.1%	22.5%

Diagram of Option A:

B. *Most Schooling in Youth with Several Rotations Between Work and Free Time Throughout the Remainder of Life:* A life pattern in which most schooling and pre-work training is accomplished in youth or early adulthood, where one primarily works full time during middle adulthood but with extended periods away from work (for example 6 months) every 5 or 6 years, and increases the proportion of free time in later years until complete retirement in late 60's. Thus maximum retirement would be exchanged for extended free time periods in mid-life.	37.7%	37.7%	41.7%

Diagram of Option B:

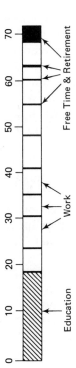

Education   Work   Free Time & Retirement

29.8%   15.2%   25.8%

C. *Basic Schooling in Early Youth with Continuous Rotations Between Education, Work and Free Time Throughout the Remainder of Life:*
A life pattern in which basic education in essential skills (reading, math, etc.) ends early, where most persons leave school periodically starting in mid-teens for limited periods of work, and then finish high school and other education in the course of lifelong rotations between work, school and free time. Thus time spent for education in youth and time spent for retirement in later years would be reduced in exchange for extended periods of education and free time during the middle years of life.

Diagram of Option C:

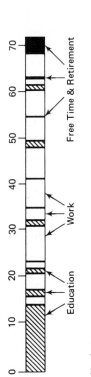

Education   Work   Free Time & Retirement

D. No Answer

11.3%   10.0%   9.9%

Fred Best, "Changing Values toward Material Wealth and Leisure," Policy Research Paper prepared for the Office of the U.S. Assistant Secretary for Education, Washington, D.C. (Contract No. P00–75–0221), January 1976.

results are interesting, and while these data provide only cursory insight into lifetime planning, over 67 percent of the respondents, in terms of both personal preferences and societal well-being, did choose one of the two cyclic life plans.

Organizational Constraints and Options. The actual acceptance of cyclic life patterns is inherently tied to the economic work cycle. Since the desire of a growing number of workers and nonsalaried people is apparently for more cyclic life patterns, work organizations must ultimately make necessary adjustments for the majority of people to realize such new options. Of course, there are many obstacles, among which are administrative acceptance, conversion of organizations to a variety of working patterns, administrative costs tied to coordinating noncontinuous employees, organizational discontinuity, and threats of losing trained personnel to competition.

The ability of organizations to adapt to either moderate or fully developed cyclic patterns could result, for example, in extended nonwork time to allow both self-renewal and retraining of employees, in improved worker morale and productivity, and in the creation of more suitable jobs for nonproductive and "dead-ended" workers which could benefit themselves and their organizations. Certainly one must account for the variability in organizational structures when considering the constraints and options of adapting work organizations to cyclic life patterns. Some organizations can possibly handle work schedule flexibility better if they are concerned with continuous, year-around production as distinguished from more seasonal, short-term production. Similarly, a small firm will face different constraints and options than a large corporation or business.

While there exists no systematic overview of adaptability of work organizations to cyclic patterns of life, there are certain indications that suggest widespread adaptations may in fact be possible. Some of these include: the general growth in progressively longer vacations (which suggests a large number of organizations are finding it possible to adapt to extended absences by their employees); such work scheduling innovations as "flextime": (1) four-day, 40-hour workweeks; (2) leaves of absence without pay, extended vacations up to three months (3) "cafeteria" time-income tradeoff options (a plan operating in Santa Clara County, California, in which employees have their choice between their current hours and pay or one of three additional pay-hour options: (a) 5 percent of current income traded for 10½ days off, (b) 10 percent of current income traded for 21 days off, and (c) 20 percent of income traded for two periods of 21 days off); (4) a variety of work sabbatical programs.[64]

SUMMARY

The delineation between work and leisure has traditionally associated work with productive and leisure with nonproductive activity. This has contributed to the "problem" of leisure. Work-leisure theories were discussed, with particular focus on spillover theory (the continuation of work-related experience and attitudes in leisure), compensatory theory (nonwork-like leisure activity), and personal community theory (influence of one's social circle on leisure choices). Additionally, various work-leisure paradigms were presented by Parker, Kando and Summers, Kelly, and Neulinger, introducing elements of perceived freedom and constraint and other sociopsychological factors which affect the relationship.

Leisure has had different ascribed meanings throughout history, with current recognition that worker satisfaction is linked with inexorable change in the rhythm of industrial life and with the desire for more personal movement in all of one's daily life spheres: family, education, work, and leisure. Various experiments with reduced workweeks were presented, as well as efforts at improving the context of the work place and content of the job—through the redesign of work and through a lifetime redistribution of work, education, and leisure in a cyclic life plan.

[64]Refer to Fred Best, "Flexible Work Scheduling: Beyond the 40 Hour Impasse," in *The Future of Work,* ed. Fred Best (Englewood Cliffs, N.J.: Prentice-Hall, Inc., 1973), pp. 93–99; Janice Hedges, "New Patterns of Working Time," *Monthly Labor Review,* February 1973, pp. 3–8; Janice Hedges, "A Look at the 4-Day Workweek," *Monthly Labor Review,* October 1971, pp. 33–37; Riva Poor, *4-Days, 40-Hours,* 2nd ed. (New York: New American Library, 1973); Fred Best, "Changing Values," in *The Future of Work,* ed. Best, pp. 41–46; James O'Toole, ed., *Work in America,* pp. 123–138; "Xerox Sabbaticals," *Time,* September 20, 1971, p. 98; "Doing Good Works on Company Time: IBM Leave-for-Public-Service Program," *Business World,* May 13, 1972, pp. 166–168.

4

Leisure
and
Time

A time framework serves as an important criterion by which lei-sure, and for that matter all behavior, can be measured. The purpose of this chapter is to discuss various historical roots of time, conceptions of time, ways of perceiving the world, bimodal consciousness and split brain theory, traditional ways of measuring time, and some thoughts about the future of time.

HISTORICAL ROOTS OF TIME

The ancient Greeks conceived of physical time as *chronos.* Aristotle[1] spoke of elliptic motion of the celestial bodies as "eternal." In this sense "eternal" means periodic or recurring. Similarly, the nomadic hunting life was conditioned largely by the rising and setting of the sun. There were no clocks to divide the day into hours, minutes, and seconds. Tribal life was oriented around daily, monthly, and seasonal rhythms of the natural universe. Nomads understood the summer soltice and the vernal equinox, the spring, summer, fall, and winter seasons to be circular conceptions of time which were *constant* and *recurring.* Thomas F. Green states:

> According to this image, time is measured in relation to the constant and recurring passage of the sun, the fluctuations of the tides, the stages of the moon, or even the cycles of the seasons.[2]

[1]Aristotle. *Physics,* trans. P. H. Wickshead and F. M. Conford (New York:Loeb Classical Library, 1929).

[2]Thomas F. Green. *Work, Leisure, and the American Schools* (New York: Random House, 1968), p. 49.

Time was never lost or wasted; according to this conception of time the periods of the day were not seen as linear, sequential divisions. The image of time was based on the repetition of activities, both social and natural.

> In this case, time repeats itself, so that one cannot speak of "wasting" time. The time that has passed is never really lost; it will come again. . . . Time is not cumulative—that is, the idea that one might now undertake something that will reach its completion at some time in the distant future is not dominant.[3]

Circular, eternally returning time gives Homo sapiens a strong sense of belief and commitment to the natural world. Ecologically, a person understood his or her relationship to the physical world and was able to live harmoniously in his or her natural surroundings. DeGrazia notes that the ancient Greeks delightedly accepted the eternal harmonious order that could be discovered through contemplation.[4]

The Hebrew term *chronos* was quite different from the Greek and traditional nomadic concept of time, although it also referred to mechanical clock time. It measured the hours of the day. However, the Greeks used *chronos* as a parameter or secondary concept as the planets projected their images in the receptacle (the order of things) in constant recurrence. The Hebrews used *chronos* as a primary term, a series of successive linear moments. The "coming age" comes as an expected, urgent, important future, but it comes only in the fullness of time. Time alone described the length of Hezekiah's life and all his deeds; his confrontation with Isaiah in the fuller's field was in history (Isa. 36:2). In opposition to *chronos,* the term *kairos* refers to a special time, the time of a very special *chronos.* It is not "eternity" as suggested by the Platonic model in which nature gave all things their regulatory structure. It is a *chronos* that has a content which is different from other moments of *chronos.* Jesus tells us that no man knows the time *(chronos)* or the seasons *(kairos)* of salvation (Acts 1:17).

The Greek metaphysical perception of time tried to locate time in the order of things, in the "receptacle." The Hebrews tried to locate things in the "world of space moving through time, from the beginning to the end of days."[5]

MECHANICAL TIME

Hunting, food gathering, play, and rest occupied the daily lives of nomads and pre-industrial people in a total life rhythm. The gover-

[3] *Ibid.,* p. 49.

[4] DeGrazia, *Of Time, Work and Leisure* (New York: The Twentieth Century Fund, 1962), p. 26.

[5] A. J. Herschel. *The Sabbath* (New York: Farrar, Strauss and Young, 1951), p. 97.

nance of cyclical, natural time was inherently introspective. The mechanization of time occurred when nomads and food-gatherers with specific work tasks needed to meet other men and engage in barter and trade of goods and wares. This required a more finite division of time between sunrise and noon, noon and sunset. The death of cyclical time and the notion of recurrence vanished with the triumph of Christianity.

Mechanical clocks are known to have existed in the thirteenth century, but the earliest survivors belong to the fourteenth century.[6] The week is an arbitrary division, simply a convenient time period between the day and the month. The Greeks divided the month into three ten-day periods and the Romans had an eight-day week between market days.

In the industrial world time is generally viewed as *linear,* without beginning or end, never pausing or veering off course. Nels Anderson states, "The time by which most of us regulate our lives is called *mechanical* because it reflects the interdependence of man and the rhythm of his machines."[7] According to this image of time being regulated by the clock, it becomes possible to speak of "wasting" time, letting time "escape," and "putting in" time.

> In this conception, time is linear rather than circular; every moment of time is new, and therefore also contains the possibility of something new. A time can pass, and when it passes it cannot be recovered. One can therefore plan to achieve something in the future that is indeed genuinely new.... One *must* plan for the future, for the span of a lifetime is brief enough, and what shape it will take is not given, but can be contrived.[8]

The acceptance of artificial timekeeping devices diluted Homo sapiens' inner biological rhythm of movement through space and oriented it to the mechanical beat of the clock. By varying the years, months, and days, it seemed possible to arrange for more optimum work and play schedules.

Would the industrial worker be happier, after a long and more rewarding period of working at the job, to have an ampler weekend in which to enjoy leisure at his or her own pace? Is it possible for the contemporary industrial workers to decide for themselves when they want to work or play, and in fact ignore the official week?[9] According to DeGrazia, technology is no friend of leisure.

[6]J. B. Priestley. *Man and Time* (New York: Dell Publishing Co., 1968), p. 27.

[7]Nels Anderson. *Dimensions of Work* (New York: David McKay Co., 1964), p. 106.

[8]Green, *Work, Leisure, Schools,* p. 52.

[9]See Phillip Bosserman, "Implications for Youth," in *Technology, Human Values and Leisure,* ed. Max Kaplan and Phillip Bosserman (Nashville: Abingdon Press, 1971), pp. 162–163, for examples of alternative work schedules.

The machine, the hero of a dream, the bestower of free time to men, brings a neutralized idea of time that makes it seem free, and then chains it to another machine, the clock. . . . Clock time cannot be free. . . . Clocked time requires activities and decisions that must always be referred back to and synchronized with the machine and its ramifications in an industrial culture.[10]

Mechanical time came into existence because, among other reasons, the industrial civilization has demanded more precision, promptness, and regularity than natural time can provide. Anderson comments:

It is mechanical time the engineer must use in planning or directing a project, and the same time must be used by the mechanic to measure the speed or output of a machine or the co-ordination of machines in a series. When the scientist would measure relationships between durations and other abstractions (space, distance, momentum, volume) he must use mechanical time.[11]

It is interesting to note that the environment of mechanical time, which demands precision, punctuality, regularity, and reliability as well as the networks of interdependence regulated by the clocks, is largely human-made: buildings, paved streets, water systems, sewage systems, lighting and communications networks, even parks, recreation centers, and human service establishments, are all made by human beings. In this environment the rhythms of natural time are disregarded and typically suppressed. Each of the natural types of time has its own tempo and environmental orientation.

Clocks appeared as early as the ninth century, although these were not mechanical clocks. They were sand clocks or water clocks and were seen as novelties. Anderson writes about the first clocks.

What is said to have been the first clock with wheels was made in Paris by Heinrich Von Wick and presented to Charles V in 1364, and the first pocket clock appeared in 1510. Before the fourteenth century clocks were mechanical devices without face or hands, which marked the time when church bells were to be tolled. The second hand was not achieved until 1609.[12]

The clock without its wheel system, its hands and face, and power stored within it is the forerunner of all work-performing machines. Its product is information which it measures and announces in precise duration. Mumford related how time became the arbiter of efficiency

---

[10]DeGrazia, *Of Time, Work and Leisure* p. 310.

[11]Anderson, *Dimensions of Work*, p. 107.

[12]*Ibid.*, p. 108.

for all other mechanisms, and the efficiency with which it abstracts time makes it the prime necessity for all human uses.[13]

The human-made environment of mechanical clock time reinforces the artificial rhythms of the industrial workday, communications networks, transportation systems, and scheduled routines of schools, churches, offices, and recreation facilities. Without the clock, free time as we know it in industrial society would not have emerged. Work and leisure, fused in pre-industrial society, have become *opposing* conceptions in our highly industrialized North American cultures. The contemporary arrangement of time has become rigorously circumscribed by industrial work time. Because work time needs to be filled with productive occupation, leisure time is seen largely as empty time, not innately meaningful.

COSMIC TIME

Cosmic time derives from the Hebrew word *cosmos,* meaning world-place or universe. The word denotes a spatial array of things, and thus cosmos is subordinated to time. Some people are said to be guided by magnetic fields from the universe and their body rhythms said to reflect this arrangement of things in the world. The work of Dr. Frank Brown has been most influential in developing this theory, suggesting that an independent internal timing system for rhythms is not necessary to life since the environment is always generating rhythmic signals. These include variations in terrestrial magnetism, electric fields, and background radiation and other signal sources, such as gravitation, from which no creature on earth can be completely isolated.[14] His research suggests human beings may unconsciously use a variety of subtle cosmic cues rather than depending upon inherited choices for their physiological rhythms.

Another concept of time, in relation to social process and social change, has been developed by Gioscia. A fourfold paradigm reflects the part-whole metaphor and the space-time metaphor as shown in Figure 4–1.[15]

Cell I refers to the particle point of view, in which events, processes, or changes are construed as the resultant configuration of individual particles. Processes and changes are ascribed to the addition or subtraction of parts. Cell II refers to the Gestalt point of view, in which things,

---

[13]Lewis Mumford. *Technics and Civilization* (New York: Harcourt, 1934), pp. 14–17.

[14]Gay Luce, "Biological Rhythms," in *The Nature of Human Consciousness,* ed. Robert E. Ornstein (San Francisco: W. H. Freeman & Co., 1973), pp. 439–442.

[15]Victor Gioscia, "On Social Time," in H. Yaker, H. Osmond, and F. Cheek, *The Future of Time* (Garden City, N.Y.: Anchor Books, 1972), p. 79.

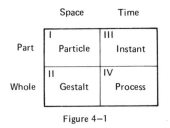

Figure 4—1

events, processes, and changes are construed as self-defined wholes. Gestaltists insist that analysis must consider the wholeness of such units of inquiry or else the results if broken into component parts will be distorted and reductionist. Cell III is the instant point of view, having particular reference to clock time. In cell IV the process point of view is presented; this view holds that the whole time of events, physical and/or social, must be perceived in its entirety.

The traditional Western conceptualization of time is linear; it uses past, present, and future terminologies and includes, birth, life, death, thesis, antithesis, systhesis, origin, process, recapitulation, etc. But it must be realized that this linearization of time is *only one* possible conceptualization of social process. The traditional Chinese view of time, for example, a cyclical temporal pattern, would not fit our Western models at all. Time is not an absolute, a constant, proceeding at some fixed rate. There are alternative views of the human experiencing of time,[16] and rates of behavior have variant speeds, variant accelerations and decelerations, and variations in the uniformity of these patterns.

PERSONALITY AND TIME

Time may be viewed in relation to the psychological classification system which describes differences in temperament among normal individuals. Jung[17] first described these personality types. His typological system states that there are eight different but equally normal ways of perceiving or experiencing the world. There are four functional types: *thinking, feelings, sensation,* and *intuition;* and two attitudinal types: *introversion* and *extraversion.* Since the functional types exist in each of the attitudes, eight major types result: extraverted thinking, introverted thinking, extraverted feeling, introverted feeling, extra-

---

[16]*Ibid.,* 73–141.

[17]C. C. Jung. *Psychological Types* (London: Pantheon Books, 1923).

Table 4–1
Personality Function

Sensation Type	Tells us something exists
Thinking Type	Tells us what that something is
Feeling Type	Enables us to make a value judgment about this object
Intuition Type	Enables us to see the possibilities inherent in the object

verted sensation, introverted sensation, extraverted intuition and introverted intuition. The functions are described in Table 4–1.

Thinking and feeling are opposed: both are ways of *evaluating* an object or a situation. Thinking accomplishes this through principles such as "true" or "false"; feeling evaluates through emotional responses such as "pleasing" or "distressing." Accordingly, it is not probable that a person would evaluate simultaneously in two conflicting ways; a person having a primary thinking function would tend to be weak in the area of feeling, and vice versa. Intuition and sensation are also opposites, both ways of perceiving the world. Sensation is the relating function, in which the sensory mechanism is used to determine the presence or absence of an object. Intuition is perceived by the consciousness and is a method of relating to the world through hunches and guesses. As with the other opposing functions, those people having sensation as a primary function would tend to be weak in intuition, and vice versa.

These functions can be either predominantly extraverted or introverted. All extroverts have in common their willingness to respond *quickly* to external stimuli, although the *way* in which they respond will depend on their primary function. Such people tend to be gregarious, and on the whole they are oriented toward action rather than toward introspection or reflection. All introverts tend to exhibit a certain *hesitancy* about responding too quickly to external stimuli, requiring time to integrate them before responding overtly. Introverts enjoy being alone and find satisfaction from occasional seclusion.

Any typology is an abstraction of reality. Everyone has the potential for all four functions.

However, each person has a hierarchy in functions and a natural predisposition to one of the attitudes. The more nearly balanced the two attitudes are, the greater the individual's potential for experiencing both the joys which derive from the inner spheres and the pleasures which come from the external world. . . . bringing all four functions into conscious control is extremely helpful for optimal functioning.[18]

[18]Harriet Mann, Miriam Siegler, and Humphrey Osmond, "The Psychotypology of Time," in Yaker et al., *The Future of Time,* p. 147.

One might argue that the skills of the feeling type and those of the intuitive type will become important ingredients of a well-balanced society as the amount of free time increases, with their orientation toward process, time flowing, and inspiration of the anticipated future. Western society has largely been oriented toward the functions of sensation and thinking and has tended to undervalue the skills of those who relate primarily through either feeling or intuition. Some important conflicts need to be resolved relative to personality types utilizing Jungian typology: (1) there is a need to differentiate and quantify these experiential worlds (refer to Chapter 7 for a discussion of the psychology of leisure) and (2) a method should be derived by which individuals can be taught about and sensitized to experiential worlds which are markedly different from their own.

Many people feel constrained by the one-way temporal process epitomized by industrial time clocks. They yearn to escape the artificial entanglements of work time and to explore more fully the natural world unbound by stoplights, the six o'clock news, school buzzers, alarm clocks, sirens, and factory time clocks. Psychological time is concerned not with the specificity of quantitative time, but rather with quality.

> No matter how the empirical self adapts itself to the concept of passing time, a one-way horizontal track, the essential self (which expects something different and better) tries to escape from the contradictions, the ruthless opposites, and knows nothing but a sense of frustration, a profound dissatisfaction.[19]

Mechanical, chronological time conveys the idea that within time there can be no sense of completeness, no enduring satisfactions. Everything in mechanical time, no matter what its scale, is here today and gone tomorrow. The continuous passage of time includes only fragments of ourselves. This one-way track of passing time fosters a curious apathy, a boredom, a lack of zest, a flavorless sense of living. Unfortunately, the passing time is all we have. The individual must learn to perceive time and space as an opportunity to add experience and knowledge, through a broadening and deepening consciousness.

Attempting to escape time's limitations, frustrations, and contradictions, people in Western culture often find themselves devouring everything around them. The Eastern philosophy of time and the universe refuses to be devoured by events and time. Eastern cultures believe in a self that does not waste away, a detachment that allows them to "behave as if they believed, paradoxically, that in this world

---

[19]Priestley, *Man and Time,* p. 173.

everything is important and nothing is important."[20] Although psychological time is little help to the scientist or computer analyst surrounded by clocks, calendars, and precise instruments, Priestley states the outer or mechanical time measured by those instruments is essentially unreal; reality can be found only in our inner sense of duration or psychological time.[21] *The basis of leisure in post-industrial society clearly gains significance when its meaning is attached to the industrial rhythm of life, but its attributes and character emerge only when interpreted by the individual who makes of it what is pertinent and valuable to his or her personal life regimen.*

FOUR MODES OF TIME EXPERIENCE

Ornstein[22] states that there are four modes of time experience: (1) the present, short-term time (represented by perception of short intervals and rhythmic-motor aspect of time known as rhythm or timing); (2) duration, the past, long-term memory; (3) temporal perspective—philosophical, social, cultural constructions of the world and their effects on the interpretation of time experience; and (4) simultaneity and succession.

Present, short-term time studies are divided into perception or apprehension of short intervals and rhythmic-motor aspects of time. The apprehension of brief intervals of time is most often studied by presenting the observer with the interval and then obtaining his or her estimate of the length of that interval. Timing is usually studied using sequential stimuli and a key-tapping device.

The duration is our normal experience of time passing, of hours lengthening or shortening, of one interval passing more quickly for one person than another or more quickly for the same person in one instance than in another. The experience of duration seems most keyed to remembrance of things past—to retrospection.

The third mode of time experience is more socially determined than the two previously discussed. Our general temporal perspective is derived from the kind of culture we live in. As with any other mode of experience, the direct experience of time is subject to personal and social as well as intellectual interpretation. In the West we are precise; everything is broken up into small units. This approach has been quite useful in a technological society. Other cultures that are not so technically oriented have different basic units of time. For example, one

---

[20]*Ibid.,* p. 176.

[21]*Ibid.,* p. 45.

[22]Robert E. Ornstein. *On the Experience of Time* (Baltimore: Penguin Books, 1969), pp. 15–24.

Indian culture uses the time to boil rice as its "basic unit." To study temporal perspective, one must study other cultures to determine the distinctions between these differing time conceptions. And within a given culture, there are time concepts of differing social classes (e.g., a traditional black time expression, "colored people's time") and those of differing philosophical orientations.

The final dimension of time experience described by Ornstein is that of simultaneity and succession. This is an extremely esoteric psychological approach stimulated by the idea of the "perceptual moment."

BIMODAL CONSCIOUSNESS

When considering the psychological and physiological variations that occur from day to day and from minute to minute as we work, have leisure, study, and engage in community activities, one must recognize the existence of two basic organismic states or modes that are coordinated to conduct a particular function. These modes have both biological and psychological components.

The two primary modes of organization of the human organism are an *action* mode and a *receptive* mode. The action mode is a state organized to *manipulate* the environment. "The action mode is a state of striving, oriented toward achieving personal goals that range from nutrition to defense to obtaining social rewards; plus a variety of symbolic and sensual pleasures, as well as the avoidance of a comparable variety of pain."[23] In contrast, the receptive mode is a state organized around *intake* of the environment rather than manipulation. For maximum intake of the environment, the sensory-perceptual system is dominant over the formal, rational functions in this mode.

These two modes are not to be equated with activity and passivity. "The functional orientation that determines the mode has to do with the *goal* of the organism's activity: whether or not the environment is to be acted upon or whether stimuli or nutriment are to be taken in."[24]

For example, a woman working in her garden operates in the action mode only to the extent needed to conduct her work activity; the receptive mode can still play a prominent role in her conscious experience. Often the leisure researcher does not accurately calculate the full underlying meaning of investigated leisure experiences, because the researcher's perceptions may be oriented only to one mode or the other.

[23]Arthur J. Deikman. "Bimodal Consciousness," in *The Nature of Human Consciousness,* ed. Robert E. Ornstein (San Francisco: W. H. Freeman & Co., 1973), p. 68.

[24]*Ibid.,* pp. 70–71.

The action mode dominates our consciousness. This often results in the overlooking of other alternative states of consciousness which do not fit readily into "action" mode survey techniques and methods of analysis. In Zen Buddhism, meditation is a principal form of achieving the goals of "enlightenment." A person meditating is "not supposed to do" anything except to *be* sitting. That state of beingness is enlightenment itself. This approach of consciousness is aimed at specifically doing away with categorizing and classifying, an activity that is believed to intervene between the subject and his or her experience. In meditation, the sense of time can be altered to what might be referred to as timelessness. During meditation the subject may experience a sense of total satisfaction with his or her moment-to-moment experience so that the need to strive for a distant satisfaction is diminished. "Thus, the emphasis on experiencing, or enduring, and on being—rather than on avoiding pain or seeking pleasure—provides the groundwork for a mode of consciousness that Zen texts describe as nondualistic, timeless, and nonverbal."[25] This mode of organism being just described is categorized as being part of the receptive mode. Sexual activity that is satisfactory is oriented toward the receptive mode and makes sex less obsessive and overcompensation less necessary.

Because Western culture has failed to cultivate the receptive mode, most psychological models and even leisure service orientations and research inquiries have tended to view the object world as the standard by which to judge the realism of perception and cognition. However, the receptive mode, as well as other modes yet to be discerned or utilized, can be conceptualized as modes by which the organism addresses itself to reality dimensions other than those of the object world now associated with the action mode and logical thinking. "The 'thinking' of the receptive mode may be organized in terms of a *different* logic in pursuit of aims located along different dimensions of reality than those to which we ordinarily address ourselves."[26]

It has been suggested by some bimodal consciousness groups that a change in values is necessary to combat the threat to human survival which has occurred as a result of allowing our action mode of consciousness to dominate our existence. The success achieved by Western culture in the manipulation of the environment and acting on others has resulted in pollution, racism, sexism, discrimination against the handicapped and the aged, unending wars, and so on. A shift in values, in self-definition and a more unified view of the world on the part of

[25]*Ibid.*, pp. 78–79.
[26]*Ibid.*, p. 84.

each individual, would help eliminate these obstacles to realizing our collective and individual potential. A first step toward resolving the discrepancies in those life styles which "appear" to be unsuited or outside the framework of mainstream society would be to recognize the relativity of different modes of consciousness, rather than to assign an absolute primacy and validity to the action mode.

SPLIT BRAIN THEORY

The human brain has two hemispheres, each with its own method of thought. While each hemisphere has its own function—the left being primarily responsible for speech and logic, and the right for expression and symbolism—they must inevitably work together. A result of the development of such brain hemispheric research is an increased understanding of the full range of human abilities in an integrated way.

As a result of the pioneering work of Roger Sperry and Ronald Meyers, and later Robert Ornstein, who translated their research into human consciousness, the discovery of two independently functioning parts of the brain took place. The left hemisphere of the brain processes information in a linear, logical fashion and carries on verbal and mathematical reasoning. It is verbal and uses language to communicate with the outside world. The right hemisphere perceives images holistically in gestalts. It thinks abstractly, processes information in a spatial and intuitive way, and appears to be the locus of our creative and artistic capabilities and our appreciation of forms and music.[27]

Sperry's findings and the work of Ornstein and others have opened up a whole new arena in psychology and have tremendous possibilities for leisure research and the delivery of leisure services. It challenges the priorities of our educational system, including leisure education, which is almost totally geared to the development of the left hemisphere. Leisure programs that subscribe to the linear, materialistic, discretionary time orientation may be missing tremendous untapped potential of the right hemisphere. We may in fact be discriminating against one whole half of the brain in our educational and leisure service delivery organizations where the knowledge base, instruction, program organization, and bases for evaluation are almost totally biased toward systematic, linear, logical thought and behavior. If there are critical periods for the development of the right hemisphere's spe-

[27]Refer to Wayne Sage, "The Split Brain Lab," *Human Behavior* 5:26, June 1976.

cial traits, it may be necessary to train it at that age or lose forever the possibility of realizing its full potential.

METHODS OF MEASURING LEISURE AS TIME

The nature of leisure participation has commonly been researched by the use of time-budget studies. In this method people keep structured diaries in which they record what they experience during regular (hourly) intervals, typically over the course of a day or week. These temporal intervals represent conceptual aspects of daily life which vary from culture to culture.

> In industrial societies, the productive processes at the core of the dominant economic institutions have encouraged great cultural emphasis on temporal matters. The extent to which daily life for many persons is segmented with reference to time is greater in such societies than in others. Because leisure activities are part of culture, it seems reasonable to expect that they might be ordered, as are other activities, in some temporal manner.[28]

The time-budget studies aid in assessing the time apportioned to different categories of activities. Such data assist in answering empirically how certain categories vary in certain populations. A study conducted by the National Opinion Research Center at the University of Chicago in 1973, reported by Cheek and Burch,[29] included some questions relating to the amount of estimated free time that was usually available to the respondents during a weekday and also on a weekend. The study (depicted in Table 4–2) shows that the modal category for free time during the weekday is *less than four hours and more than two.* Additionally, the majority of respondents report less than four hours per weekday as free time. On weekends (refer to Table 4–3) the modal category is ten or more hours, yet the majority of the respondents report less than eight hours as free time. The availability of free time is more compact for the majority of respondents during the weekdays than on weekends. It can be seen, for example, that the number of respondents is smaller in the weekday distribution than in the weekend distribution.

The data suggest the existence of an empirical regularity with respect to temporal orderings of availability of free time. Cheek and Burch comment: "Weekdays differ from weekend days in terms of the

---

[28]Neil H. Cheek and William R. Burch. *The Social Organization of Leisure in Human Society* (New York: Harper and Row, Publishers, 1976), p. 33.

[29]*Ibid.,* pp. 34–36.

Table 4–2
Comparison of Weekday Free Time Available to Adults
During Differing Time Periods of Reporting, Percent*

LENGTH OF AVAILABLE TIME	TIME FRAME OF REPORTING PARTICIPATION (PERCENTAGE)	
	WEEKLY	MONTHLY
Less than ½ hour	7.6	8.0
Less than 1 hour, more than ½	7.2	8.0
Less than 2 hours, more than 1	18.8	18.6
Less than 4 hours, more than 2	32.6	29.1
Less than 6 hours, more than 4	15.9	17.2
Less than 8 hours, more than 6	6.7	6.6
Less than 10 hours, more than 8	2.8	3.6
10 hours or more	8.1	8.9
Total	99.7	100.0

Neil H. Cheek and William R. Burch, The Social Organization of Leisure in Human Society (New York: Harper and Row, Publishers, 1976), p. 24.

amount of free time available as well as in the distribution of such time. The weekday is more sharply constrained than is the weekend day.[30]

Temporal orderings do not allow one to show how this is directly related to leisure activity participation. Also the amount of time available seems not to be as important as the manner in which it is distributed. In the United States and Canada a common characteristic is that the week (seven days) is typically segmented into two divisions—weekdays and weekends. While most previous studies were organized around the notion of a prescriptive work orientation for the weekday and free time orientation for the weekend, new innovations in work (as reported in the previous chapter) suggest that such a design for time-budget studies will have to be reconstructed.

Godbey and Parker comment on the relative merits and shortcomings of time-budget studies.

One major advantage of the time budget is that it allows different categorizations of leisure and nonleisure activity to be made while using the same data. [Some shortcomings are] ... many people [as high as 90 percent] ... are not willing to participate in such a study.... Additionally, time budgets are dependent upon the memory of the individual involved. People are likely to remember some leisure activities longer than others, especially those that are the most enjoyable, and to underestimate the amount of time spent in activities that they consider to be of "low status." Illegal activities, or those considered immoral, are likely to be omitted as well. Another problem is the actual recording of the activities [which arises from a person having to choose between several options to describe what a person may have engaged in doing].[31]

[30] *Ibid.,* p. 36.

[31] Geoffrey Godbey and Stanley Parker, *Leisure Studies and Services: An Overview* (Philadelphia: W. B. Saunders Co., 1976), p. 16.

Table 4-3
Comparison of Weekend Day Free Time Available to
Adults During Differing Time Periods of
Reporting, Percent*

LENGTH OF TIME	TIME FRAME OF REPORTING PARTICIPATION (PERCENTAGE)	
	WEEKLY	MONTHLY
Less than ½ hour	2.9	3.3
Less than 1 hour, more than ½	2.4	2.7
Less than 2 hours, more than 1	5.6	5.4
Less than 4 hours, more than 2	14.5	13.1
Less than 6 hours, more than 4	18.5	18.7
Less than 8 hours, more than 6	15.1	16.1
Less than 10 hours, more than 8	14.1	11.8
10 or more hours	26.8	29.1
Total	99.9	100.2

*Neil H. Cheek and William R. Burch, The Social Organization of Leisure in Human Society (New York: Harper and Row. Publishers, 1976), p. 36.

COMPARATIVE MULTINATIONAL TIME-BUDGET STUDY

An exhaustive twelve-nation comparative time-budget study, under the direction of Alexander Szalai, was carried out under the aegis of the European Coordination Centre for Research and Documentation on Social Sciences. The study surveyed daily activities of urban and suburban populations in: Belgium, France, Federal Republic of Germany, German Democratic Republic, Czechoslovakia, Hungary, Yugoslavia, Bulgaria, Poland, European part of the Soviet Union, Peru, and the United States.[32]

The study marked the first time that such a massive amount of data on how time budgets are utilized by various socioeconomic groups from socialist and capitalist countries was gathered and interpreted. The materials obtained allowed not only an identification of what is common and particular in the time budgets of the various populations, but also an examination of the impact of industrialization and urbanization in these nations on their way of life, on the nature of their everyday activities, and on the duration and patterns of their leisure. This study was an improvement over most previous such studies in that it incorporated the use of data from several countries; in addition to considering the duration of one component of human activity on the average person of a particular socio-economic group, it showed the way of life and behavior of people, family budgets, contents of particular activities and so on.

[32]Alexander Szalai, ed. The Use of Time (The Hague: European Coordination Centre for Research and Documentation in the Social Sciences, 1972) 868 pages.

Undoubtedly, taking into account not only primary but also secondary activities, performed simultaneously with the former (and the subsequent examination of them), the place where they occur, and the social environment, is a great contribution to the time budget methodology.[33]

Some of the findings are: Employed women devote over 3 hours to housework and household obligations, while employed men contribute only 1 hour. On days off, employed women spend 5.1 hours on such tasks; as a result they have almost a similar work shift when they are away from work. This "second shift" of employed women, after having worked a full shift in her working place, may be a significant factor which hinders development of her human potentialities and talents other than those which can unfold themselves in the household and in the family circle.[34] Additionally it was found that the available free time for employed women as compared with their male partners was less and similarly women had less free time than men in respect to the cultural use and the choice of opportunities for leisure.

The study shows that nations in the early stages of industrialization have more of the population working longer. Overall, there is a remarkable similarity in time budgets related to the general uses of leisure time, although Russians devote a little more time to educational pursuits, Americans to organizational activities and nonwork trips, Bulgarians to spectacles, and Germans to sports. The study revealed that the mass media (radio, television, and reading) consume most free time of working people in all the countries surveyed.

The distribution of the activities during the course of the week pertains to the rhythm of working people. Since in most Eastern European countries Saturday is typically a normal working day, the character of Sunday is dependent upon the uses of Saturday. Sunday is only partly a day of rest. Interestingly, night work on a regular basis contributes to more free time; afternoon work decreases free time in all countries.

The introduction and use of household labor-saving devices (refrigerators, washing machines, dishwashers, etc.) were thought to be a savior in freeing people, particularly women, from the drudgery and time commitment to housework. Actually, there has been only a small reduction in household work. Szalai comments on two reasons for the surprisingly small time savings:

Firstly, the demands of husbands and children on the quality and quantity of household services and comforts have risen together with the

---

[33]B. P. Kutyriov and V. D. Patrushev, "The Use of Time," Book Review, *Society and Leisure* 7:169–170, 1975.

[34]A. Szalai, "Continental Report," *Free Time and Self-Fulfillment* (Antwerpen: Foundation Van Cle, 1977), p. 49.

development of labour-saving household technologies.... Secondly, some of the most time-consuming types of household work and especially of child care do not lend themselves easily to technological modernization.[35]

The nature of nonwork behavior as it pertains to intragroup interaction is an important index of interpreting leisure behavior. Cheek and Burch comment on the insight gained from the multinational time-budget study and the support of their contention that gender is an important determinant of leisure behavior.

Women—whether in hunter-gatherer or industrial societies, communist or capitalist societies, rich or poor societies—consistently have different locales and patterns of work-nonwork cycles. But when viewed with the ethnographic studies, the multinational data clearly suggest that the nonwork realm is most significant in maintaining the intragroup bond. And regardless of the complexity, size, or density of a society, this pattern remains consistent.[36]

They infer that the intragroup bond formed in nonwork activities is essential for maintaining the larger intergroup solidarity.

THE DYNAMICS OF TIME IN
FOUR INDUSTRIAL SOCIETIES

The findings of a study on the allocation of time in four countries (Great Britain, France, Czechoslovakia, and the United States) were reported in *Society and Leisure.*[37] The primary question related to the reduction in work and the allocation of freed time in these advanced capitalist and socialist industrial societies. The study sought to identify what part was played by the growth of free time, by the multiplying of leisure activities, and by the development of new values in the processes of change to a post-industrial (scientific-technological) society.

The reports of the allocation of time in these four countries revealed these general characteristics as reported by Bosserman[38]:

1. Growth in the quantity of time freed from work during a person's life cycle has been a significant evolutionary development over the past 100 years, especially since World War I.

[35]Szalai, *The Use of Time,* pp. 49–50.

[36]Cheek and Burch, *Social Organization of Leisure* p. 90.

[37]*Society and Leisure,* vol. VII, no. 1, 1975.

[38]Phillip Bosserman, "Some Interpretations on the Dynamics of Time on Industrial Society," *Society and Leisure* 7:155–164, 1975.

2. The growth of these block periods of freed time has accelerated over the last 25 years.

3. The freeing of time from work has been the result of economic, political, and sociocultural processes.

4. The length of vacation periods have become the most important time blocks for people during the major years of their work life. The life styles they are developing within these vacation weeks are what they long to continue when they retire. The holiday periods at Christmas and in the spring are beginning to resemble the vacation.

5. The pressures on transportation, vocation, housing, etc., resulting from the massive trend toward lengthening of vacations are multiple and interrelated. Sociocultural desires, added income and abundance through greater productivity, and union activity have combined to produce greater annual leaves and more holidays falling in such a way as to extend weekends or vacations.

6. The dynamics of the development of pop-mass culture (cultural centers in France; symphony orchestras, community arts councils, cultural programs, outlets in general for artistic, sport, recreational, and intellectual expression in the United States; and similar development in Britain) have contributed to the socio-political-cultural pressure to free time from work.

7. Greater longevity with better health and more social security have influenced the demand for earlier retirement in France, Great Britain, Czechoslovakia, and the United States. Older people increasingly desire leisure and view it as a *legitimate* function of old age.

8. Youths are being delayed entry into the labor market because the economy requires greater skills, especially the services. The result is longer education in order to have the requisite training to contribute to the needs of the economy. Youth, presently disengaged from the labor market, is creating within it new values and life styles which have as their fundamental source *leisure* in all its dimensions. Hence, retired people—adding to the vacation life styles of the work life—and youth —creating subcultures of "leisuring"—together become the two groups which are in the vanguard of post-industrial society.

9. There is an increasing interest in different, more fluid rhythms to work and education with more consideration being given to the idea of sabbaticals and educational leaves to "retool" or retrain for present or different careers.

10. Accompanying the increasing desire by people to exercise more control over their natural life rhythms throughout their entire life span, the pressures of population density, transportation to and from work and leisure, energy shortages, and environmental misuse all have influenced governments, firms, and institutions in every society to consider flexible work and leisure schedules.

11. The dialectics of freed time and work time have been instrumental in creating a new set of values which sometimes conflict with, sometimes are complimentary to the work ethic. In some ways, the spillover hypothesis of work influencing leisure is being supported with many workers seeking fulfillment of many of the work ethic purposes through leisure itself.

12. Productivity is a key to freed time from work, with differing expectations of workers in the countries studied. Notably, in the United States workers seem less motivated to work, eying possible ways of translating their interests into the availability of more free time. In France, where productivity has been steadily increasing, workers are desiring more income and larger blocks of free time. In Great Britain workers seem to desire more income but are desirous of more flexible work arrangements translated into annual leave and earlier retirement. In Czechoslovakia, the state-run government has reduced work hours, lengthened holiday time (which is not always taken), and, with the combination of increasing tourism abroad and earlier eligibility for retirement, expanded people's opportunity for leisure.

13. In all four societies manual workers have longer hours, work years, and work lives. The fact that inflation in the Western European countries and in the United States has been high in recent years suggests that more workers are opting for additional work time to stay even with the level of living they have come to enjoy.

14. Family size and situation have an effect on the length of the work week. Workers, particularly women because of certain labor shortages, are encouraged to stay in the work force more and for longer periods of time.

DISCERNING SOCIAL PHENOMENA

Social role, like time, is a product of social interaction and social reality. It has a number of depth levels, which proceed from obvious, easily observed and described social phenomena to deeper modes which are more difficult to discern and less regularized in their behavior. However, there is a unity, a "total social phenomenon" of these forms of behavior, and Bosserman offers a diagram to illustrate two main divisions of social phenomena (Figure 4–2).

The social phenomena which are above the horizontal line in Bosserman's diagram have a much more organized, regular, routinized, patterned character. They are the most commonly studied in the social sciences (including leisure) as they are amenable to survey research, statistical operations, and multivariate analysis, all methods effective in getting at the more rational, more "deterministic" phenomena. Below the horizontal line exist those social "facts" which are less dis-

```
                          Surface

                    Institutional      Discernable
     Organized       Patterned          Primarily by
     Social          Rational           Quantitative
     Phenomena       Visible            Methodologies
     ────────────────────────────────────────────────
                         Underground

                    Noninstitutional   Discernable
     Unorganized     Fluid Patterning   Primarily by
     Social          Nonrational        Qualitative
     Phenomena       Invisible          Methodologies
```

Figure 4–2*
Divisions of Social Phenomena

*Phillip Bosserman, "Some Theoretical Dimensions to
the Study of Social Time," Society and Leisure 7:29,
1975.

cernible by quantitative methods and require other means to get at them. Such qualitative approaches of cultural anthropology—participant observation, the variation on this theme utilized by ethnologists, in-depth case studies, and broadly based community studies—have been employed and refined to grasp the essential nature of these relatively nonrational, less visible, noninstitutionalized, unorganized phenomena.

The horizontal line represents the social frameworks such as groups, social bonds, a global society in which the total social phenomena live and manifest themselves. There is a constant tension and conflict among the various depth levels, within each level itself, and between the social phenomena on the vertical scale and the frameworks themselves.

It must be further realized that this diagram of social phenomena is intended to suggest that those elements which make up the social structure have distinct nonmaterial properties. Tiryakian has noted:

Social reality is not reducible to physical reality.... The *meaning* of human actors' behavior and orientation ... cannot be deduced from the biological, chemical, or physical properties of their situational objects.[39]

The "underground of social being" referred to by Bosserman when speaking of the deepest layers of social reality represent latent and potential expressions or possibilities of expression which are always present, always in some sense contesting and seeking to "surface," to

[39]Edward Tiryakian, "Towards the Sociology of Esoteric Culture," *American Journal of Sociology* 78:171, November 1972.

become visible.[40] Tiryakian comments on the subtlety of nonorganized, nonrational phenomena, serving as the wellspring of societal change.

> Society as an ongoing phenomenon is in a state of dynamic tension, between institutionalized phenomena which characterize "public life," and noninstitutionalized ones which fall outside the pale of publicly legitimated and rewarded activity. Institutional phenomena are by and large the visible layer of society. Noninstitutional phenomena, which fall outside of and even go counter to the rationalization of conduct, are not all of the same order nor do they spring from the same depth level of societal structure, but tend to be concealed from public view, in part because they are "unpleasant" and in opposition to the value-orientations embodied in the ongoing institutional system.[41]

The nature of social reality that is suggested from the above comments and paradigm reveal the complexity and dialectical basis of social life. Bosserman interprets religious, cultic, artistic, recreational, and play-oriented activities thus as being experience and affect-oriented.

> They are more than just outlets for tension and strains. Religious and cultic activities, artistic, recreational and play forms are more than tension managers, pattern-maintainers—they evoke a pluralism of possibilities in instant conflict with what is accepted and patent.[42]

The changing allocation of time has and will continue to have an impact on the way priorities are ordered. In periods of societal crisis, the nonpublic forms become manifest and contribute to the changes in public, rational society. Work as an economic function no longer is the single largest source of *meaning* for life. The activities of nonwork and the noneconomic aspects of work have radically altered and continue to alter the normative underpinnings of social reality.

Bosserman suggests that the changes in the social structure in relation to work may be less significant than they appear. Work will not decrease significantly in the near future. Because of the need to give jobs to administrative types in order that they can consume, work will continue to be important. The occupational profile (see Tables 4–4 and 4–5) is changing dramatically—the "inefficient" services are expanding, the "ombudsmen" person-related jobs especially are becoming more important, the growing interest in handcrafts, the wares of artisans, indicate that work is far from decreasing. It does not appear in a global sense that we are moving toward a life free from work. The *nature* of

---

[40]Bosserman, "Some Interpretations," p. 30.

[41]Tiryakian, "Esoteric Culture," p. 122.

[42]Bosserman, "Some Interpretations," p. 31.

Table 4-4*
Service-Producing Industries (in thousands)
At the onset of the 1970's service-producing industries accounted for more than 6 out of every 10 people who work for a wage or salary.

	1947	1969
Transportation and Public Utilities	4,166	4,448
Trade	8,955	14,644
Finance, Insurance, and Real Estate	1,754	5,559
Service	5,050	11,103
Government	5,474	12,227
Total	25,399	47,981

Goods-Producing Industries (in thousands)

	1947	1969
Mining	955	628
Construction	1,982	3,411
Manufacturing	15,545	20,121
Agriculture	7,891	3,606
Total	26,373	27,766

*Seymour Wolfbein, Work in American Society (Glenview, Ill.: Scott, Foresman & Co., 1971), pp. 33–34.

work is changing as the demands for more personalized service increase.

Additionally, while time is being freed from work in greater block periods, it has the built-in constraints of a consumption society and service economy.

First, it takes time to consume which means money and time must be weighed against money in a calculating way. Secondly, services are person-related and for many types of jobs, time cannot be easily calculated in small segments and must be seen as performing tasks until they are completed. However, the time segments are longer and hence, there is greater latitude with them.[43]

The occupational profile can be shown more visibly by referring to Table 4–5.

It can be seen that work is still important, if not central to Americans, but the importance of freed time, especially the opportunity for leisure, is a new dimension which is a *reality* for a growing number of people. There appears to be an increase in American society in general of the development of a service economy with many of person-caring services fusing leisure and work and giving an ambivalent

[43]Phillip Bosserman, "The Evolution of and Trends in Work and Non-Work Time in United States Society, 1920–1970," *Society and Leisure* 7:112–113.

Table 4-5*
Occupational Distribution of the Employed
Population 1900–1969

MAJOR OCCUPATIONAL GROUP	1900	1947	1960	1967	1969
Total	100%	100%	100%	100%	100%
White Collar	18	35	43	46	47
Professional workers	4	7	11	13	14
Proprietors, managers, officers	6	10	11	10	10
Clerical workers	3	12	15	17	17
Sales workers	5	6	6	6	6
Blue Collar	36	41	37	37	36
Craftsmen	10	14	13	13	13
Operators	13	21	18	19	18
Laborers	13	6	6	5	5
Service	9	10	12	12	12
Private household workers	5	3	3	2	2
Other service workers	4	7	9	10	10
Farm	37	14	8	5	5
Farmers and farm managers	20	9	4	3	3
Farm laborers and foremen	17	5	4	2	2

*Seymour Wolfbein, Work in American Society (Glenview, Ill.: Scott, Foresman & Co., 1971), p. 46.

quality to the dichotomy between work and leisure. It has been suggested that the rhythm of life used to be principally directed by work time and now the rhythm of life is in a state of flux, perhaps with free time becoming an important determinant of the flow of life (with leisure playing a significant part).

Godbey and Parker present arguments as to why leisure might be increasing and, conversely, why leisure might be decreasing in a post-industrial society such as that of North America.[44] Post-industrial society is characterized by:

A technology of cybernetics and automation.

A shift from food and goods production to a service economy.

Mass society, production, culture, leisure, and education.

A more fluid system of human relationships.

Reasons contributing to increased leisure are:

[44]Godbey and Parker, *Leisure Studies and Services* pp. 20–24.

1. Technological advancement has allowed for more time off the job. It has contributed to material self-sufficiency and thus enabled us to engage in a wide variety of leisure activities. Industrial society set aside certain segments of free time, such as evenings, weekends, holidays, and vacations, and made them available for leisure.

2. Technology has boosted earnings, particularly discretionary money which has reached upwards of $200 billion.

3. Added to the availability of more time and money has been the marked decline in puritanism. We are less stressful of pleasure.

The belief that leisure is sinful and must be earned and re-earned through work is losing its popularity in the new welfare state. A growing sense of social freedom makes it possible to seek leisure as a desirable end in itself without feelings of guilt. The greater acceptance of differing life styles and "do your own thing" attitude frees the individual to do as he wishes—restrictions pertaining to sexual activity are diminishing, resulting in greater acceptance of pre- and extra-marital sex, homosexuality and nudity.... We're becoming seekers of pleasure as many of the old prohibitions disappear.[45]

4. Finally, it is argued that leisure may be increasing in importance because work is losing its hold as a central life interest and is becoming meaningless to many employees. These employees are increasingly identifying themselves in terms of their leisure pursuits rather than their work.

Reasons why leisure might not be increasing are:

1. The actual gains in "free time" accrued in the past 130 years are relatively minimal according to DeGrazia. He has argued that the worker spends the additional hours gained from the reduced workweek moonlighting, engaging in do-it-yourself activities around the house, commuting to and from work, and converting extra hours into household chores, minimizing the gain in free time.

2. If our economy continues to shift from a goods to a service economy, further reductions in the workweek are unlikely. It has even been argued by R. Carter that there might be an overall increase in the amount of work activities, rather than a decrease: The reasons are:

(1) the recent attempts of managers of large corporations to make work more meaningful through job enrichment, job rotation and a human relations approach to decision making; and (2) the relatively low productivity of the service occupations (government, trade, finance and personal services).[46]

---

[45]*Ibid.,* p. 21.

[46]R. Carter, "The Myth of Increasing Non-Work Versus Work," *Social Problems* 18:52–67, 1970.

Additionally, it is argued by Burck[47] that services are devourers of time because service workers are less efficient, live performance and personal contact are involved, and capital cannot be substituted for such labor. Also the production of goods is increasingly dependent upon the production of services and this fact, combined with the government's commitment to improving the quality of life, will cause more time to be spent at work, not less (although the high unemployment and increasing accountability of governmental services may cause a shift in this trend).

3. Studies have indicated that the total time of individuals engaged in household responsibilities has not been reduced significantly despite the presence of labor-saving devices.

4. Time becomes scarce as our work values spill over into our leisure values.

Just as we desire to be efficient and productive in our work, we also desire to be efficient and productive in our leisure. This attitude toward leisure, with its emphasis upon accomplishment, efficiency and mastery through technique and incremental improvement, places us in a situation in which we often feel that we do not have to do or to accomplish our leisure goals.[48]

Thus from a psychological perspective we have less leisure.

5. Being able to actualize the "leisure potential" made available through technology requires restructuring the very societal institutions that gave us this potential and dealing with the problems that they created.

SUMMARY

Circular conceptions of time developed in ancient Greece around a constant and recurring rhythm of life—defined as chronos. This eternal, recurring view of time gave way to a mechanical, clock orientation in the social order which emerged on a larger scale in the fourteenth century. Mechanical time provided the industrializing civilization more precision and regularity. It is argued by DeGrazia that a mechanical rhythm of life applied to contemporary society dilutes the ability of the individual to achieve a true state of leisure.

Other orientations to time include a cosmic view; part-whole and space-time concept; a personality perspective, which describes temperament and differences in perceptions among people; bimodal consciousness, which represents two modes of human organization (a receptive

---

[47]G. Burck, "There'll Be Less Leisure Than You Think," *Fortune,* March 1970, pp. 87–89, 162, 165–166.

[48]Godbey and Parker, *Leisure Studies and Services,* p. 23.

and an action mode); and split brain (hemisphere) orientation emphasizing the need to develop a full range of human expression.

Time-budget studies serve as a traditional method of recording human activities at various regular intervals (e.g., day, week, year). Data have consistently shown an empirical regularity to temporal orderings of availability of free time. However, time-budget studies have disadvantages which include an unwillingness of people to participate, omission of certain activities such as illegal activities, and confusion of respondents over activity choices offered on questionnaires.

A comprehensive twelve-nation study was undertaken to assess the utilization of time by various people in different cultures. It represented the first time that a massive amount of data were gathered and interpreted regarding how time was utilized by various socioeconomic groups from socialist and capitalist countries. A similar study of the allocation of time was undertaken in four countries. Some of the findings revealed: (1) there has been a growth in the quantity of time freed from work, particularly since World War I; (2) the freeing of time from work has been the result of economic, political, and sociocultural processes; (3) length of vacation periods have become the most important time blocks during the major years of work life; (4) the dynamics of the development of pop mass culture has contributed to the sociopolitical-cultural pressure to free time from work; (5) there is an increasing interest in different, more fluid rhythms of work and education; (6) there is an increasing desire to exercise more control over one's natural life rhythms throughout the life span; and (7) manual workers have long hours, work years, and work lives.

There is a changing allocation of time and work. As an economic function work is no longer the single largest source of meaning for life. Some reasons contributing to increased leisure are technological advancement leading to higher earnings and more time off the job, decline in Puritan Work Ethic, and the lessening of work as a central-life interest. Conversely, some reasons why leisure might not be increasing are minimal actual gains in "free time," continued consumption of goods necessitating an overall increase in the amount of work activities, little gains in time freed from household responsibilities, spillover of work values into our leisure values, and necessity to restructure societal institutions to actualize the "leisure potential."

PART THREE

FUNCTIONAL AND ENVIRONMENTAL PERSPECTIVES OF LEISURE

5

Leisure
and
Life Style

Viewing leisure via life style incorporates a broad interpretation of a person's life choices, personal interests, and engagement in group behavior. In this chapter life style patterns will be explored along with the influence of the human life cycle and stages of development in the human life span. A discussion of social groupings and the implications for leisure will be presented. The social worlds of leisure, the influence of family interaction patterns and taste as a reflector of values, preferences, and identity will be explored in relationship to contemporary culture.

The term "life style" is used as a synthesizing perspective, an important emerging sociopsychological indicator for delineating the nature of human behavior in general, which is partly expressed through leisure interests and tastes. It represents a person's pattern of behavior. It is considered by Rapoport and Rapoport[1] that life style surpasses the various single-criterion conceptualizations of leisure (such as its definition as free time or as a function of psychological, social and/or environmental aspects, etc.) as leisure interests are apparently tied less to gross occupational, gender, income, and educational characteristics and are more determined by a wide range of personal and social experiences; leisure is more a part of life than merely something antithetical to work or only a release of tension.

[1]Rhona and Robert N. Rapoport. *Leisure and the Family Life Cycle* (Boston: Routledge and Kegan Paul, 1975).

Feldman and Thielbar define life style by stating that it:

1. is a group phenomenon, influenced by a person's participation in various social groups,

2. pervades many aspects of life and spills over into many areas of social contact, e.g., work, play, school, family, church, etc.,

3. implies a central life interest in which a single activity (avocational pursuits, work, religion, cultural heritage, etc.) pervades a person's other interests and unrelated activities.[2]

Life style, then, represents various elements, such as social class, ethnic-religious background, occupational characteristics and involvements, social and cultural affiliations, and specific job situations and experiences which represent family life cycle stage, age, and gender. These elements integrated with work, family, and community interests to form an amalgam of different patterns which fluctuate throughout the life cycle.

Wilensky has reported that both social class and this new range of sociopsychological determinants exist in today's society. This is occurring because of the heterogeneity of life situations and the unevenness with which modern changes affect different parts of society. Wilensky offers three essential patterns in relation to leisure and life style:

1. *Class-determined patterns*—essentially relevant for lower status workers whose occupational life approximates most closely to the nineteenth-century picture of the monotonous and dehumanized work setting contributing to an anomic leisure pattern portrayed by Marx and Engels.

2. *Individualized personality-determined patterns*—representative of deviant, solitary, alienated, fluid patterns. These are noted in various contexts, including the compensatory contra-system type evidenced by delinquents, counter-culture types, etc.

3. *Family-home localism*—representative of less deviant, less solitary, less alienated, more habitual individuals who are less inclined to be retreating away from society but *towards* the comfort and security of the family circle.[3]

[2]Saul D. Feldman and Gerald W. Thielbar, eds. *Life Styles: Diversity in American Society* (Boston: Little, Brown and Co., 1972), pp. 1–3.

[3]Harold L. Wilensky, "Work, Careers and Social Integration," *International Social Science Journal* 12:543–560, 1960.

LEISURE AND THE FAMILY LIFE CYCLE

According to the Rapoports the perspective of the human life cycle may lead to a greater understanding of people's needs. Since the life cycle is based on relatively constant preoccupations arising from psychobiological maturational processes, this perspective cuts across and underlies class and subcultural patterns.

The life cycle usually plays itself out in the framework of family living; and while leisure in its most essential properties may be fundamentally individual and personal, the family is a major link to the social and cultural world. The type and meaning of leisure and other interests enjoyed by an individual are *dependent* on the stage of the life cycle and on the pressures, influences, and opportunities exerted by various others in these stages (for a brief explanation of six generally recognized periods of growth and change in human development, refer to stages of development in the human life span, Table 5–1).

According to the Rapoports, individuals develop their lives along at least three lines: work, family, and leisure. Individuals integrate influences and experiences in all of these life spheres as they create and live out a life career (specific life sectors or blocks of experience). While the three separate planes are conceptually distinct, individuals combine them in characteristic ways to form whole-life-style patterns (see Figure 5–1).

Each strand of life experience—work, family, and leisure interests—is viewed as having a semi-autonomous career of its own. Though each has different properties, there is a sense in which a structure (as depicted in Figure 5–1) is erected by a spiral process of later experiences being partly built on earlier ones. Life revision occurs, consciously or unconsciously, as each stage is entered into and a new integration

Table 5–1
Stages of Development in Human Life Span

1. Generalized stage of childhood, in which the individual seeks to learn rudimentary skills.
2. The stage of adolescence, in which the major concerns shift toward the development of identity and psychological severence from parents.
3. Early middle years, in which the individual seeks a place in the adult world in terms of mature relationships and economic autonomy.
4. Mid-life, where the individual confronts aging and reevaluates his or her general course in life.
5. Late middle years, in which the individual confronts what he or she has become and is likely to become.
6. Old age, with the realization of death and the necessity for finding and maintaining ongoing interests and engaging purposes.

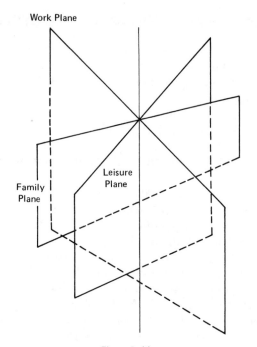

Figure 5–1*
Three Planes Representing Sectors Based on
the Individual Lifeline

*Rhona Rapoport, R.N. Rapoport, and Z.
Sterlitz, "Leisure and the Family Life Cycle: A Map of the Territory," Sport and Leisure in Contemporary Society, eds. Stanley
Parker, Nikki Ventris, John Haworth, and
Michael Smith. (London: School of the Environment, Polytechnic of Central London,
1975), p. 35.

brought about. Each career strand thus forms a *helix* at each critical status transition (e.g., getting married), when people go back over previous critical experiences associated with the event.

Changes in job, changes in interests, moves of home, and other such events constitute critical turning points in the life cycle. While each such event tends to originate in the role structure of a single strand, the interlocking nature of the strands is such, in the Rapoports' view, that the life career as a whole—the summation of the life styles at all points through the life cycle—comprises a "triple helix."

The Rapoport's thesis is that underlying observable life-style patterns there are sociopsychological dimensions of motivations that are

important to appreciate if one is to understand people's life requirements. They propose that at *any* stage in the life cycle:

1. Persons have *preoccupations* derived from their basic biological, social,
    and developmental tasks.

2. These *preoccupations,* in turn, lead to certain *interests* in the kinds of
    occupation and relationships that will predominate in that period.
    Through the life career these *interests* change as *preoccupations* and
    social expectations change.

3. Finally, the opportunity structure presents *activities* that provide
    spheres of action to carry out these *interests.*

The "preoccupations-interests-activities" scheme suggests that leisure interests are not some separate segment of life that may be altered
at will. What a person "wants" in leisure complements identity and
social-role development through the life career. Leisure is not determined by work, education, family, and community roles; but neither
is leisure separate from them. Activities (such as taking a walk in the
park) would ideally be chosen to satisfy needs integral to biological,
personal, and social development just as employment, marriage, and
community relationships may be chosen to enhance leisure roles that
are valued. The key concepts reflecting the developmental nature of the
changes that occur in the course of the cycle are the following:[4]

PREOCCUPATIONS	INTERESTS	ACTIVITIES
Are mental absorptions, or less conscious, which arise from psychological, matur-ation, and aging processes as they interact with social environmental conditions.	Arise in people's awareness as ideas and feelings about what they want or would like to have or do, about which they are cu-rious, to which they are drawn, through which they feel they might derive satisfaction.	Are spheres of ac-tion—such as car driving, dancing, participating in or watching sports, attending clubs, etc.

It is argued from this perspective that the variety of life styles
emerging is less likely than previously to justify a leisure concept
which is based, for example, on a residual counterpart with work. The
enrichment of the quality of the working life, the intensification of
family and home-centered activities, the normative acceptance of social
variation along the blurring of class strata all contribute to a picture of
life style, so the Rapoports contend, in which work, family, and leisure
are fused in amalgams of different patterns.

[4]Rhona Rapoport, Robert N. Rapoport, and Z. Sterlitz, "Leisure and the Family Life Cycle: A Map
of the Territory," *Sport and Leisure in Contemporary Society*, ed. Stanley Parker et al. (London: School
of the Environment, Polytechnic of Central London, 1975), p. 34.

SOCIAL GROUPINGS AND THEIR IMPLICATIONS
FOR LEISURE

It has been noted by a number of leisure scholars, including Cheek, Field, and Burdge[5] that leisure activities tend to be group experiences, with a minimum of 90 percent (of persons studied) engaged in leisure activities with others. The family represents the most common social unit in which leisure participation takes place. Therefore, it is of interest to note how people organize into groups.

The use of the social group as an empirical model for statistically explaining variation in leisure activity in a study reported by Cheek, Field, and Burdge[6] helped to explain the intensity of participation in water-based recreation. Typically social aggregate variables (socioeconomic-status variables) are used to demonstrate differences among users of recreation settings; these variables include occupation, education, income, age, ages of family members, size of family, marital status, sex, size of town. While education and income still continue to distinguish participants, Cheek, et al. state that social aggregate variables fail to explain the differences that arise in the frequency of participation.

While the ORRRC (Outdoor Recreation Resources Review Commission) studies remain the standard reference on the influence of aggregate variables upon recreation behavior, it and many similar studies failed to exclude the nonparticipants before using some method of multivariable analysis to explain recreation participation. Further, when nonparticipants are excluded from the ORRRC studies pertaining to seven variables, less than 12 percent of the variation is explained. This indicates that other factors, not included in main aggregate variables, are responsible for explaining over 85 percent of observed differences in outdoor recreation participation. While state and federal outdoor recreation studies for years have attempted to assess or predict demand for outdoor recreation in general and for selected activities specifically, the conclusions reached about users are often *invalid* because of an incomplete analysis strategy.[7] Social characteristics, it has been found, do not adequately predict leisure behavior. The activity profiles generally tend to inflate the strength of the statistical relationships. But when the social group on which participation occurs is added to the analysis, the ability to explain the intensity of participation is greatly enhanced.

[5]Neil H. Cheek, Jr., Donald R. Field, and Rabel J. Burdge. *Leisure and Recreation Places* (Ann Arbor, Mich.: Ann Arbor Science Publishers, 1976), p. 63.

[6]*Ibid.,* pp. 61–73.

[7]*Ibid.,* p. 71.

TYPES OF SOCIAL GROUPS

There are three major types of leisure involvement in social groups: (1) leisure interests cause one to join an existing group with similar interests; (2) leisure behavior is central to life style, and group formation is based on this leisure interest; and (3) group membership is based on other factors and dictates leisure interests and activities.

In the *first* type of group formation related to leisure involvement, similar *taste* is the basis for a person's choosing membership in an existing group with similar interests. Taste is defined by the dictionary as an individual's esthetic preference or liking. However, sociologists typically define taste as preference exercised in response to felt normative pressures. Taste serves as a boundary for group maintenance and is also the cohesive factor in holding the group together. Taste, then, is an important element which influences life style and leisure choice.

Cheek, Field, and Burdge suggest that leisure taste is formed in childhood and is carried over into adulthood. Thus adults would tend to participate in activities similar to those they experienced as children.[8] Similarly, evidence suggests that inactivity during childhood may create inactivity as adults. These findings support Burch's[9] explanation of leisure behavior, the "personal community theory," which states that one's inner social circle of acquaintances is a great influence on leisure behavior, as opposed to the "familiarity theory" and the "compensatory theory." The familiarity theory suggests that a person's leisure (camping) activity style reflects one's familiar pattern of living. The compensatory approach suggests that leisure (camping) style reflects sharp departures from the user's at-home routine.

Taste arises within the small social group based upon kinship and friendship.

They are transient in the sense that they govern preference among a limited set of individuals for a limited set of time. When individuals move out of their original social groups to form new groups, they may modify the content or discontinue conforming to such norms. However, norms peculiar to the new group tend to emerge for reasons previously considered, and these norms usually govern substantive patterns similarly as did the norms.[10]

Taste, therefore, may provide social boundaries, but in order to ensure intergroup solidarity, its boundaries are permeable. It is inher-

[8]*Ibid.*, pp. 75–87.

[9]William R. Burch, "The Social Circles of Leisure: Competing Explanations," *Journal of Leisure Research* 1:125, 1969.

[10]Neil H. Cheek and William R. Burch. *The Social Organization of Leisure in Human Society* (New York: Harper and Row, Publishers, 1976), p. 130.

ently social in character, arising from affect-laden matters and typically connected with the biosocial properties of the human race.

A significant small social group—the family—provides the early requisite skills in the formative years which enable continued development in later phases of the life cycle. However, human beings do not spend all of their lives in the same social group, except perhaps symbolically. Membership in a social circle is generally dictated by taste and common interests, such as leisure activities. While social circles are informally organized and much of the interaction is indirect, they still provide a sense of identity for the individual and sanction a particular style of leisure behavior.

According to Charles Kadushin's theory,[11] a *social circle* is a collection of people who share common interests and who are informally organized (there is a low degree of institutionalization, and a high proportion of the interaction is indirect). Social circles have four fundamental properties: (1) They are based on *free choice,* lending to the possibility that they can eliminate other forms of social bonding, e.g., tribal and neighborhood types of organization; (2) they are formed around six focal points—age and sex statuses, self-interest, family, religion, and others; (3) people in modern society tend to belong to a number of social circles; and (4) they have both integrative and conflict-producing properties.[12]

Cheek and Burch comment on a study by Russell Lynes[13] on the emerging taste strata of low-, middle-, and high-brows which suggests a certain personal competence underlies the system.

> Thus a purely social creation such as taste, in which standards ambiguously float without any objective means for testing and about which a range of professional taste-makers issue contradictory pronouncements as to the absolutely right standard, still becomes a creation which can erect the strongest boundaries for regulating social relations.[14]

In the *second* type of leisure involvement, groups' leisure preferences and behavior serve as a central life interest for such social entities. It might be argued at this juncture in the development of modern technological society that such group formations represent an extreme example of life styles. Such groups manifest themselves around rejection of work norms (craft guild people), surfers, etc. Groups are formed because of the differential association of participants in a particular

---

[11]Charles Kadushin, "The Friends and Supporters of Psychotherapy: On Social Circles in Urban Life," *American Sociological Review* 31: 786–802, 1966.

[12]*Ibid.,* p. 788.

[13]Russell Lynes, *The Taste Makers* (London: Hamish Hamilton, 1949).

[14]Cheek and Burch, *Social Organization,* p. 141.

behavior. Complete social worlds are organized around leisure interests. These social worlds will be represented by language, rules of behavior, dress code, and even group literature in some cases. People become members of this type of group because of the particular meaning an activity has for them. Such leisure-dominant life-style groups are still regarded as cult or counterculture in type, and so research based on groups from mainstream society cannot be aptly applied to them.

Since work is still the principal gauge of social organization in modern technological society, the underlying meaning of activity preferences and bases for group membership remain elusive. Certainly, while all social groups are elastic and permeable, new cultural vogues will probably result in changes within such social circles, similar to those representative of the cultural norm.

The *third* type of leisure involvement is based on group membership dictated by various nonleisure factors. Essentially these types of social groups are based on the formation of:

1. *Social action systems*—family and friendship groups in which a basic component is a large amount of interpersonal interaction.

2. *Social aggregate systems*—groups that are based on the statistical sharing of a common trait, e.g., age and gender, but that do not include a lot of interpersonal interaction.[15]

Social action systems are structured with roles and statuses and governed by norms and standards—matters of taste are learned as an aspect of social bonding or socialization of the group. Within this type of group, families are the most common social unit in which leisure tends to occur. A *social aggregate system*—for example, a social aggregate of females 20–29 years of age who collect antiques—works in conjunction with social action systems to influence leisure behavior. However, because of our social structure these systems are seldom found without the added influence of a social action group. For example, age group and gender do determine categories of leisure interest, but they are further modified by family influences or peer group pressure. Cheek, Field, and Burdge amplify:

It is not the individual properties such as statuses and roles of family and friendship groups but the points of intersection between systems that offer leisure researchers a new direction in activity studies. For example, the relationship between occupation, sex, age, or educational attainment (social aggregate system) and the family or friendship groups (social action system) represents a point of intersection for analyzing participation.[16]

[15]Cheek, Field, and Burdge, *Leisure and Recreation Places*, pp. 62–65.

[16]*Ibid.*, p. 65.

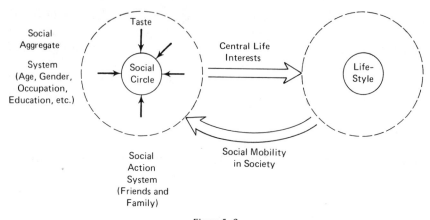

Figure 5–2
The Influence of Taste on Social Circles and Life Style

In summary, social circles are the *fundamental* social mechanism for maintaining life style and it is the combination of life style and social circle that ensures the maintenance of a given form of permeability in the wider society. Taste and social circles, since they cut across social strata or private boundaries, can maintain either an open class structure or a very closed one. The amount of permeability in a social class system will have a definite effect on leisure opportunities and available avenues of expression and participation in leisure activities.

SOCIAL WORLDS OF LEISURE

Participation in leisure ranges from a one-time type through regular weekend and holiday participation to commitment to the activity as a central life interest. Social worlds serve as the environments of social interaction among social groups. They are made up of norms, expectations, roles, and special schemes elaborated by participants through a special communication system. Social worlds may also have special meanings and symbols which further accentuate difference and increase social distance from outsiders.[17]

The social worlds of leisure are perhaps best illustrative of the second type of social group formation related to leisure involvement. Such configurations serve as increasingly important reference groups in contemporary societies. Cheek, Field, and Burdge have noted that mountain climbers and surfers, for example, members of two types of leisure social worlds, have come into conflict with other recreation groups and

[17]*Ibid.,* p. 133.

118

with political agencies over a variety of issues ranging from rules for climbing and surfing to "life-style" issues—clothing, looks, and manners.[18] Cleavages between the advocates of these leisure social worlds and the larger society have developed into conflicts. Such cleavages exist between what might be referred to as surfing "purists" (those espousing communion with nature, highly individualistic experience, sometimes mystical search for nirvana) and "innovators" (those involved with developing marinas, hotels, and special spectator facilities to enhance the sport's commercial potential), or between "orthodox" climbers (a cultic sect of climbers who believe in the individualistic, noncompetitive nature of the activity) and "reformists" (who are seeking to glamorize the sport through promotion of climbing gear, climbing classes, and "stunts," even attempts to make mountaineering more ecologically relevant).

The morass of societal and scholarly data from the analysis of leisure social worlds has tended to focus on highly institutionalized sports such as football, basketball, and baseball. However, there are numerous other social worlds including sailing, scuba diving, antique collecting, clam digging, and others, which are emerging as major areas needing investigation. As Cheek, Field, and Burdge have suggested, the norms of leisure behavior become reinforced in social worlds, and eventually certain codes of behavior evolve. The social worlds can come into conflict with other recreationists and with administrators of recreation areas. As special leisure worlds become more numerous, the management of recreation areas, particularly those with multiple objectives, will be faced with finding ways to balance the demands of unique leisure groups with the needs of the more conventional recreationists.

LEISURE AND THE FAMILY

The family, the primary source of an individual's socialization, provides an important setting in which the attitudes of children are developed toward all major institutions, including leisure. As has been previously stated, the family serves as the primary context for leisure expression. In addition, it has been postulated by Orthner[19] that persons select leisure activities that are compatible with the kind of interaction they prefer in their marriages, and that the activities reinforce this marital pattern. It has been suggested that leisure plays

[18]*Ibid.,* pp. 133–142.

[19]Dennis K. Orthner, "Leisure Styles and Family Styles: The Need for Integration," *Leisure Today,* October/November 1974, pp. 11–13.

a role in marital cohesion: family members valuing the mutual enjoyment of certain activities was indicative of marital satisfaction while valuing separate interests was more likely to predict dissatisfaction. Traditional families were less dependent on leisure for cohesion than egalitarian families. Orthner[20] found that higher proportions of time spent in joint activities with the spouse were associated with marital satisfaction for both husbands and wives. He also reported that high proportions of time spent in solitary pursuit were negatively related to marital satisfaction, especially for wives. This evidence suggests that marital partners establish mutually reinforcing leisure and marital interaction patterns. Further, it seems clear from studies on marital cohesiveness and satisfaction that these patterns may not always function in equilibrium or supportively, and that differences may vary according to sex, social class, degree of family traditionalism, and stage of the family life cycle.

Orthner[21] investigated the ways in which different leisure activities function to support different types of interaction in marriage, in order to understand and measure more effectively the marital consequences of leisure participation. He developed an activity framework (refer to Figure 5–3) which draws upon patterns of interaction, ranging from little or no interaction or symbolic feedback to extensive contact and interaction. They are:

1. *Individual Activities.* Activities that are carried out alone and that do not directly influence the feedback mechanisms of a relationship. If they are dominant patterns, they can break down interdependency between family members and encourage each person to develop his or her own world with its own satisfactions.

2. *Parallel Activities.* Activities which are shared but with limited opportunities for interaction, such as watching television, going to the theater, or gardening. There are few requirements for direct communication.

3. *Joint Activities.* Activities, such as game playing, partying, or camping, which require significant interaction and require each person to recognize the needs of others and in which dialogue becomes necessary for successful participation. Joint activities encourage more open communication, provide feedback, and may develop alternate role relationships for the participants. "Joint activities, if desired, may also increase interpersonal satisfaction to the extent that a better understanding of the other increases his or her significance in the interactive process."[22]

---

[20] *Ibid.,* pp. 11–13.

[21] Dennis K. Orthner, "Patterns of Leisure and Marital Interaction," *Journal of Leisure Research* 8:98–111, 1976.

[22] *Ibid.,* p. 102.

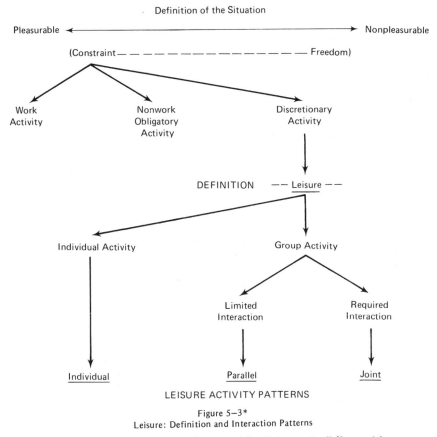

Definition of the Situation

Pleasurable ⟵————————————————————⟶ Nonpleasurable

(Constraint — — — — — — — — — — — — — — Freedom)

Work Activity

Nonwork Obligatory Activity

Discretionary Activity

DEFINITION   — — Leisure — —

Individual Activity

Group Activity

Limited Interaction

Required Interaction

Individual

Parallel

Joint

LEISURE ACTIVITY PATTERNS

Figure 5—3*
Leisure: Definition and Interaction Patterns

*Dennis K. Orthner, "Toward a Theory of Leisure and Family Interaction," (Prepared for the annual meeting of the Pacific Sociological Association, San Jose, Calif., March 1974), p. 26.

Orthner's study showed that the degree of interaction in leisure activities is positively related to the degree of interaction in nonleisure settings only to the extent that the participants give exclusive attention to each other. While he only partially demonstrated that there is a relationship between type of leisure activity and amount of marital interaction, his study does show the decline over time in joint activity which parallels decline in marital satisfaction.

The family serves as the primary staging area for a substantial portion of leisure activities, except for adolescents and single individuals. Adolescents share less of the home-centered family life of their parents.

Table 5-2
Listing of Parallel and Joint Leisure Activities*

PARALLEL ACTIVITIES

Shopping for pleasure	Constructing models	Bicycling for pleasure
Going to library	Writing poems, stories	Fishing
Attending racetracks	Family needlework	Swimming
Visiting museums or galleries	Art modeling, painting	Hunting
Attending movie theater	Sewing for pleasure	Hiking
Attending wrestling or boxing matches	Writing letters	Playing pencil and paper games
Attending athletic events or spectator events	Reading books, magazines, newspapers	Attending musical concerts
Caring for pets	Playing musical instruments	Attending lectures and debates
Studying nature	Listening to records or tapes	Attending plays and other drama
Collecting (stamps, coins, etc.)	Watching television	Taking college class
Gardening and yard work for pleasure	Listening to radio (primary activity)	Attending church
Tinkering in workshop	Skin or scuba diving	Taking naps or relaxing
	Roller skating	Creatively cooking (beyond meal preparation)
	Ice skating	

JOINT ACTIVITIES

Going to parks or playgrounds	Motor boating	Playground games
Visiting zoo	Flying for pleasure	Playing Ping-Pong
Attending drive-in theater	Playing handball	Taking part in amateur dramatics, debates, discussion groups
Spending time in taverns, nightclubs, lounges	Attending organized camps	Community service groups
Visiting amusement parks	Going on hayrides	Parent teacher activities
Attending parties	Playing badminton	Political activities
Picnicking away from home	Playing shuffleboard	Attending: craft or adult education classes, fraternal organization meetings, community social events, church suppers, family or club reunions, other socials outside the home
Eating meals out	Riding horses	
Riding in auto for pleasure	Playing miniature golf	
Playing billiards or pool	Playing golf	
Playing basketball, baseball, volleyball	Camping (organized area)	
Playing tennis	Camping (backwoods)	
Water skiing	Playing backyard or lawn games	
Snow skiing	Dancing or attending dances	Playing informally with the children
Bowling	Playing football	Engaging in affectional or sexual activity
Sailing	Canoeing, rowing	Casual conversation
	Playing card games	

*Dennis K. Orthner, "Patterns of Leisure and Marital Interaction," Journal of Leisure Research 8:104, 1976.

Larson[23] discusses some of the use and availability of leisure for marriage and family relationships:

1. Families of differing occupational levels within and across social class categories use leisure in differing ways.

2. The use of free time for leisure is most often individual or couple-oriented rather than family-oriented. Television viewing is often used as an excuse for family interaction. The contact of the family unit with the community militates against *family* activities. Religious and educational institutions seldom organize their family night activities around family units, tending instead to segregate family members into differing groups and activities.

3. Conjugal satisfaction is related to the mutual enjoyment of leisure activities. Larson cites a Bull and Johannis study[24] which found that wives expect husbands to use their nonwork time in family maintenance rather than for self or extra-family activities.

4. Family use of free time for leisure is subjected to severe competition from alternative responsibilities and opportunities. Family members, fathers in particular, are able to find resolution of personal needs through extra-family relationships.

5. The involvement of children and youth in extracurricular afterschool activities, proliferation of organizations and clubs, and community recreation provisions is increasingly removing the child from the influence of the family.

Leisure service, while not an essential ingredient in family stability, nonetheless plays an important role in bringing family members together outside of their responsibilities and commitments. Some future considerations related to the family implications for leisure service outlined by Larson are as follows[25]:

1. The primacy of the conjugal (marital) relationship is apparent. With more married couples in Canada and the United States deciding not to have children, the average couple will spend more time alone together during the life span without the presence of children. Also, there will be more childless marriages. These trends suggest the need for more adult programming during the life span—in particular, a couple focus.

[23]Lyle E. Larson, "The Family and Leisure in Post-Industrial Society," *Work and Leisure in Canada*, ed. S. Hameed and D. Cullen (Edmonton: University of Alberta, 1972), pp. 132–142.

[24]Neil C. Bull and Theodore B. Johannis, Jr., "Wife's Perception of Aim and Spouse's Non-work and Leisure Behavior," Paper presented at the Annual Meeting of the Canadian Sociology and Anthropology Association, 1970.

[25]Lyle E. Larson, "Recreation Programming and the Family," *Seminar Proceedings* (Seebe, Alberta: Recreation Administrators Seminar, Paper presented to the Recreation and Park Association of Alberta, Canada, January 1978), pp. 194–201.

2. As divorce rates continue to rise (48 percent in the United States, 33 percent in Canada), there will be more single parents (particularly more mothers) and more motherless and fatherless children. Single parenthood is a source of stress, and parenting problems are more complicated than ever. Substitute and supplementary day care will become more common and indeed more necessary. As a result, leisure service programs will need to adjust to the interests and needs of the single-parent family. Family activities may need to be more oriented to one-parent families. Activities may need to be scheduled to provide both alternative activities to day care and recuperative periods to single parents during their nonwork time. Joint recreation and day care facilities need to be explored in the future.

    Additionally, an important emphasis of adult programs could be on male and female companions for single parents. Coeducational activities in weekend camping events, competitive sports, and related activities in the interest of promoting companionship among unattached, and frequently frustrated, single parents can be both memorable and self-evoking.

3. Dual-career marriages will likely continue to increase. While dual-career marriages can be fulfilling for both wives and husbands, the evidence suggests that this form of marriage pattern is quite problematic. A large number of working women, particularly the better educated, will have children. The implication of working motherhood is that (1) the roles of husbands and wives must change in order to equalize the housekeeping responsibilities, and (2) the time with children, among couples who have children, must involve unusual effort and commitment to ensure quality time. Dual-career families typically have greater difficulty scheduling compatible holiday times and evenings together. While leisure service programming may not appeal to the dual-career family, effective programs which are adaptable to intensive weekend use, day care programs, early evening programs, or "on-the-way-home-stopover" activities might be attractive to them.

4. Existing male-female segregation in many facilities and activities will increasingly be unnecessary and even inappropriate. Sex roles will continue to become more androgynous. Coeducational activities will become more acceptable and thus more viable. Sex-typed appointments in leisure service should become a thing of the past, with respect to both administration and leadership in all leisure facilities.

5. Leisure service agencies will be confronted with alternative life styles (including group marriages, communal living, common-law marriages, homosexual relationships). Since much of the foregoing is related to strengthening the marriage and family, assisting alternative-arrangement couples to achieve a more satisfying life together could pose moral problems for all public agencies.

LEISURE AND HUMAN DEVELOPMENT

A major theory of human development is psychosocial theory developed by Erikson.[26] It is based on four organizing concepts: (1) stages of development, (2) developmental tasks, (3) the psychosocial crises, and (4) the process of coping.

Stages of Development

Erickson's theory suggested eight stages of psychosocial development through the life cycle. For clarification purposes Newman and Newman[27] expanded it to nine stages (Table 5–3) and enlarged the perspective treated earlier in the chapter.

Developmental Tasks

The developmental tasks consist of a set of skills and competencies that are acquired by the individual as he or she gains increased mastery over the environment. The tasks may reflect gains in motor skills, intellectual skills, social skills, and emotional skills. Acquisition of earlier fundamental skills is crucial to the mastery of tasks at later stages of development. A person's orientation or view of the world at any one time depends on his or her ability to utilize intellectual, emotional, and social skills.

The Psychosocial Crisis

The psychosocial crisis refers to the person's psychological effort to adjust to the demands of his or her social environment at each stage of development. The term "crisis" here refers to a normal set of stresses and strains rather than to an extraordinary set of events. At each stage of development, society makes certain psychic demands upon the individual. These demands are experienced by the individual as mild, in relation to persistent guidelines and expectations of behavior. Near the culmination of each stage of development the individual must make some form of resolution, adjusting to the demands of society while simultaneously translating the societal demands into personal terms. This process produces a stage of tension within the individual which must be reduced for the person to proceed to the next stage.

[26]E. H. Erikson. *Childhood and Society* (New York: Norton, 1950).

[27]Barbara M. Newman and Philip R. Newman. *Development Through Life* (Homewood, Ill.: The Dorsey Press, 1975).

It is this tension stage which is called the psychosocial crisis. The psychosocial crisis of a stage forces the person to utilize developmental skills which have only recently been mastered. There is, therefore, an interrelationship between the developmental tasks of each stage and the psychosocial crisis of that stage.[28]

The Process of Coping

The coping process refers to active efforts on the person's part to resolve stress and to create new solutions to the problems that face the individual at each developmental stage. Coping can be understood as behaviors that allow for the development and growth of the individual, not merely the maintenance of equilibrium in the face of threat.

The tension itself is not a result of personal inadequacies, but failure to resolve the tension can result in serious limitations to future growth. The concept of psychosocial crisis at each life stage does serve to legitimate the anxiety and tension that many people experience as they mature. It also implies that some degree of conscious attention is required, particularly in the later life stages, in order for growth to continue.

The essential approach of Erikson's theory is that it spans the life cycle and captures the essence of psychological work that takes place during critical life stages. There certainly are other life stage approaches which could be articulated, particularly which identify the pressures of the process of change. However, the whole realm of theory related to human development identifies the contribution of individual maturation, culture, and the immediate social environment to the process of personal development. Human developmental theory seems to be an area essential to the understanding of the nature of leisure expression *throughout* the life span, in order to identify how at each life stage the individual comes into contact with informal groups and more formal institutions which attempt to influence a person's motives, values, and behavior (a primary determining influence for the formulation of leisure tastes and selection of life style).

LEISURE AND POPULAR AND HIGH CULTURE

There is considerable argument on the merits of popular culture (representing the esthetic and other wants of middle-class people) and high culture (representing the arts, music, literature, and other symbolic products of the upper-class and well-educated elite). According to

---

[28]*Ibid.*, p. 19.

Table 5–3
Development Through Life: A Psychological Approach*

LIFE STAGE	DEVELOPMENTAL TASKS	PSYCHOSOCIAL CRISIS
Infancy (birth to 2 years)	1. Social attachment 2. Object permanence 3. Sensory motor inteligence and primitive causality 4. Maturation of motor functions	Trust v. Mistrust
Toddlerhood (2–4)	1. Self-control 2. Language development 3. Fantasy and play 4. Elaboration of locomotion	Autonomy v. Shame and Doubt
Early School Age (5–7)	1. Sex role identification 2. Early moral development 3. Concrete operations 4. Group play	Initiative v. Guilt
Middle School Age (8–12)	1. Social cooperation 2. Self-evaluation 3. Skill learning 4. Team play	Industry v. Inferiority
Early Adolescence (13–17)	1. Physical maturation 2. Formal operations 3. Membership in the peer group 4. Heterosexual relationships	Group Identity v. Alienation
Later Adolescence (18–22)	1. Autonomy from parents 2. Sex role identity 3. Internalized morality 4. Career choice	Individual Identity v. Role Diffusion
Early Adulthood (23–30)	1. Marriage 2. Childbearing 3. Work 4. Life style	Intimacy v. Isolation
Middle Adulthood (31–50)	1. Management of the household 2. Child-rearing 3. Management of a career	Generativity v. Stagnation
Later Adulthood (51–)	1. Redirection of energy to new roles 2. Acceptance of one's life 3. Developing a point of view about death	Integrity v. Despair

*Adapted from Newman and Newman, Development Through Life, p. 24.

Gans[29] both of these forms of cultural expression represent *taste culture* which functions to entertain, inform, and beautify life, and which expresses values and standards of taste and esthetics. Gans believes that America is actually made up of a number of taste cultures, each with its own arts, literature, music, and so on, which differ mainly in that

[29]Herbert J. Gans. *Popular Culture and High Culture* (New York: Basic Books, 1974), p. 10.

they express different esthetic standards. Essentially, the underlying assumption of this analysis is that *all* taste cultures are of equal worth. Because taste cultures reflect the class and particularly educational attributes of their adherents, low culture is as valid for poorly educated Americans or Canadians as high culture is for well-educated ones, even if the higher cultures are, in the abstract, better or more comprehensive than the lower cultures. This principle suggests two policy alternatives identified by Gans:

> (1) "Cultural mobility," which would provide every American [and Canadian] with the economic and educational prerequisites for choosing high culture; and (2) "subcultural programming," which encourages all taste cultures, high or low.[30]

According to Gans, taste cultures can be identified in three forms:

1. They consist of values and the cultural forms which express these values: music, art, design, literature, drama, comedy, poetry, criticism, news and the media in which these are expressed—books, magazines, newspapers, records, films and television programs, paintings and sculpture, architecture, and, insofar as ordinary consumer goods also express esthetic values or functions, furnishings, clothes, appliances, and automobiles as well.

2. Taste cultures include the values, forms, and media of the natural and social sciences and philosophy—including the commercial populations.

3. Finally, taste cultures have political values; although they do not often express them explicitly, they do so implicitly, and even when not, they frequently have political implications.[31]

Taste culture is related to the culture of leisure but it is not restricted to leisure values but is intertwined with nonleisure values too. Taste culture has to do with those values and products about which people have some choice. Taste culture is only a *partial* culture; it tends not to be viewed as *total* way of life. But it is tied to the rest of culture, because the values of taste culture are often similar to other values people hold, for example, about work or family life. "Indeed, one reason for the existence of many taste cultures is the fact that America is culturally pluralist, made up of a number of subcultures which coexist around a common core—'American culture' "[32]

Because the core is so vague, taste cultures are probably more correctly described as subcultures. The main source of differentiation between taste cultures and their populations is socioeconomic level or

[30] *Ibid.,* p. XI.
[31] *Ibid.,* pp. 10–11.
[32] *Ibid.,* p. 13.

class. This is seen by Gans to be representative of the customary income, occupation, and education level of the public. The subcultures are delineated by taste cultures according to high culture, upper-middle culture, lower-middle culture, low culture (culture of the working classes or proletariat, or "prole"), and quasi-folk culture (culture which is transmitted through direct and oral communication as in tribal or folk societies). Additionally, there are subcultures of youth, blacks, Chicanos, Chinese and Japanese Americans, Puerto Ricans, elderly, and disabled. Finally, there are a number of ethnic cultures—for example, Italian, Greek, Polish, and Irish—who are representative primarily of European immigrant groups seeking revival of cultural ways that were brought over from the "old country," found in family life, festivals, and religion, but that have been partially eroded through assimilation and acculturation.

Gans outlines two possible policy alternatives which would permit people to maximize their educational and other opportunities to choose from higher taste cultures or would enable people to pursue the differential esthetic tastes of their own culture.[33] Essentially, these two policy approaches to cultural mobility and subcultural pluralism (programming) have implications for leisure service. Cultural mobility implies that every individual would have access to the income, education, and other background characteristics of the class level necessary to choose the taste culture they decide to embrace. The second policy alternative, subcultural programming, implies that the good life can be *lived at all levels of taste* and that the overall taste level of a society is not as significant a criterion for the goodness of that society as the welfare of its members. In essence, while cultural reform or improvement is necessary, the more basic purpose of the culture of a people, according to the latter perspective, is to achieve human self-realization and to enhance the leisure potential of each individual.[34]

According to the subcultural programming perspective (the provision of cultural content to express and satisfy the specific standards of every public taste) the following is relevant: (1) it would enable people to find content best suited to their wants and needs, thus increasing their esthetic and other satisfaction as well as the relevance of their lives; (2) it would considerably increase cultural diversity, enhancing and enriching American culture as a whole (certainly television programs like *Roots, Centennial,* and *Holocaust* have heightened the pride

---

[33]The term subculture refers to any identifiable segment of society. T. Kando. *Leisure and Popular Culture in Transition* (St. Louis: The C. V. Mosby Co., 1975) p. 43, makes reference to contraculture, having to do with a subculture, which stands in opposition to important aspects of the dominant culture.

[34]See Gans, *Popular Culture and High Culture,* p. 131.

and importance of various subcultures and contributed to the society's overall well-being); and (3) it would also identify and then serve the taste of other subcultural and ethnic populations which are served poorly today.

According to Kando, popular culture permeates all of the classes, although it is primarily associated with middle-class culture. It is distinguished from mass culture in that it is the "better of the two" and is the *"typical cultural and recreational activities of typical segments of a society."*[35] High culture is defined by Kando as *"the recreational, cultural, and artistic activities traditionally not included in mass culture, such as theater, ballet, classical music, and the fine arts."*[36] As one can see, though, such a definition permits high culture to be popular. *"Mass culture consists of cultural elements traditionally not included in high culture, and transmitted by the printed press, the electronic media, or by other forms of mass communication."*[37] While mass culture defines the concept, mass leisure tells us what it means as it expresses *"the typical recreational activities in modern society."*[38] The terms *prole culture* and *prole leisure* refer to "the cultural and recreational activities of the proletariat."[39] Proletariat refers to the lower class, typified in Marxian terms as the ordinary wage earners who do not own the means of production but instead sell their labor. It might be said that many of the traditional leisure service offerings ignore the prole leisure audience representing the lower-class population, as well as various subcultures and life-style groups whose cultural and leisure activities may not be a reflection of social class—they are isolated *outside* the core culture, not as its top, middle, or bottom. Kando makes reference to activities of artists, jazz musicians, sectarian religious groups, rodeo people, poker or billiards players, and a variety of alternative sexual life-style groups, including mate swappers and homosexual and trasvestite communities.

The counterculture is a subculture which stands in opposition to important aspects of the dominant culture and is exemplified in the Sixties by the hippie retreatist, rebellious youth movement and perhaps the Black Panthers during the reign of Eldridge Cleaver and Huey Newton. Folk culture advocates direct interpersonal contact, much like the tribal culture of the Tassaday community in the Philippines.

To Kando the future of work and leisure in our society is a type of society in which spectator-performer distinction (star-audience) fades

[35]T. Kando, *Leisure and Popular Culture in Transition*, p. 41.

[36]*Ibid.*, p. 42.

[37]*Ibid.*, p. 42.

[38]*Ibid.*, p. 42.

[39]*Ibid.*, p. 43.

Popular Culture and Alternative Culture Relationships*				
Conventional Society, with Pluralistic and Mass Characteristics				Alternative Society, with Folk Characteristics
Orientation: Rational and Purposeful (Pragmatic) Values: Materialistic				Orientation: Affective Values: Idealistic
Work	Nonwork			Work–Nonwork Distinction Vanishes
		Popular Culture		The Counterculture
		Upper Class High Culture		Social Classes Vanish
Mass Production	Mass Consumption	Middle Class Mass Mass Leisure Culture	Subcultures	Folk Culture
		Lower Class Prole Prole Leisure Culture		

Figure 5—4*

*Adapted from T. Kando, Leisure and Popular Culture in Transition, p. 45.

and a more participatory culture emerges. Rapoport and Rapoport suggest that much of the leisure analysis has occurred at either the *macro-social* or the *micro-social* level but rarely the relationship between the two. At the macro-social level, the analyst surveys the increase in time off, increase in disposable income, increase in technological products available for mass consumption, increase in transport technology, increase in equalization of education, etc., trends which contribute to an increase in *aggregate* demand for leisure facilities. At this level there has been an increase in provision—of parks, miles of coastline set aside for recreation, numbers of tennis courts, racquetball courts, sports stadiums, museums, art galleries, theaters, symphony orchestras, pop festivals, tours, swimming pools, etc. There has been an institutionalization of roles and activities dealing with these phenomena. These are representative of leisure industries: departments of leisure and recreation in local, national, regional, and provincial government; and councils and departments in sport and leisure and in the arts, and countryside commissions. There are leisure journals, research and scholarly publications, institutes, professors, committees, and projects. This macro-social level may be referred to as the leisure sector, as differentiated from other spheres of life in contemporary society.

Then at the micro-social or individual level, leisure has meaning in reference to individual phenomenology, individual life styles that are highly varied and perhaps becoming more so. While it is important that a separate leisure sphere of administrative authority exist to assume responsibility for the creation of facilities, the individual users need not, and in fact typically do not, think of a separate sphere in their own lives in the same way. It is important that there be provisions to be used if wanted. Macro-social processes are not simply extrapolations of micro-social ones; and micro-social processes are not simply ones that are small. The diversification of life styles contributes to the minimization that a single definition of leisure is possible. There is need for focusing on issues of social integration and the relationship of the individual to society. *It might be expected that in the future more attention will be given to how individuals achieve a balance in their patterns of social participation among the different spheres of work, family, education, leisure, and other interests.*

SUMMARY

Life style is seen as a concept which expands our understanding of leisure beyond a single-criterion perspective. It represents a person's participation in a social group, the tastes, values, interests, and personality which permeate one's total life space, and it can imply a central life interest. According to the Rapoports, individuals develop their lives along three spheres of life—work, family, and leisure. Each of these strands of life experience is seen as having a semi-autonomous career of its own. Underlying observable life-style patterns are socio-psychological dimensions of motivations which are represented in a "preoccupation-interests-activities" scheme. This perspective of life style suggests that what a person "wants" in leisure complements identity and social-role development throughout the life career.

Most leisure activities take place in a social group. The family represents the most common social unit in which leisure participation takes place. Higher proportion of time spent in joint leisure activities with one's spouse has been associated with marital satisfaction for both husbands and wives. The three major types of leisure involvement in social groups are: (1) leisure interests cause one to join an existing group with similar interests; (2) leisure behavior is central to life style, and group formation is based on this leisure interest; and (3) group membership is based on other factors and dictates leisure interests and activities.

A human developmental approach to viewing human behavior aids in understanding the totality of individual maturation, culture, and the immediate social environment to the process of personal development. Such a perspective seems to be essential in understanding the nature of leisure expression throughout the life span.

High culture, popular (mass) culture, and counterculture serve as representations of values and standards of taste esthetics. Such taste cultures are related partially to leisure life styles. Gans suggests two policy perspectives relative to enabling people to select differential tastes of their own culture: *Cultural mobility,* providing people with the economic and educational prerequisites for choosing high culture, and another approach supporting *subcultural programming,* which would enable people to achieve self-realization and to enhance the leisure potential of each individual.

6

Socioeconomic-Status Perspectives of Leisure

A historically important area of leisure investigation at the micro-social level has been the analysis of social aggregate variables and their relationship to leisure participation. A number of studies have indicated that a person's social class position, racial and family background, gender, age, income education, and/or occupation seem to be associated with some forms of leisure expression.

CONSPICUOUS LEISURE

Leisure, particularly in the Greco-Roman concept, has been most often associated with an elite social class. In earlier, less industrialized societies, leisure was available in great quantity only to aristocrats, ruling classes, and privileged, who were immune from labor. Thorstein Veblen demonstrated that through various periods of history the wealthy elite have been identified through their possession of leisure.[1] Veblen's book profoundly affected social scientists, leading to a conceptualization of leisure as representing free time and social class in economics. Veblen's treatise admonishes the elitist "leisure class" for exploiting others while themselves engaging in "conspicuous consumption." This is possible because they are economically self-sufficient and can afford to be unproductive and to fill their free time with consumption of goods. Veblen's identification of the "idle rich" led to the concept of *leisure class.* Richard Kraus states:

[1]Thorstein Veblen. *The Theory of the Leisure Class* (New York: New American Library, 1953).

134

Veblen's major work, *The Theory of the Leisure Class,* pointed out that in Europe, during the feudal and Renaissance periods and finally in the industrial age, the possession and visible use of leisure became the hallmark of the upper class. Abstention from labor became the evidence of wealth and social standing.[2]

The concept of social class views leisure as a way of life for the rich elite. Leisure and life-style orientation have become increasingly an area of concern and interest, although Veblen's interpretation of the rigid dichotomy of social class is no longer relevant. The diffusion of culture, the spread of wealth, and increases in free time for the working class have resulted in increased access for the masses of material possession and forms of relaxation and entertainment.

Kenneth Roberts notes that as leisure "has gradually established a definite place in people's lives its autonomy from the influence of other institutions has correspondingly increased."[3] In the nineteenth and early twentieth century a person's social class was central to the pattern of his or her life. As leisure has become an increasingly differentiated institution and integral aspect of the social structure, activities people elect during leisure have become independent from other social roles. While class, occupational, racial, and other social determinants play an important role in determining one's leisure pattern, they have become less significant elements in advanced industrial and technological societies.

SOCIAL CLASS DIFFERENCES AND LEISURE

A number of studies have investigated class differences in the use of leisure. Many activities have been found to be correlated to class level, "particularly those in which participation requires a certain level of education; others, such as television, are not distinctly related."[4] Clyde R. White,[5] Saxon Graham,[6] Joel Gerstl,[7] Leonard Ressman,[8] and

[2]Richard Kraus. *Recreation and Leisure in Modern Society,* 1st ed. (New York: Appleton-Century-Crofts, 1971), p. 255.

[3]Kenneth Roberts. *Leisure* (London: Longmans Green and Co., 1970), p. 91.

[4]Rolf Meyersohn, "The Sociology of Leisure in the United States: Introduction and Bibliography, 1945–1965," *Journal of Leisure Research* 1 (Winter 1969) 56.

[5]Clyde R. White, "Social Class Differences in the Uses of Leisure," *American Journal of Sociology* 61 (September 1955), 145–150.

[6]Saxon Graham, "Social Correlates of Adult Leisure-Time Behavior," in *Community Structure Analysis,* ed. Marvin B. Sussman (New York: Thomas Y. Crowell Co., 1959), pp. 331–354.

[7]Joel Gerstl, "Leisure, Taste, and Occupational Milieu," *Social Problems* (Summer 1961), pp. 56–58.

[8]Leonard Ressman, "Class, Leisure and Social Participation," *American Sociological Review* 19 (February 1954), 75–84.

Lawrence C. Thomas[9] have investigated the relationship between social class differences and the uses of leisure, and have found clear distinctions among the various social class levels.

White's study analyzed the relationship between social class differences and the uses of leisure by identifying four social classes in several census tracts in Cuyahoga County, Ohio: upper-middle, lower-middle, upper-lower, and lower-lower. He identified several major categories of leisure use and grouped them under headings related to settings for leisure activity. They included: (1) public recreation facilities, (2) group-work agencies, (3) church, (4) museums, (5) libraries, (6) commercial amusements, and (7) other. He found that lower classes made much greater use of public facilities than upper classes, and the home was the most frequent setting for their leisure involvement, with commercial amusements a close second. Differences between lower and upper class in leisure participation sharpened with age.

Max Kaplan[10] cautions that social class determinants are no longer effective in predicting leisure interests and needs because the diffusion of culture, increased mobility, the mass media, and rising affluence have brought varied forms of leisure within reach of almost everyone. Meyersohn also reveals that social class differences may not be as crucial as other variables.

> Of greater interest are the more detailed examinations of leisure usage within educational, occupational, and income groups, such as Gerstl and Hecksher and DeGrazia. These studies make clear that even though socioeconomic level is an important variable, the kind of work, defined more subtly, constitutes a significant variable as well.[11]

OCCUPATIONAL DIFFERENCES AND LEISURE

Leisure appears to be related to people's working lives. Roberts notes that several writers have attempted to analyze the role of leisure in society and its relationship to occupational positions and the functioning of the economy. Roberts gives three essential reasons for the relationship, as revealed by various authors: (1) Marx saw that leisure offered the worker under capitalism a means whereby the labor force could rejuvenate itself; (2) subsequent writers have shown leisure to be based on values and interests generalized at work; and (3) for others,

[9]Lawrence C. Thomas, "Leisure Pursuits by Socio-Economic Strata," *Journal of Educational Sociology* 29 (May 1956), 367–377.

[10]Max Kaplan. *Leisure in America: A Social Inquiry* (New York: John Wiley and Sons, 1960).

[11]Meyersohn, "Sociology of Leisure," p. 56.

leisure offers an opportunity to compensate for the frustrations and monotony involved in work in modern industry.[12]

Occupations appear to have strong influence on leisure, and while generalizations are often misleading, most research reveals that working classes tend to spend their leisure passively, seeking entertainment through spectator events, television, or relaxation. Middle classes are most inclined to adopt active leisure pursuits, participating in and running associations, meeting and entertaining friends, or becoming involved in pursuits that demand some degree of mental or physical activity. These differences widen as people grow older and progressively adapt themselves to the patterns of their social strata.

Roberts offers seven reasons for different types of leisure pursuits among individuals of various occupations.

1. Manual occupations demand a great deal of time and energy, leaving such people unable to cultivate active leisure pursuits.

2. Manual occupations are physically arduous and therefore may result in a need to spend leisure simply by relaxing or recuperating.

3. Less financially well-off persons do not have substantial incomes to invest in leisure interests outside the home and do not have discretionary money to spare for club subscriptions, trips to the theater, sports equipment, and the like.

4. White-collar families have a greater opportunity to travel abroad and this exposure may stimulate another leisure interest. Certain leisure activities appear to trigger off others.

5. Education awakens white-collar people to leisure interests outside the sphere of the manual worker.

6. A white-collar worker's job may create more opportunities to acquire skills than can be exploited during leisure.

7. Leisure habits emerge as status and attitudes which are generated at work spill over into and influence people's leisure lives.[13]

However, a study by David A. Cunningham et al.[14] found few significant relationships between occupational groups and participation in active leisure activities. This study suggests the need for community recreation authorites to make various types of leisure opportunities available to all occupational groups.

Work has dictated to a large degree when, how, and where the industrial employee spent his or her leisure. "The rhythm of the indi-

---

[12]Roberts, *Leisure,* pp. 23–24.

[13]*Ibid.,* pp. 28–29.

[14]David A. Cunningham, Henry J. Montoye, Helen L. Metzner, and Jacob B. Keller, "Active Leisure Activities as Related to Occupation," *Journal of Leisure Research,* 2 (Spring 1970), 104–111.

vidual's life is largely determined by the interplay between the demands made by work upon the individual and the demands upon his leisure."[15] Roberts suggests that research on employee behavior and its relationship to various leisure interests would be more fruitful if researchers used the life styles and attitudes that employees have developed outside to explain their behavior at work. The dominant work rhythm of life and leisure is no longer determined by the demands of the economy. Leisure behavior appears to have become an important influence on industrial behavior.

Neulinger indicates that often studies relative to leisure activity patterns show a difference arising from social class rather than educational discrepancies. Typically, data reveal that the *more* educated person has a higher affinity for leisure and work, which may only indicate that the more educated person has a longer vacation or a more meaningful job.[16] Similarly, the higher a person's income, the more likely that individual is to be identified through work; this perhaps suggests that such persons have jobs which allow ego satisfaction. Most measurements of social class combine income, education, and occupation as an index of leisure activities. However, while these three variables are useful in correlating leisure activity patterns, the significance of occupation as an independent variable for distinguishing one's job and one's free time activities is diminishing as blue-collar and white-collar classifications become more diffuse. There have been a number of studies attempting to determine whether leisure participation does vary as a function of social class and/or occupation; while there continues to be debate on this question, it does appear that doubts are being increasingly raised, particularly as noted by Burdge, [17] Cunningham et al.,[18] and Cheek and Burch.[19]

Cheek and Burch explored the research which has analyzed the traditional distinction between work and nonwork, its rewards in wealth and prestige, and its social structure as the antecedents of a life style. They found that many of the traditional variables did not account for much of the observed variance. Certain universal characteristics of blue-collar culture (the stages of individual and family life cycles and the rhythms of industrial time) *shape* the meaning of work, and certain

[15]Roberts, *Leisure*, p. 34.

[16]John Neulinger. *The Psychology of Leisure* (Springfield, Ill.: Charles C. Thomas, 1974), pp. 97–98.

[17]Rabel J. Burdge, "Levels of Occupational Prestige and Leisure Activity," *Journal of Leisure Research* 3:262–274, 1969.

[18]Cunningham et al., "Active Leisure Activities," pp. 104–111.

[19]Neil H. Cheek and William R. Burch. *The Social Organization of Leisure in Human Society* (New York: Harper and Row, Publishers, 1976), pp. 102–121.

occupational groups, such as academics and printers, had a life style that spilled over into their work. They go on to state:

Indeed we begin to see what elites and many subordinate groups—women, blacks, and hippies—have known all along; that often style of life determines occupation. Our membership in human groups—extended kin, peers and social circles—largely sets the occupational pattern we follow.[20]

Thus, a reciprocal process seems to occur between work and non-work. Therefore, one may conjecture that life is *multivalent* and this process suggests much more complex and much different causal connection than the usual interpretation that the nature of nonwork is totally dependent upon the nature of work.

LEISURE AND LEVEL OF EDUCATION

It is increasingly recognized among researchers of leisure behavior that educational attainment seems the best predictor of nonwork behavior. The august research document of outdoor recreation participation patterns in the 1960's, the Outdoor Recreation Resources Review Commission study, is a report by Meuller and Gurin[21] which found that different rates of outdoor recreation participation by different occupational groups become minor when education is held constant.

Neulinger comments that the amount of education a person obtains may, and most likely will, determine the nature of both one's work and leisure activities.

Certain avenues of both work and leisure remain closed to those with little formal education. Thus, not only is a college degree required for many positions in government and industry, but equally a college background is necessary to give the person access to certain social circles which in turn determine his life and leisure style. And even though our present educational system does not yet provide "an education for leisure," it is true that the educated person has a greater potential for leisure, since he is better equipped to do what he wants to do, both on his job and in his free time.[22]

---

[20] *Ibid.,* pp. 102–103.

[21] Eva Mueller and Gerald Gurin. *Participation in Outdoor Recreation: Factors Affecting Demand Among American Adults* (Washington, D.C.: U.S. Government Printing Office, 1962).

[22] Neulinger, *Psychology of Leisure*, p. 97.

John Hendee and his colleagues, in a series of studies,[23] consistently confirm the importance of educational attainment related to wilderness camping and nature exploration. Wippler, after analyzing various socioeconomic status variables related to leisure behavior in the Netherlands, also found level of education most important.

> Of the three measures of social stratification (education level, income level, level of occupational prestige) the educational level is the most important predictor; although the level of occupational prestige plays an independent part; the income level, on the contrary, makes no independent contribution toward explanation of variance when the influence of the other two measures of social stratification is kept constant.[24]

Education may be the single most important social determinant of one's leisure behavior; this seems particularly true given the greater accessibility of two other areas of social indicators: occupation and income.

AGE AND LEISURE BEHAVIOR

According to Neulinger, age becomes a determining factor affecting leisure behavior depending on two factors: a person's life history, and the external factors imposed on a individual. He states the two kinds of effects of age:

> One reflects the person's life history, the time and place of his growing up, his particular development and the state of his physical and mental well-being. The other relates to external factors that are imposed upon the person and about which he has little control. Examples of the latter type are the legal drinking age, age limitations for driver's licenses, hunting licenses, mandatory retirement ages, etc.[25]

He cautions that since the second type of age effects are based on chronological age alone, they may have quite different consequences for people with different life histories. Schmitz-Scherzer and Strodel[26] commented that "chronological age is not necessarily the key variable

---

[23]John Hendee et al., "Wilderness Users in the Northwest—Their Characteristics, Values, and Management Preferences" (Portland: U.S. Forest Service Research Paper PNW-61, 1968); Joseph Harry, Richard Gale and John Hendee, "Conservation: An Upper-Middle Class Social Environment" *Journal of Leisure Research* 1:246–254, 1969; John Hendee, Richard Gale, and William Catton, "A Typology of Outdoor Recreation Activity Preferences," *Journal of Environmental Education* 3:28–34.

[24]Reinhard Wippler. *Social Determinants of Leisure Behavior.* English Summary (Assin: Van Gorcum, 1968).

[25]Neulinger, *Psychology of Leisure*, p. 95.

[26]R. Schmitz-Scherzer and I. Strodel, "Age-Dependency of Leisure-Time Activities," *Human Development* 14:47–50, 1971.

with regard to leisure-time activities. Rather, social variables, personality traits, and health status seem to influence greatly the use of leisure time."

While the preponderances of research corroborates the Schmitz-Scherzer and Strodel study, Babchuck and Gorden[27] have noted that similar patterns of continuity seem to occur in voluntary associations. Specifically, as age increases, affiliation and participation change from one type of association to another. Children, they note, tend to affiliate and participate in expressive organizations, whereas the mature adult, particularly the male, is more likely to affiliate with instrumental and instrumental-expressive organizations. An older person is less likely to participate in instrumental activities but increases involvement in expressive groups and activities. They conclude that a cycle of associationally typed participation parallels the life cycle and points to variation in the obtained integration for the individual at different stages.

Cheek and Burch comment on an assumption of what seems to be overlooked in relation to age grading as one of the natural bases of interaction for *all* ages.

> Secondary schools are age ghettos of the adolescent; swinging singles bars for young adults are as age graded as the retired people's trailer community. What should be clear is the importance that nonwork has in maintaining continuity, and because one's friends, kin and associates are aging at the same rate, there is a certain age segregation.[28]

Age cannot always be uniformly applied to various cultures, since social age varies according to the unique patterns of each society. Cheek comments on social age as applied to the stages of our social development.

> ... among many primate species, clear social distinctions exist among infants, juveniles, subadults and adults with respect to the individual's appropriateness as a playmate, hunting partner, warrior, copulatory partner, parent, and so on. This general pattern also appears to be characteristic of Homo sapiens ... in short, human aging, while continuous as with most other forms of life, is experienced by many individuals as discontinuous. Particular segments of the continuous process tend to take on differential social meanings, symbols, and significance for both the individual and the larger group.[29]

[27]Nicholas Babchuck and C. Wayne Gorden. *The Voluntary Association in the Slum* (Lincoln: University of Nebraska Press, 1962).

[28]Cheek and Burch, *Social Organization of Leisure*, p. 112.

[29]Neil H. Cheek, Jr., "Aspects of Social Age," Unpublished paper presented for Rural Sociological Association Annual Meetings, 1972.

Social age, then, is seen by Cheek as an imputation of meaning to a chronological age of a particular individual. Further, recognition of the appropriate chronological age is based upon characteristic biological and physiological transformations experienced during life. Cheek and Burch elaborate this perspective:

> There are changes in the appearance of secondary characteristics, variations in muscle tones, changes in overall stature, variation in dentition, changes in pelage—both quantitatively and in coloration. These variations are often the features that enable a conspecific [a member of the same species] to quickly structure cultural expectations of the way in which social interactions will proceed. Indeed, within a given culture, knowledge of others' social age and sex enable age to most accurately predict how a transaction may proceed without any other information being initially available. Of course, the manner in which symbolization occurs varies among life-styles, and this information is also available to participants, which enables even more accurate expectations to be formulated.[30]

There are various categories of social age (as previously discussed in Chapter 3) and taken together they describe the elemental social ages of human social orders. In different cultures the related symbols attached to particular chronological ages will vary. But it is seen by most social scientists that it is possible to recognize the various sociopsychological distinctions in the life process of human beings.

GENDER AND LEISURE

Gender-related aspects of leisure behavior have traditionally been an important separating determinant which has delineated nonwork patterns among males and females. While sexual identity, like age, has a biological component, its reality in society emerges only through its social component. Every individual member of a social group similarly is also a possessor of a sexual identity.[31]

Western society has drawn a sharp delineation between the roles of men and women, in both work and nonwork. While there have been exceptions, the rule of thumb is that men have held higher status and better-paying jobs in work and women have had more home-centered responsibilities. These different roles imply different work patterns and in turn result in different free time allocations. They also can be expected to affect both the meaning and function of leisure. Robinson[32]

[30]Cheek and Burch, *Social Organization of Leisure,* p. 100.

[31]*Ibid.,* p. 96.

[32]John P. Robinson, "Social Change as Measured by Time Budgets," *Journal of Leisure Research* 1:75–77, 1969.

has noted that while work has consumed a much greater proportion of the males' time than the females', there is a small difference between the total leisure activity hours. More recently Robinson and Godbey stated that working women have more free time available for leisure activity than housewives.[33]

The relationship of gender to the life cycle appears to be an important consideration. Many researchers now argue that single-criterion categories, such as age, work status, gender, and occupation, provide only gross distinctions. Angrist[34] found in a study of female college alumni that the *amount* of leisure participation was similar for all her respondents, although the nature of that participation produced extensive variation. Cheek and Burch comment on the complexity, evident in Angrist's study, which exists in work-nonwork associations:

> Her well-educated, female respondents clearly indicate that for a significant segment of industrial populations the nature of work is *dependent* upon nonwork social relations—marital status, ages of children, and access to domestic help. Further variations in the nature of nonwork activities are not matters of personal whim but are rather clearly determined by the role networks associated with given stages of the life cycle.[35]

Tinsley and Kass[36] studied 95 undergraduate college students to identify the need-satisfying characteristics of ten commonly related leisure activities; they found that sex was *not* significantly related to scores on any of the 445 need-satisfier dimensions investigated. Therefore, it appears that male and female participants in a given activity agree in their perception of the needs which participation in that activity satisfies. Theobald[37] found that females were heavily discriminated against in their participation in recreation programs he studied in nineteen communities in Ontario, Canada; these programs tended to reinforce sex-segregated stereotypes. Specifically, Theobald found that sport activities were heavily dominated by males. Females tended to participate in no-contact, individual and dual sports. Females dominated cultural and arts and crafts programs, with the majority of formal recreation programs being conducted on a sex-segregated basis. Part of the inequitable resource allocation for women was found to be due to

[33]John Robinson and Geoffrey Godbey, "Work and Leisure in America: How We Spend Our Time," *Leisure Today,* October 1978, p. 7.

[34]Shirley Angrist, "Role Constellations as a Variable in Women's Leisure Activities," *Social Forces* 45:423–431, 1967.

[35]Cheek and Burch, Social Organization.

[36]Howard E. A. Tinsley and Richard A. Kass, "Leisure Activities and Need Satisfaction: A Replication and Extension," *Journal of Leisure Research* 10:191–202, 1978.

[37]William F. Theobald, "Discrimination in Public Recreation: Attitudes Toward and Participation of Females," *Leisure Sciences* 1:231–240, 1978.

the women's not requesting (demanding) changes in resource allocation in areas traditionally serviced for men.

Weyl-Willett[38] found that the leisure attitudes of married employed women differed significantly in three aspects from the leisure attitudes of married housewives:

1. Married housewives perceived that they had more leisure than married employed women.
2. Married housewives found self-definition through leisure.
3. Employed married women found self-definition through work.

Additionally, Weyl-Willett's study showed that a significant difference existed between married employed women and married housewives in the meaning of the concepts of leisure and work. Her study revealed that married employed women wanted more free time, yet work activities appeared to be more satisfying than leisure activities. Talents could be *better* expressed, and personal ambitions be better realized, through work. Married housewives reported that leisure activities were satisfying and possibly expressed their talents better than work, although they were undecided about wanting more free time. Work and leisure were concepts that appeared to be very similar in meaning although leisure was considered to be necessary. Part-time employed married women, being both housewives and employed women, displayed the attitudes toward leisure of both groups.

INCOME AND LEISURE

Income has long served as a discriminant variable in measuring leisure activity participation. People with more income have tended to have higher participation rates in nearly all nonwork activities. However, Cheek and Burch note that income seems to operate more as a constraint,[39] and Lucas concurs: "Income seems to be more necessary than sufficient as an explanation of recreation choices. Money does not form taste, it limits their expression"[40]

Neulinger cautions that the effect of income as a variable in the collection and evaluation of findings from the study of leisure participation may be either overstated or understated for many reasons. Some of these reasons are:

[38]Margaret Weyl-Willett, "Leisure Attitudes of a Selected Sample of Married Women in Santa Clara County, California," Unpublished Master's Thesis, San Jose State University, San Jose, California, December 1977.

[39]Cheek and Burch, *Social Organization of Leisure*, p. 46.

[40]Robert C. Lucas, "Wilderness Perception and Use: The Example of the Boundary Waters Canoe Area," *Natural Resources Journal* 3:394–411, 1964.

1. The difference between gross and net income can be considerable.
2. Family earnings may not be reported by the respondent, and thus only one's own income and not that of one's spouse or living partner, or a boarder, may be reflected in the survey.
3. Income from a second job or odd job may not be represented; this could make a big difference in terms of what an individual can afford to spend during leisure.
4. Finally, one's frame of reference could make an important difference in the subjective perception of one's income. For example, if a person with a meager income lives in a reasonably affluent section of town, then his or her earnings will seem quite paltry compared with neighbors. Yet the same income in a poor neighborhood, where demands and aspirations might be lower, could be interpreted differently.[41]

LEISURE AND RACE

The public provision of leisure service has traditionally been most prevalent in white middle-class communities. While the early efforts of the recreation movement in America were oriented to the needs of the urban underprivileged, this concern was basically limited to white youth. The delivery of public recreation and leisure service has been scrutinized as a result of investigations of impoverished conditions in urban communities, stimulated by civil unrest during the 1960's.

Public servants have assumed that all groups of people have an equal need for recreation and that recreation is a universally voluntary experience. Oppressed racial groups, including blacks, Chicanos, Puerto Ricans, Chinese and Japanese Americans, and Indians, have rarely been able to engage in leisure pursuits as freely as the advantaged Anglo citizen, whatever their social class or occupation, because of discriminatory practices, insufficient discretionary money, and inadequate leisure opportunities and services available in their communities.

The failure of organized public recreation and leisure service to effectively serve nonwhite Americans attracted some attention in the late 1960's. Kraus[42] states that not until the 1960's did the recreation profession begin to give special attention to the leisure needs of the poor, especially the nonwhite poor, in urban slums. The federal government's antipoverty program, which provided funding to aid disadvantaged groups, gained impetus from a wave of urban rioting which erupted throughout the nation in 1964 and 1965. Only after these civil

[41]Neulinger, *Psychology of Leisure,* pp. 98–99.
[42]Richard Kraus, *Recreation and Leisure in Modern Society,* p. 388.

disturbances were the needs of inner-city residents brought forcefully to the attention of the public.

The extent to which public recreation and leisure service provides egalitarian leisure opportunities for various nonwhite groups was vigorously questioned at the height of the urban disorders in the late 1960's. It is generally believed that participation by nonwhites in community associations, clubs, and other cultural and leisure activities represents a significant step toward their integration into mainstream American life.

A National League of Cities study, cosponsored by the old Bureau of Outdoor Recreation and Department of Interior, found that "in most cities surveyed, officials readily admitted that the needs of all population groups were not being adequately met. Only in recent years have cities begun to recognize the obligation to provide recreation for the handicapped and deprived."[43] The study revealed that recreation and leisure-service programs and facilities are considered a high-priority item among the deprived. "Residents of deprived urban neighborhoods are almost entirely dependent upon public recreation facilities, whereas residents of more affluent neighborhoods have a wide range of recreational opportunities."[44]

Although many city officials claimed that the leisure needs of disadvantaged persons are essentially the same as those of the rest of the community, studies by Shirley Jenkins[45] and Edwin J. Staley[46] document the dependency of the poor on public recreation and leisure-service facilities and programs. Jenkins and Staley conclude that the deprived, particularly nonwhite inner-city poor, require greater opportunities for leisure and cultural experiences than do the economically and socially advantaged.

James F. Murphy's study of public recreation and leisure service delivery approaches for blacks indicates that the provision of public service at the national level has had effects similar to municipal-level recreation:

1. The black community has been and is today largely isolated from the mainstream interests of American society. The relationship between the two communities, black and white, has not been one of interdependence but one of a dominant majority, dependent minority relationship.

[43]Department of Urban Studies, *Recreation in the Nation's Cities: Problems and Approaches* (Washington, D.C.: National League of Cities, 1968), p. 2.

[44]*Ibid.*

[45]Shirley Jenkins. *Comparative Recreation Needs and Services in New York City Neighborhoods* (New York: Community Council of Greater New York, 1963).

[46]Edwin J. Staley. *An Instrument for Determining Comparative Priority of Need for Neighborhood Recreation Services in the City of Los Angeles* (Los Angeles: Recreation and Youth Services Planning Council, 1968).

2. The socializing function of recreation in both black and white communities has been largely to establish the legitimacy of the values, ideals and interests of the dominant majority.

3. Because the black minority has been thwarted in the pursuit of those values, ideals and interests, it was socialized to accept and did accept [that] the socializing function of recreation in the black community has been dysfunctional with regard to the real needs and interests of the black minority.[47]

The convergence of the last two perspectives has resulted in an incomplete democratization process in public recreation and leisure service. Blacks, as well as Chicanos, Puerto Ricans, Asian-Americans, and Indians, have been partially circumscribed by a society that has permitted them only limited outlets and opportunities for leisure expression. Most racial minorities have historically been barred from places of white amusement—theaters, movie houses, amusement parks, pool halls, bowling alleys, parks, and zoos—even when these were supported by public funds. Discrimination and the lack of access to public leisure facilities and programs has encouraged certain racial minorities, particularly blacks, Chinese-Americans and Chicanos, to develop their own music, life style, dress, and sanctions for fun.

In his study of the leisure participation of blacks of all ages in 24 suburban communities in New York, New Jersey, and Connecticut and the five boroughs of New York City, Kraus[48] found a sharp contrast between the reported recreation involvements of black and white participants in such activities as sports, cultural programs, and activities for specific age groups in public recreation, park, and school programs. Blacks dominated such sport activities as track and field, swimming, basketball, and various forms of combative activity, particularly boxing. Blacks participated far less in activities such as tennis, golf, and archery, which have traditionally been considered white middle-class pastimes. Black children and youth were found to participate widely in the areas of music, drama, and dance. Also, black families tended to make extensive use of picnicking, fishing, and biking facilities, which are relatively inexpensive. Contrarily, they were found to make only limited use of more expensive activities, such as boating, skiing, and riflery. White participants dominated those activities that represent "upper-class" cultural tastes. In cultural programs in which blacks did become involved, activity was typically segregated. The patterns reported by Kraus were recognized by recreation directors to be charac-

[47]James F. Murphy, "Egalitarianism and Separatism: A History of Approaches in t he Provision of Public Recreation and Leisure Service for Blacks, 1906–1972," Ph.D. thesis, Oregon State University, 1972, p. 197.

[48]Richard Kraus. *Public Recreation and the Negro: A Study of Participation and Administrative Practices* (New York: Center for Urban Education, 1968), pp. 31–32.

teristic both in terms of activities in which they participated and their involvement by age group.

Typically, blacks, Puerto Ricans, Chicanos, Indians, and Asian-Americans grow up in environments characterized by isolation, constriction, and rejection. They often live in encapsulated communities which shelter and at the same time separate them from the wider society. Tensions and opposing forces bear heavily on them from within and without their communities. The environment of the poor, particularly of deprived racial minority groups, tends to influence the development and support of recreation and leisure efforts, and to evoke participation patterns characteristic of the particular milieu. According to Moore,[49] the problem of adequate social development of many of the nation's poor is compounded by their inadequate leisure potential.

1. Coping with sustenance difficulties produces a pragmatic orientation; goals tend to be short term and abilities to defer gratification are limited. Thus, leisure rewards must be relatively immediate and concrete; and they must accompany income security, or else futility is reiterated.

2. Restricted childhood play experiences—a possible characteristic of low-income areas—implies an underdeveloped recreation repertoire. The disadvantaged population seldom has the opportunity to gain leisure "know-how" in the realms of the dominant society's positively sanctioned leisure and play activities.

3. Disadvantaged neighborhoods are distinguished by their lack of recreation services—whether they be public, semi-public, private, nonprofit, or commercial.

4. Disadvantaged populations, though often residentially mobile within their own neighborhoods, infrequently travel outside this context on their own volition. This may be due to the deficiencies in transportation, income, knowledge, and/or self-confidence: this factor considerably lessens the extent and degree of potential recreation experience and resources.

5. Cultural differences may be the source of leisure habits that are inappropriate to the urban setting or contradictory to values and norms of the larger society.

6. Minority membership may deter participation in available leisure activities because of social pressures and discrimination by other groups of the society.

Chicanos, like many other nonwhite racial minorities in North America, subscribe to a different set of beliefs from the dominant white

---

[49]Velva Moore, "Recreation Leadership with Socioculturally Handicapped Clientele," in *Recreation and Leisure Service for the Disadvantaged,* ed. John A. Nesbitt, Paul D. Brown, and James F. Murphy (Philadephia: Lea & Febiger, 1970), p. 16.

culture and this has carryover in the leisure domain. Jackson,[50] in a study of Anglo and Mexican-American teachers and custodians, measured the relationship of socioeconomic status and ethnic background to leisure values and attitudes. He found that:

1. Mexican-American teachers were positively oriented toward vacations and free time.
2. Both Mexican-American teachers and custodians had a greater measure of self-definition in leisure than did Anglo teachers and custodians.
3. Anglo custodians perceived leisure and the need for it in the most negative light while Mexican-American teachers were most positively inclined.
4. No group favored a strong role for society in leisure planning.

Jackson suggests the following implications for the provision of leisure opportunities as they apply to variant ethnic value orientations toward leisure:

1. An implicit endorsement of the existence and need for cultural uniformity in American society does not provide adequate guidelines for leisure planning.
2. Many of those responsible for lending direction and substance to leisure programs and services are committed to values of the dominant culture—the middle class.[51]

Jackson's research has been echoed by other studies. In leisure planning there is a common fallacy that a uniform attitude and value system exists within any given community; there is only a tacit consideration for varying needs, attitudes, and values of various social class, age, gender, and ethnic subgroups. These studies indicate the imperative need, in designing leisure service programs, to recognize the values and attitudes of subgroups which do not conform to the dominant middle-class expectations. There is more than one cultural norm in leisure within any community. Typically the white middle-class image is the one most often portrayed by community leisure service planners, and as the findings in Jackson's study indicate, there are differentiated attitudes such as affinity to leisure, self-definition through leisure, amount of vacation desired, and society's role in leisure planning which deviate *qualitatively* from the traditionally held model for leisure consumption (future orientation, doing, mastery-

---

[50]Royal G. Jackson, "A Preliminary Bicultural Study of Value Orientations and Leisure Attitudes," *Journal of Leisure Research* 5:10–22, 1973.

[51]*Ibid.,* p. 20.

over-nature, and individualism), particularly by lower-income Mexican-Americans (present, doing, subjugation-to-nature, and lineality).

According to Cheek, Field, and Burdge,[52] there are few differences in the leisure activities of blacks and whites after controls have been made for social class. In other words, middle-class blacks are more like middle-class whites than they are like lower-class blacks. But within a particular social class grouping blacks and whites do not always participate similarly with respect to particular leisure activities.

> First, it appears that blacks, particularly those who are in lower social and economic grouping, are members of more closed or cohesive groups. . . . For example, blacks are more likely to entertain their friends in the more closed and familiar settings of home and neighborhood than are whites. Among lower class blacks, not only is the level of participation relatively high, but we have also found that there is a particularly strong tendency for lower class blacks to participate in a sport with the same people each time they play.
>
> It was also found that with evening activities, sports participation, activities with friends and participation in voluntary associations the relationship between social and economic status and variation in leisure activities is stronger among whites than among blacks.[53]

It has been revealed that blacks (and other racial minority groups) engage in leisure among a more closely knit group and that black leisure is less differentiated. These patterns may reflect some of the consequences of racial discrimination upon the life style of blacks. Racial discrimination may, in effect, have caused the increase in the level of cohesion within the black community and may serve a similar role for other oppressed racial minority groups. Discrimination has limited the life space of blacks, Chicanos, native Americans, Puerto Ricans, and Asian-Americans, resulting in a more restricted field of experiences.

To a large extent leisure choices, preferences, and forms of ethnic and racial expression have been significantly influenced, even dictated, by the dominant society. Confronted with discriminatory treatment by the dominant white society, minority members in America have shown various patterns of responses.

> Some have been eager to assimilate (a group wishing to be absorbed or merged into the dominant group) in order to lose their minority stigma and/or original identity. Others have sought equality with separation

---

[52]Neil H. Cheek, Donald R. Field, and Rabel J. Burdge. *Leisure and Recreation Places* (Ann Arbor, Mich.: Ann Arbor Science Publishers, 1976), pp. 99–129.

[53]*Ibid.*, p. 105.

(accommodation) and still others accept the status of inequality (and an inferior status). There are some minority members who have rejected both the segregated role and inferior image, and have demanded integration.[54]

While ethnicity per se may not be a major determinant of leisure behavior, it seems clear from the previously discussed studies that recreation and leisure service managers and white individuals charged with the development of leisure programs will need to become more familiar with the influence of ethnicity on life styles of various non-white subcultures. Additionally, because there are few differences between whites and blacks or other racial minority groups, male and female, able-bodied and disabled individuals, special or totally new and different programs are not necessary for such groups. *What is important is that programs are made available, accessible, and pertinent to the needs and expressed desires of all people.*

SUMMARY

Leisure's association with the upper classes, expressed by Veblen's "conspicuous leisure" concept, has been greatly altered since the turn of the century. A number of different socioeconomic-status variables have served as a basis for interpreting differences in leisure behavior.

Social class appears to be a less significant factor influencing leisure. Upper-, middle- and lower-class identifications appear to have less meaning as predictors of leisure expression because of diffusion of culture, increased mobility, the mass media, and increased affluence which has brought leisure within the reach of most people.

Leisure does appear to be related to people's occupation, particularly as expressed in compensatory activities for manual workers and spill-over influences for white-collar employees. However, it is argued that there is less influence of work than in previous eras dominated by a survival economy.

One of the best predictors of leisure behavior seems to be education. Educated individuals appear to have a greater potential for leisure since they are better equipped to do what they want, both on the job and in free time, and are given greater accessibility to two other leisure predictors: occupation and income. The influence of age, gender, and race have less apparent effect on leisure choices now because various forms

[54]James F. Murphy and Dennis R. Howard. *Delivery of Community Leisure Services: An Holistic Approach* (Philadelphia: Lea & Febiger, 1977), p. 45.

of discrimination based on these social indices are being changed. This change has resulted in a growing equalization of leisure expression for all individuals in society. To ensure increased, unabridged leisure participation, leisure service practitioners will need to design programs to recognize and appreciate the values and attitudes of subgroups which do not conform to the dominant middle-class expectations.

7

Psychological Perspectives of Leisure

Various leisure activity patterns and their relationship to need dimensions of the individual will be presented. Psychological aspects of the "leisure problem" and sociopsychological leisure concerns are discussed. The chapter then views the concept of flow, an internal state of playfulness, and concludes with a paradigm of play behavior which provides a basis for understanding the dynamics of the process which facilitates individual expression and the motivation which results in leisure behavior.

Most recent research developments in the study of leisure behavior have centered primarily on the psychological domain of the human being. Such an inquiry places emphasis on the "needs" of the individual which are represented in the human personality in all of its varied forms.

Perhaps the earliest, most forceful perspective in explaining needs as related to human motivation was articulated by Henry Murray,[1] who suggested that human beings are set in motion by a complex series of some 20 needs. When a need is aroused, the individual is in a state of tension, and satisfaction of the need involves reduction of the tension. The human organism, then, learns to attend to objects and perform the acts it has found in the past to be associated with tension reduction. Therefore, the individual not only learns to respond consistently in such a manner as to reduce tension and thus experience satisfaction,

---

[1]Henry Murray. *Explorations in Personality* (New York: Oxford University Press, 1938).

but also learns to respond in such a manner as to develop tension so that it can later be reduced. Applying this to leisure, the individual chooses specific leisure activities on the basis of their ability to satisfy certain needs. One might expect a person to select those activities whose inherent values are consistent with one's personality style or the sum total of all that one is and does, to one's characteristic patterns of perceiving and responding. From this perspective it is assumed that some leisure activities satisfy the needs of individuals better than others, and that the individual's own unique personality determines what is appropriate for him or her.

More recently, several leisure researchers—Bishop and Witt[2]; London, Crandall, and Fitzgibbons[3]; Neulinger and Breit[4]; O'Conner[5]; Tinsley, Barrett, and Kass[6]; and Howard[7] —have reported empirical differences in leisure behavior activities in terms of the needs which they fulfill. These researchers have demonstrated that there are stable dimensions of leisure activities that can be used to describe individual patterns of leisure behavior. Bishop[8] analyzed adult reports of leisure activity participation and found three similar factors in four different communities. They were activities labeled: (1) *Active-Diversionary,* including several sports, dancing, and listening to records; (2) *Potency,* consisting of such activities as attending sports events, bowling, and swimming indoors; and (3) *Status,* representative of reading books, adult education, movies, and attending plays, concerts, and art shows. Witt[9] analyzed data collected from high school students in three of the four communities used by Bishop. He found four factors labeled *Sports, Outdoor-Nature, Adolescent-Social,* and *Aesthetic-Sophisticate.*

O'Connor, in administering the Edwards Personal Preference Schedule to active members of nine different leisure interest groups, found differences between each group and a general adult sample. Neulinger

[2]Doyle W. Bishop and Peter A. Witt, "Sources of Behavioral Variance during Leisure Time," *Journal of Personality and Social Psychology* 16:352–360, 1970.

[3]Manuel London, Rich Crandall, and Dale Fitzgibbons, "The Psychological Structure of Leisure: Attitudes, Needs, People," *Journal of Leisure Research* 9:252–263, 1977.

[4]John A. Neulinger and Melinda Breit, "Attitude Dimensions of Leisure: A Replication Study," *Journal of Leisure Research* 3:108–115, 1971.

[5]Constance O'Connor, "A Study of Personality Needs Involved in the Selection of Specific Leisure Interest Groups," Unpublished Doctoral Dissertation, University of Southern California, 1971.

[6]Howard Tinsley, Tom Barrett, and Richard Kass, "Leisure Activities and Need Satisfaction," *Journal of Leisure Research* 9:110–120, 1977.

[7]Dennis R. Howard, "Multivariate Relationships Between Leisure Activities and Personality," Unpublished Doctoral Dissertation, Oregon State University, Corvallis, Oregon, June 1973.

[8]Doyle Bishop, "Stability of the Factor Structure of Leisure Behavior: Analysis of Four Communities," *Journal of Leisure Research* 2:160–170, 1970.

[9]Peter A. Witt, "Factor Structure of Leisure Behavior for High School Age Youth in Three Communities," *Journal of Leisure Research* 3:213–220, 1971.

and Breit, in a survey of 335 full-time employed adults, found that younger people were more likely than their older counterparts to look toward leisure activities rather than work to find meaning in their lives. London, Crandall, and Fitzgibbons surveyed 83 predominately male undergraduates in relation to their perception of the need-satisfying attributes of 30 leisure activities. London, Crandall and Fitzgibbons found that the respondents could be grouped according to how they perceived three types of activities: *Sports* (playing baseball, basketball, football, and tennis), *Cultural-Passive* (attending concerts, going to movies, visiting museums, reading, listening to records, etc.), and *Productive-Intellectual* (involves painting and drawing, knitting, playing chess, cooking, etc.), when the leisure activities were viewed on the basis of their ability to satisfy three need dimensions; *Liking* (how much an individual would like to perform an activity if the opportunity arose), *Feedback* (knowledge of results of one's performance in an activity), and *Positive Interpersonal Involvement* (representative of the satisfaction of social and security needs and affecting the lives and well-being of others and the feeling of being special).

Tinsley, Barrett, and Kass, in an initial study on the extent to which various need dimensions were relevant among five leisure activities (watching TV; attending plays, concerts, and lectures; reading books and magazines; bicycling; and drinking and socializing), found 45 need-satisfier dimensions which might potentially be satisfied through participation in leisure activities. They found that 42 of the need-satisfier dimensions significantly differentiated among the five activities. The need-satisfier dimensions showing the greatest discrimination among the activities were: sex; catharsis; independence; understanding; affiliation, and getting along with others. In a later replication study Tinsley and Kass[10] found that the needs for catharsis, independence, advancement, getting along with others, reward, understanding, activity, ability utilization, exhibition, sex, and supervision-technical appear to be activity specific (that is, they can be satisfied to a significantly greater degree through participation in some leisure activities than in others).

The study by London et al.[11] demonstrated that it is possible to differentiate individuals within a group on the basis of their perceptions of as well as their participation in leisure activities. Their study suggests that differences in the perceptions of needs potentially satisfied by leisure activities have implications for the delivery of leisure services. They comment:

[10]Howard Tinsley and Richard Kass, "Leisure Activities and Need Satisfaction: A Replication and Extension," *Journal of Leisure Research* 10:191–202, 1978.

[11]London et al., "Psychological Structure of Leisure."

In general, people should be asked why they chose to get involved in particular leisure programs or activities. Their reasons should provide an estimate of needs which they wish to fulfill by their participation in such activities. Understanding people's needs can be used to guide program development or implementation. For example, if a segment of the population served expects information on how well they performed compared to other individuals in sports events, such information should be made available. If feedback is of little concern to most individuals, investing in an electric scoring device which displays games statistics may be a waste of money and may not enhance the attractiveness of the sports facility to members of the community. As another example, when individuals associate the satisfaction of social needs with participation in leisure programs or activities, they will respond best when they are offered activities involving group participation. In this case facilities for group sports may be utilized more than facilities for individual sports.[12]

Thus, according to London et al., planners and managers of recreation and leisure facilities need to understand how the population served by these facilities differ in their views of the needs fulfilled by leisure activities and experiences. Knowledge of what needs individuals wish to satisfy when they engage in various types of activities may be sufficient for designing leisure delivery systems that will be of value to, and will be used by, most individuals. Of course, the particular set of leisure activities and attributes examined will depend upon the situation. London et al. suggest that there are simpler techniques than three-mode factor analysis (as used in their study) which can be used to analyze such information. For example, mean differences in ratings of needs that people desire to fulfill by their participation in different leisure activities may provide sufficient data for such purposes. They state that such information would go beyond the rates of participation data typically collected in order to understand why individuals engage in particular activities. "For example, knowledge about the needs of both users and non-users of leisure facilities can be used to modify leisure services to maximize need fulfillment, and as a consequence, participation."[13]

PSYCHOLOGICAL ASPECTS OF THE "LEISURE PROBLEM"

According to Neulinger, leisure is indeed a problem. The difficulty is, however, in trying to determine what the problem really is. He suggests that free time is not a problem per se, it is how we experience

---

[12]*Ibid.,* p. 261.
[13]*Ibid.,* p. 262.

it that makes it a problem. The psychological nature of the "leisure problem" stems from the ways of coping with conditions brought about by technology. Neulinger offers three distinct but interrelated aspects of this problem.[14]

The Threat and Frustration of Free Time

New amounts of bulk free time have been gained by people, principally as a result of technology. This increased need to make decisions is not only a result of greater amounts of free time but is also brought about by the erosion of tradition and prescribed rules of behavior. Members of today's leisure class (representative of the masses, unlike the old aristocratic, nonproductive leisure class) have been trained in productive behavior and are led to believe that engaging in the continuous consumption of goods and services is necessary and important to maintain a highly productive life style. However, increasingly they are also being asked to engage in nonproductive behavior in their free time and are expected to know how to enjoy it.

This problem presents itself in an ironic way. Neulinger comments:

> Thus, not only is the person threatened by the prospect of free time because of a lack of inner resources and the capacity to handle choice, but the situation is made worse by dangling in front of him a set of demanding options created by a society whose only interest is to make him spend his last dollar, or better still, a dollar he has not even earned yet. . . . The freedom of free time is once more taken away from him by prescribing socially approved ways of spending his time which force him into a frenzy of galloping consumption.[15]

The Fear of Hell

The individual is made to feel even more incapacitated by the abundance of free time with the existence of the antiquated Protestant Work Ethic which still exerts a persistent pull on one's feelings about free time and nonproductive activity. This ethic, of course, made work an ultimate value and fostered an attitude of shame and guilt toward nonproductive activity. Neulinger suggests that what is needed is a new *Leisure Ethic* that will provide people with the assurance that by far the greatest virtue is to engage in leisure, to be oneself and freely actualize one's fullest potential.

[14]John A. Neulinger, "Into Leisure With Dignity: Social and Psychological Problems of Leisure," *Society and Leisure* 6:133–137, 1974.

[15]*Ibid.*, p. 135.

The Loss of Self

Because work has been traditionally seen as the basis for self-esteem and identity formation, the shortening of the workweek/year and indeed work career poses new problems for the individuals engaged in meaningless jobs. New developments in industry and management suggest the need for all activity to be accepted as purposeful, whether in work or in other aspects of life, including leisure. In this sense, leisure is greeted with a tremendous challenge and afforded great importance and relevance for contemporary life.

SOCIOPSYCHOLOGICAL LEISURE CONCERNS

There are areas of leisure which are considered to be "problems" or issues which stem from various sociopsychological maladies either endemic in the individual or emanating from a combination of societal and human orientations. While none of the following problems should be considered abnormal per se, they bring about manifestation of behavior—overt or covert, simple or complex, rational or irrational—which is seen as needing change for the sake of the health and well-being of both the individual and society. Some of these issues are alcoholism, drug addiction, sex-role stereotyping, and handicapping conditions affecting disabled individuals.

Alcoholism

Alcoholism is a pervasive life style, separate from a nonalcoholic life pattern. According to Sessoms,[16] the alcoholic's life style is considered to be destructive and pathological. For close to 10 million alcoholics, taking a drink is the central, dominant interest which influences all other activity, including social relationships.

Sessoms suggests that there are three groups for whom alcoholic beverages play a significant role in the life style. First, there is the alcoholic, whose life is totally encompassed by drinking. Second, there are the oenophilists or wine lovers, who plan vacations around their interest in wine, join wine clubs, subscribe to wine and gourmet journals, and so on. Third, for the social drinker alcohol is considered to be a part of the social processes; there is an expectation to have a cocktail or a beer. Many groups consider the neighborhood bar as a recreation center; their central interests are related to the activities and relationships which take place in that setting. The latter two life style groups are representative of leisure behavior apparently free of alcoholism.

[16]H. Douglas Sessoms, "Alcoholism: A Separate Life Style," *Leisure Today,* 1974, pp. 27–28.

"For the wine connoisseur, drinking is both a social and intellectual activity. For the social drinker, it is a social lubricant. For the alcoholic, it is a necessity."[17] Sessoms suggests that life styles are not good or bad in themselves. Society makes judgments about their worth according to prevailing social mores.

Drinking is important to North American culture. It represents an accepted ritual for various leisure festive occasions such as marriage, christenings, funerals, banquets, receptions, and holiday gatherings of family and friends. It is taken for granted as a way to relax and to reduce tension and anxiety. It does, however, often produce exaggerated behavior, including aggression toward others, extreme extroverted behavior, and loud and boisterous activity.

Drinking typically takes place in the leisure setting, and even takes on cultic overtones, as users teach the less skillful the rituals of use, increasing the allure to the beginner. This often takes place for youth around the school setting. The most prevalent problem related to drinking is the social aspect of its addiction. Sessoms comments: "Once a drug has become socially acceptable and may be used legally for purposes of pleasure, the public seems to ignore it as a drug regardless of its negative consequences. The question becomes one of drug abuse rather than drug use."[18]

Most theories of alcoholism regard the most important precondition to be stress and the inability of the organism to adapt to it. Many leisure programs can be important, socially acceptable ways of channeling energy and creative potential. Leisure, and particularly organized public recreation, becomes an essential vehicle whereby people may reduce tension, fulfill personal aims, and exercise control over their actions; these opportunities are not always available in the more demanding aspects of their life.

Drug Addiction

Growing drug use and abuse has tremendous implications for leisure, particularly as apparently more and more young people seek to find satisfaction from altered states of consciousness and even retreat into oblivion. There is increased used of PCP (angel dust), marijuana (relaxed state laws have resulted in greater usage among all population groups), cocaine (the "in" drug of the jet set, political circles, and others), LSD, hashish, and other drugs.

Some writers and analysts have suggested that as work and leisure

[17] *Ibid.,* p. 28.

[18] H. Douglas Sessoms and Thomas A. Stein. *Recreation and Special Populations*, 2nd ed. (Boston: Holbrook Press, 1977), p. 173.

in our society become less exciting, more boring, and generally less participatory, more people will seek a variety of thrills and challenges to provide stimulation through risk-taking pursuits, including the use of addicting and dangerous drugs. The role of leisure becomes one of providing important emotional and physical outlets for people who have little opportunity during their daily routine for self-expression, direct participation in decision-making, or reward from recognition of meaningful contribution to the completion of tasks. The benefits of drugs are seen by the user to outweigh the costs of personal injury or other accidents that may occur.

Of course, some people seek release through more acceptable risk activities. Miles comments:

> After the risk has passed and the challenge met, a great physical and spiritual satisfaction is the reward. It is an intense emotion, and this is another value of risk recreation. Routine living and too many amenities may dull one's emotions. Tied up with multiple demands and bombarded by multiple stimuli, a person withdraws and struggles to maintain an equilibrium, always striving to control the swing of emotions. Away from the routine and in a risk situation, emotions surge up and are given a release.[19]

It has been recognized that in recent years more and more people have become tremendously dependent on drugs, both as a form of medication and as a tranquilizer. A 1976 report cited in *New York Magazine*[20] indicated that Americans spend $11 billion a year on prescription drugs and another $26 billion on over-the-counter pharmaceuticals. It was also stated that over 75 million people regularly consume drugs (almost 57 percent of the American population).

As Kraus[21] has indicated, while most adults profess to being shocked by the growing statistics of drug use among children and youth, the fact is that adults themselves are extremely heavy users of tranquilizers and other legal or prescribed stimulants. It must be realized by adults that their noontime cocktails or socially accepted small doses of "pot" are no different than their children's newly formed habit of cigarettes or alcohol.

Sex-Role Stereotyping

Traditionally sexual identification has played a significant role in leisure. Most of the early studies of leisure participation and interests

---

[19]John C. Miles, "The Value of High Adventure Activities," *Leisure Today,* April 1977, p. 3.

[20]*New York Magazine,* August 23, 1976, p. 48.

[21] Richard Kraus. *Therapeutic Recreation Service,* 2nd ed. (Philadelphia: W. B. Saunders Co., 1978), p. 282.

used a methodology which primarily took gender as the significant demographic variable for distinguishing patterns of participation. It is now recognized that the activities and statuses of boys playing cowboys, engineers, doctors, truck drivers, and soldiers, and of girls playing dolls, housemaker, secretary, cook, and nurse, have been arbitrary, discriminatory, and a form of brainwashing, limiting the potential forms of expression and personal expectations for both boys and girls.

There is increased need on the part of leisure service personnel to recognize the forms of discrimination and break through such stereotyping to open children's play to a wider range of possibilities and eliminate any sex-role stereotyping in leisure activities.

Conditions Affecting the Disabled

There exists in North American society a segregated segment which has been largely ignored and visibly discriminated against and which until recently had few rights and limited access to public facilities, jobs, and leisure opportunities. The fact that the able-bodied are in the mainstream while the disabled are outside this mainstream has only recently come under attack in the United States and Canada.

The disabled have either been relegated to separate classes in public schools or been placed in "special" schools. Classes catering to children and youth with specific disabilities—the visually impaired, the mentally retarded, the emotionally disturbed, and the physically disabled—are common throughout North America. The area of employment also has a separate system just for the disabled. Sheltered workshops, work activity centers, and adult development centers are available to the more severely disabled. Here, regardless of untapped capabilities, work activities may center around throwing old clothes donated to charitable agencies into parking machines, sorting buttons of different sizes, stacking clothes hangers, or assembling bicycle parts. Competitive work situations offer few alternatives. Limited opportunities exist for the qualified disabled person in skilled or professional work settings.

Housing also is restricted in our society for most individuals with disabilities. Medically oriented facilities, such as convalescent homes, as well as federally funded projects segregate the disabled from the rest of society. Because so few alternatives are accessible, many disabled adults continue to live with their parents. Most forms of transportation have traditionally been inaccessible to the disabled. As a result, we have seen the growth of a system of special vans, labeled as to their unique passenger load. So, while allowing the disabled some mobility, most able-bodied people do not have to mix with them.

Efforts to serve the disabled in recreation and leisure services historically have been manifested in clinical and medical settings. In what is termed recreation therapy, individuals in mental health, rehabilitation, and similar treatment settings often have their leisure experiences prescribed for them.

Several forces perpetuate this discriminatory condition. For example, architectural barriers are effective in limiting mobility and independence of some disabled people. Curbs, stairs, narrow doors, high counters, vending machines, telephones, water fountains, and elevator controls are designed so as to limit their use by the disabled.

Another strong force in the perpetuation of segregation is the development and maintenance of professions specializing in "working with" the disabled. Examples include special educators, rehabilitation counselors, physical and occupational therapists, and, of course, recreation therapists. People in these professions have developed organizations which have tended to promote their cause and which, ironically, may in some cases be encouraging the dependency and continued limited participation of these individuals they seek to serve, the disabled.

There are several reasons given to justify the continuing segregated professional human services for the disabled. It is said to be "for their own good" because: (1) the disabled receive individual attention, and (2) it protects them from unwarranted daily frustrations, concerns, and failures.

Rationalizations for segregation in the community are: (1) the general public may be offended or embarrassed by the disabled, (2) "normal" consumers may no longer want to use the services that are used by the disabled, and (3) generalists are not qualified to provide services to the disabled.

As a result of this segregated system which has developed over the years, members of society at large really do not have an understanding of the disabled. In fact, they may even be fearful of them. The result of segregation of the disabled individual may be even more devastating than the impairment itself.

The efforts to overcome this debilitating condition are referred to as "mainstreaming." Mainstreaming is based on the concept of normalization, which is defined by Wolfensberger[22] as "the utilization of means which are as culturally normative as possible, in order to establish and/or maintain personal behaviors and characteristics which are as normative as possible." It is also based on the philosophy of humanism, which supports the belief in the worth and dignity of the individual.

[22]W. Wolfensberger. *The Principle of Normalization in Human Services* (Toronto: National Institute on Mental Retardation, 1972), p. 29.

The individual is seen as a developmental organism, with untapped potential, who has the right to take risks, to make choices, to take the responsibility for those choices, and to experience patterns and conditions of everyday life. This view also advocates the elimination of social and physical barriers which impede the nonmainstreamed person in his or her access to opportunities for self-expression.[23]

Increased efforts need to be made to desegregate public facilities, to remove architectural and physical barriers that restrict access, and to make full provision in everyday life for plentiful and appropriate transitional services and support services so disabled persons may participate in programs of their choice.

A related issue has been the limited opportunity for disabled persons to experience risk recreation. The disabled individual, having been isolated from *all* aspects of mainstream society, have typically had few opportunities to engage in activities and experiences with an element of high risk. The disabled are able to participate like any other person in risk recreation, including downhill skiing, snowmobiling, horseback riding, motorcycling, gymnastics, mountain climbing, wilderness camping, white water canoeing, and other such activities. Architectural barriers are considered to be one of the major obstacles to allowing disabled persons to pursue feasible activities that provide an opportunity for excitement. Because disabled persons have been labeled as handicapped and typified as lacking the necessary abilities and skills to participate in certain activities, most human service providers, teachers, and leaders have lowered expectations of their performance. Because of this attitude, the disabled individuals themselves do not see themselves as capable, competent, and adventurous persons. There is a tremendous need on the part of all service providers and the disabled themselves to understand the abilities of the disabled and facilitate their involvement in all recreation pursuits.[24]

THE CONCEPT OF FLOW

As developed by Csilkzentmihalyi,[25] *flow* or the state of playfulness, is achieved whenever a person is in optimal interaction with the environment. It can occur anywhere; in a shower, while driving a car, writing a poem, or working on a job. It is not play or being engaged in

[23]J. F. Murphy. *Recreation and Leisure Service: A Humanistic Perspective.* (Dubuque, Iowa: William C. Brown Company Publishers, 1975), p. 2.

[24]Refer to Carol Ann Peterson, "The Right to Risk," *Leisure Today,* April 1978, pp. 23–24.

[25]Mihaly Csilkzentmihalyi and S. Bennett, "An Exploratory Model of Play," *American Anthropologist* 73:45–58, 1971; and M. Csilkzentmihalyi, "Play and Intrinsic Rewards," *Journal of Humanistic Psychology* 15:41–63, 1975.

an activity which matters most, it's the process. Csilkzentmihalyi has found in his studies of play behavior that individuals totally immersed in a sport or creative act lose their sense of time and the external world, and experience an altered state of being.[26]

It is Csilkzentmihalyi's contention that we need to investigate more fully the nature of intrinsic rewards. We tend to understand only extrinsic rewards, and we spend countless resources to motivate people to do things they do not enjoy doing or we keep them in line through social controls. Artificially imposed "motivation" obliges them to do things at school, work, or at play that they really don't enjoy, and so they need to "recuperate" from the meaningless routine which fails to provide intrinsic motivation. Further, Dr. Csilkzentmihalyi contends that through an understanding of how intrinsic rewards work, "it might become possible to incorporate flow into normal non-play life activities, to make the roles available in society more playful and therefore, more free and creative."[27]

Csilkzentmihalyi's research suggests that human survival might depend on our ability to conceptually incorporate synergistic forms of enjoyment into the structure of human motivation while preserving the playful quality inherent in daily events. Using such an approach might serve to enable people to learn how to be responsive to their total selves.

The concept of flow provides interesting insight into how individuals who are intrinsically involved maintain their complete involvement by processing every relevant piece of important information about the activity being performed. Levy suggests how this process occurs.

> Stimulus seeking human organisms try to maximize their enjoyment by finding an optimal relationship between their skills and the requirements of the activity. In order not to be bored (i.e., their skills are superior to the requirements of the activity) or overly anxious (i.e., their skills are inferior to the requirements of the activity), players monitor all their information—feedback mechanisms to ensure that all relevant stimuli have been processed and their impact analyzed.[28]

The individual, in carrying out this complex and necessary information-processing exercise, must delimit his or her relevant boundaries

[26]M. Csilkzentmihalyi, "The Americanization of Rock Climbing," *University of Chicago Magazine* 61:20–27, 1969.

[27]M. Csilkzentmihalyi, "What Play Says About Behavior," *The Ontario Psychologist* 8:9, June 1976.

[28]Joseph Levy. *Play Behavior* (New York: John Wiley & Sons, 1978), p. 11.

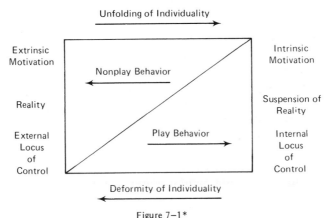

Unfolding of Individuality

Extrinsic Motivation

Nonplay Behavior

Intrinsic Motivation

Reality

Suspension of Reality

External Locus of Control

Play Behavior

Internal Locus of Control

Deformity of Individuality

Figure 7–1*
Play Behavior: The Unfolding of Individuality

*Joseph Levy, Play Behavior p. 19.

of information. This has been referred to as "epistemic,"[29] "narrowing of consciousness,"[30] "arousal,"[31] and "centering of attention."[32]

According to Levy, the following salient characteristics—in addition to intrinsic motivation (the drive to become involved in an activity originating from within the person or the activity, the reward being generated by the transaction itself)—are important properties of the play or leisure experience: *suspension of reality* (the loss of the "real self" and the temporary acceptance of an "imaginary self"), and *internal locus of control* (the degree to which individuals perceive that they are in control of their actions and outcomes). Figure 7–1 represents a schematic representation of the unfolding of individuality through play behavior.

It is suggested by Levy's diagram that play behavior incorporates a dynamic process that facilitates the unfolding of creative and profound traits of the individual—potentially a viable approach of understanding and promoting human development within the context of post-industrial society.

[29]D. E. Berlyne, "Determinants of Subjective Novelty," *Perception and Psychophysics* 3:415–423, 1960.

[30]A. H. Maslow. *The Farther Reaches of Human Nature* (New York: Viking Press, 1971).

[31]M. J. Ellis. *Why People Play* (Englewood Cliffs, N.J.: Prentice-Hall, Inc., 1973).

[32]M. Csilkzentmihalyi. *Flow: Studies of Enjoyment,* PHS Grant Report N. Rol HM 22883–02 (Chicago: The University of Chicago, 1974).

SUMMARY

The psychology of leisure focuses on the individual. As applied to leisure research, a psychological perspective suggests that the individual chooses specific leisure activities on the basis of their ability to satisfy certain needs. Bishop and Witt have reported empirical differences in leisure behavior which cluster in certain activities and which apparently fulfill similar needs. More recent research by Tinsley, Barrett, and Kass indicate 45 need-satisfier dimensions which may potentially be satisfied through participation in five cluster activities—watching TV; attending plays, concerts, and lectures; reading books and magazines; bicycling; and drinking and socializing.

It has been found that individuals within a group may be differentiated on the basis of their perceptions as well as their participation in leisure activities. This determination suggests that recreation and leisure service providers need to understand how people differ in their views of the needs fulfilled by leisure activities and experiences.

Leisure "problems" emerge because of the difficulty people have in coping with the conditions of technology as represented by free time, work ethic, and loss of identity through meaningless jobs. Some particular problem areas identified were alcoholism, drug addiction, sex-role stereotyping, and discrimination against the disabled.

The concept of flow, defined as the state of playfulness, provides an interesting conceptual approach to the study of human behavior. This concept states that such a state can be achieved when a person is in optimal interaction with the environment. What is most important for the individual is not the result of the activity but the process.

8

Environmental Perspectives of Leisure

Environmental perspectives are important considerations in under-standing the nature of leisure behavior. Leisure locales, places where people engage in nonwork behavior, are discussed in this chapter. Further, urban places and outdoor recreation settings are presented. Values, behavior, and conflict are explored with respect to anti-social acts occurring in outdoor settings. Finally, a concept of environmental management and the impact of human acitivities in relation to main-taining an environmental balance are discussed.

The environment reflective of urban places and outdoor recreation settings, contributes an important element to a holistic configuration of leisure which "may best be understood in terms of the meanings as-signed to them by particular sociocultural groups."[1] Further, the "phys-ical environment is important for maintaining orderly relationships because it serves as a repository of meanings for symbolizing relation-ships and also provides a spatial field in which social life can be orga-nized."[2] Environmental settings or physical places tend to be identified by particular qualitative characteristics which relate to particular sym-bolic, ritualistic, and/or functional meanings by various social groups.

Levy states that environments that precede leisure behavior (e.g., work, school, street, home) and those in which leisure behavior occurs

---

[1]Neil H. Cheek, Donald R. Field, and Rabel J. Burdge. *Leisure and Recreation Places* (Ann Arbor, Mich.: Ann Arbor Science Publishers, 1976), p. 31.

[2]*Ibid.,* p. 32.

(parks, theaters, playgrounds, etc.) must be conceptualized as independent determinants affecting behavior. The work of Proshansky, Ittelson, and Rivlin[3] demonstrates a comprehensive review of environmental or physical determinism of human behavior. Levy comments: "There is a growing recognition of the critical impact of such environmental quality on the individual's bio-sociopsychological functioning."[4] Levy suggests that in regard to the person-environment discussed in his paradigm, "A Conceptual Paradigm for the Study of Play Behavior," described in Chapter 8, "it must be borne in mind that *interaction between differences in individuals and variations among environments are the determinants of variation in play behavior.*"[5]

Cheek and Burch[6] developed a taxonomy of *leisure locales,* places where people engage in behavior not ordinarily associated with instrumental or work aspects of existence. Leisure locales are characterized chiefly by three main aspects.

1. *The specialized moral order.* In other words, the type of social value placed on a particular locale.

2. *The physical design.* This refers to the setup and arrangement of a locale.

3. *The social structure.* Reference here is made to the composition and social organization of the locale—whether people are in groups or alone; whether the groups are comprised of friends, kin, strangers.

Each of these factors serves to ensure particular behavioral responses. The classification of leisure locales developed by Cheek and Burch is as follows:

1. *Transitional.* This group is characterized by courtrooms, theaters, waiting lounges in transportation depots, and is representative of strangers coming together either to rejoin or dissolve human associations.

2. *Integration.* These locales are representative of club swimming pools and school playgrounds, which serve as central interaction places and symbolic focal points of certain social groups who frequent such locales; the ecology of the places allows these groups to be spatially and temporally segregated.

3. *Bonding.* This locale refers to large open-space territories—sports stadiums, zoos, parks, beaches—where large groups of strangers are organized into small intimate social groups.

---

[3]H. M. Proshansky, W. H. Ittelson, and L. G. Rivlin, eds. *Environmental Psychology* (New York: Holt, Rinehart and Winston, 1970).

[4]Joseph Levy. *Play Behavior* (New York: John Wiley & Sons, 1978), p. 62.

[5]*Ibid.,* p. 63.

[6]Neil H. Cheek and William R. Burch. *The Social Organization of Leisure in Human Society* (New York: Harper and Row, Publishers, 1976), p. 155.

4. *Solidarity.* These indoor open space locales, characteristic of museums, galleries, and specialized shows, bring together bonded pairs and organized groups, such as schoolchildren and tour groups. These locales "reaffirm the larger social order through the display of artifacts that give physical shape to collective representations of myths."[7]

5. *Custodial.* Golden-age clubs, youth clubs, scout camps, day-care centers provide recreation opportunities for social groups and serve as a means of managing certain populations by occupying them in "useful" activities.

6. *Exchange.* This is representative of a wide variety of indoor functional places, including singles' bars, shopping centers, post offices, and unemployment offices. In these locales "personal futures are traded and exaggerated claims assume a certain currency."[8]

7. *Fantasy.* Fairs, circuses, and amusement parks provide settings for make-believe and vertigo for bonded pairs and kins.

Each of these leisure locales has its own particular design and activity cycle constraints. The leisure locale provides experiences which are typically unique, emotion-filled, and set-apart occasions that differ from our normal routine of life. These experiences provide the substance for reaffirming one's identity.

In a related work by Cheek, Field, and Burdge[9] they proceeded to determine the kinds of urban places by type of use: *residences* (houses and apartments); *neighborhoods* (the network of relationships characteristic of the domestic level of interaction); *districts* (medium to large sections of cities that are identifiable by characteristic uses, such as exclusive residences, industry, or business). The type of use that organized groups make of physical spaces is important in determining the definition of the place they will share. "The number and kinds of places shared by groups will vary with the cultural and social conditions of their existence because patterns of work, consumption, recreation, worship, and mobility will be different."[10]

Cheek, Field, and Burdge classify outdoor recreation settings into four types on the basis of their social milieu and of the residential origin and image of place held by most visitors: neighborhood, district, regional, and remote outdoor places.[11]

---

[7]*Ibid.,* p. 156.

[8]*Ibid.*

[9]Cheek, Field, and Burdge, *Leisure and Recreation Places,* pp. 33–44.

[10]*Ibid.,* p. 33.

[11]*Ibid.,* p. 34.

1. *Neighborhood Outdoor Places:* They are situated in or near residential neighborhoods; most visitors reside in the neighborhood and conceive of the place as a part of the local community.

2. *District Outdoor Places:* They are representative of a larger section of a city or other residential area that is conceived of as a district.

3. *Regional Outdoor Places:* They may or may not be located in residential neighborhoods or districts. They are used by residents of an area extending throughout a cluster of towns, cities, or counties that share a common cultural identity.

4. *Remote Outdoor Places:* While they may or may not be located within the three previous outdoor recreation places, they are known for their unique features and attract visitors from the local area, outside regions, other states, and even foreign countries.

It is suggested by Cheek, Field, and Burdge that "individuals seek outdoor areas where they may share a scheme of order with others similar enough to themselves to be able to take for granted many everyday normative constraints."[12] These constraints are not necessarily absent during leisure, only representative of a very low level of awareness. It is suggested by their analysis that in a typical outdoor leisure situation a consensus exists in reference to the status of socially problematic factors.

From Cheek, Field, and Burdge's analysis of outdoor leisure environments, if socially problematic elements rather than normative constraints are reduced, then for the solution of routine problems policy makers of outdoor leisure environments need to respond more appropriately to the requirements of specific settings. Cheek, Field, and Burdge provide support for their sociopsychological interpretation of outdoor leisure environmental use by illustrating three practical problems:

First, objectives for preserving open space and creating parks might be best formulated in terms of the social functions outdoor recreation serves for specific visitor populations. With whose expectations in mind are such areas reserved, designed, and managed? Do the planners consider how differing visitor definitions of place will affect intragroup and intergroup relationships?

Second, programs such as nature interpretation might be better utilized as a means of formally introducing users to an outdoor recreational culture. Whose scheme of order do interpreters use for introducing visitors to the rules of outdoor living? Should activities be designed to help overcome social differences by encouraging the development of a sense of group identity and mutual responsibility?

[12] *Ibid.,* p. 43.

Typology of Sociocultural Use of Outdoor Leisure Environments[*]

TYPE OF OUTDOOR PLACE	MODE OF BELONGING	COGNITIVE STRUCTURE	EXPECTATIONS OF LEGITIMATE SOCIAL CONTROL
Neighborhood			
low-income	"Propertyless"; knowledge of local inhabitants, events, and situations	Occupying "territorial" or locally bounded space (hanging around street corners and store fronts, visiting, drinking, gambling, playing, dope peddlers, etc); Use park to join others for conversation, games of chance, observe local social life	Governed by rules of mutual expectations on a personal basis
middle-class	Ownership of real property	Occupy selective space in which boundary between dwelling unit and immediate environs is sharp and minimally permeable (use park only as a pathway or a setting for local ceremonies)	Governed by formalized rules of property owners
District			
low-income	Have less knowledge and make less use of district places	Picnickers, usually ethnic minorities, show greater tendency to gather in large groups and define a common territory	District parks are seen as modes of spatial behavior typical of the neighborhood park and are used to identify it as a place where others with a similar sociocultural background are welcome
middle-class	Tend to use district parks on weekends and holidays—"It belongs to white American culture"	Visitors sense of belonging to district parks is linked to the possession of a small space in a pleasant setting	
Regional			
low-income	Public places are often not perceived as being available and are typically beyond the boundaries of the familiar world of a great many low-income residents	Regional outdoor places are interpreted as being "free" and "open" by both groups	For those few visitors, rules of social contact are not organized by formalized roles
middle-class	Public places are perceived as belonging to everyone		Seen as being governed by formalized control
Remote			
low-income	Remote outdoor spaces are perceived as belonging to everyone	More idiosyncratic definitions exist among individuals and groups from all sociocultural backgrounds; selective organization among users	While formal social control persists, legitimate use extends beyond most acceptable activities, including nude bathing, pot smoking, open sexual enjoyment, in some areas where law enforcement is difficult or the numbers of participants is too large to prevent effective social control
middle-class			

[*]Adapted for use from Cheek, Field, and Burdge, Leisure and Recreation Places, pp. 36–42.

Thirdly, social controls might be designed to fit the moral order of specific user groups. Whose normative order should pertain to given recreational areas, and should it be informally or formally enforced? Should park rangers, park policemen, or local law enforcement officers perform such functions?[13]

It can be seen from the scheme articulated by Cheek, Field, and Burdge, that the social meanings of outdoor leisure environments as perceived by user groups are often different from the personal and organizational perspectives indicated by the managers and policy makers of these nonhuman settings. From a study undertaken by Webb, Campbell, Schwartz, and Seechrest, three features were discovered that typify the normative order of socially defined places in general, and can be applied to the understanding of outdoor leisure settings.

1. The mode of "belonging" or being "at home."
2. The cognitive structure or organization of the spatial environment.
3. The expectation of legitimate social control over the organization and use of space.[14]

VALUES, BEHAVIOR, AND CONFLICT

In a study by Clark, Hendee, and Campbell[15] it was reported that depreciative acts on the environment, including vandalism, theft, and nuisance behaviors, occurred most often because campers typically disagreed with managers on the types of activities appropriate to attaining the goals associated with camping. However, it was determined that campers and managers tended to subscribe to similar goals associated with camping. These differences may be attributed to the social goals and urban behavior patterns of campers compared to the more traditional, natural environment-oriented expectations of camping behavior held by outdoor leisure resource managers. Clark et al. state: "Such a disparity may produce disagreements about the appropriateness of certain camping activities and the legitimacy of campground rules and lead to misunderstandings about campground policy."[16]

---

[13]*Ibid.*

[14]E. J. Webb, D. T. Campbell, R. D. Schwartz, and L. Seechrest. *Unobtrusive Measures: Nonreactive Research in the Social Sciences* (Chicago: Rand McNally, 1966).

[15]R. Clark, J. Hendee, D. Campbell, "Values, Behavior, and Conflict in Modern Camping Culture," *Journal of Leisure Research* 3:143–169, 1971.

[16]*Ibid.*, p. 144.

Additionally, Clark et al. suggest that these conditions result from the evolutionary change in predominant camping styles and the development of separate camping cultures favoring developed as opposed to primitive outdoor places. They suggest that today's camper, insulated from the natural environment with modern fabric and convenience campers and trailers, are no longer required to forfeit many comforts of the urban environment to enjoy outdoor recreation. Further, the range of available camping behaviors, once limited by primitive conditions, has increased. Activities once possible only in the urban milieu are now pursued routinely in contemporary campgrounds.

The increased accessibility for more varied users, coupled with continued population growth and increased free time for more and more people, have produced a larger and more varied camping population. This growth has resulted in increased conflict among users and resource managers, increased contact among recreationists, and competition for scarce facilities.[17] Clark et al. discuss the findings of their study:

> First, recreationists and managers do not share the same concept of what constitutes an environmental experience. Although recreationists seem to subscribe to the traditional goals associated with camping such as contact with the environment and isolation, they apparently feel that they can pursue such values in highly developed campgrounds.

> Second, there are important differences in the way managers perceive behavioral problems in the campground. Recreationists generally find conditions common to the urban environment such as noise, litter, and the actions of other campers less important than do the managers. Further, campers do not express the same concern for illegal behavior, such as vandalism and theft, as do managers.

> Third, these data repeatedly indicate that managers' perceptions of camper views appear to be largely a reflection of the managers' own feelings in the issues and are often at variance with what the campers' expressions of sentiments are.[18]

While these data reflect only findings concerned with campers and managers of highly developed modern campgrounds, they tend to underscore the conditions arising from sociocultural differences explained by Cheek, Field, and Burdge which seem to exist in most outdoor recreation places. Traditional outdoor recreation values of natural environment appreciation appear to permeate both managers' and users' perspectives toward camping, but different means of satisfying their goals through appropriately sanctioned behavior are clearly present. Managers' view that isolation and primitive interaction with the environment are necessary is markedly different from the view of

[17] *Ibid.*
[18] *Ibid.*, p. 156.

users, who find the highly developed, structured setting of the contemporary campgrounds and its associated social environment as appropriate. It appears that managers of outdoor leisure settings are going to have to provide a wider, more diverse range of outdoor recreation opportunities to coincide with increased interest in and accessibility to the out-of-doors and varied interpretation of leisure expression manifest among users.

A CONCEPT OF ENVIRONMENTAL MANAGEMENT

It is not the management of the environment but management of all those human activities which have a significant impact on the environment. It has been suggested that the most pressing objective of environmental management is to meet basic human needs within the potentials and constraints of environmental systems, including natural resources.

This concept brings two dimensions to the development process: it broadens the concept to include environmental quality and it extends it in time to include development over the long-term on a sustainable basis. Of course, there is the issue of use versus non or limited use. In an article appearing in the *Seattle Times*[19] a city attorney who had sponsored a scenic river bill was pleased that it had been enacted into law and that control responsibility had been directed to the State Parks and Recreation Department because they are both preservation-oriented and recreation-oriented, striking an important balance. While this was a generally responsive statement, it nonetheless suggests that leisure agencies are probably not perceived as environmentally conscious, or at least are viewed as being more consumer-oriented agencies.

It even might be argued that encouragement of some forms of leisure expression serve to subvert the environment and quality of life. It has been argued by Hardin that "lifeboat ethics" endangers our survival.[20] This metaphor suggests that each nation or resource has a limited carrying capacity, and with increased population demanding greater space, there is a danger of a crunch from exceeding that capacity. There exists a world of limited resources and the increasing demand in leisure settings (based on user levels for leisure settings by recreationists) necessitates limitations being placed on the use of some areas.

Everyone cannot be accommodated in recreation areas. Managers

[19]"Reaction Mixed Over New Law That Created First Scenic River," *Seattle Times,* June 9, 1977, p. A16.

[20]Garrett Hardin, "Living on a Lifeboat," In: *Managing the Commons* ed. Garrett Hardin and John Baden, (San Francisco: W. H. Freeman and Company, 1977), pp. 261–279.

and users need to work out a plan whereby acceptable substitutable leisure settings are made available to more diverse recreationists; people need to be encouraged to become more resourceful and self-directed and to assume more direct responsibility for initiating leisure opportunities outside the formally organized leisure service delivery system. Such a management approach would move beyond dependent-laden direct approaches; it would encourage people to become more ecologically minded and sensitive to the carrying capacity of outdoor leisure settings and it would promote self-determination. This strategy will remove pressures from those areas with limited carrying capacity and expand the users' awareness, knowledge, and skill potential for moving outside the limited sphere of bureaucratic service provisions.

SUMMARY

Environmental perspectives serve to provide a more complete understanding of the factors which contribute to leisure behavior. Social groups view the physical environment from a symbolic, ritualistic, or functional point of view. The environment serves as a repository of meanings for symbolizing relationships and a spatial field in which social life is organized.

The physical environment is seen as an independent determinant affecting leisure behavior. Leisure settings, described as locales by Cheek and Burch, are characterized by their specialized moral order, physical design, and social structure. Leisure locales are classified according to seven types: transitional (e.g., waiting lounges), integration (e.g., school playgrounds), bonding (e.g., sports stadiums), solidarity (e.g., museums), custodial (e.g., golden age clubs), exchange (e.g., shopping centers), and fantasy (e.g., amusement parks).

Urban places were classified by use: residences, neighborhoods, and districts. Outdoor recreation settings were classified on the basis of their social milieu and of the residential origin and image held by visitors: neighborhood, district, regional, and remote outdoor places. The social meanings of outdoor leisure environments as perceived by user groups are different from the personal and organizational perspectives indicated by the managers and policy makers of these settings. Further, depreciative acts on the environment, including vandalism, theft, and nuisance behavior, occur most often because campers typically disagree with outdoor recreation managers on the types of activities appropriate to attaining the goals of the users.

In the future it appears there will have to be a balance struck between those who have concern for environmental quality and resource recreation users who are oriented primarily toward consumption.

PART FOUR

HOLISTIC PERSPECTIVES AND THE FUTURE OF LEISURE

9

Holistic and Multivariate Perspectives of Leisure

Leisure looked at from an integrated, whole perspective, a holistic configuration, is the basis of this chapter. Topics explored include defining the holistic leisure perspective according to three analytical and descriptive holistic models of leisure: multiple-satisfactions approach, a multivariate conceptual model of recreation behavior, and an eclectic conceptual paradigm of play behavior. Finally, three societal views are offered to provide a basis for interpreting the sociopolitical dynamics of leisure.

We have been accustomed to living in a fragmented world. At the onset of the 1980's we find ourselves considering relating to a world that is all one, interrelated planet. Nations which previously didn't recognize each other now seek peace and harmony at best, coexistence at least. The segmentation of human experience, broken down into discernible units by the calculating, mechanical pace of industrial society, appears to have reached its peak, and people have become more desirous of relating to things and people as a whole. Such a change in perspective has transformed the study of leisure in a substantive way.

According to Max Kaplan, leisure is best understood in terms of its dynamic nature, particularly when viewed from a holistic perspective, as a total way of life. Almost anything can be identified as leisure, as elements of leisure may be found in work, family, religion, and education.

Leisure, then, can be said to consist of relatively self-determined activities and experiences that are seen as leisure by participants, that are psychologically pleasant in anticipation and recollection, that potentially cover the whole range of commitment and intensity, that contain characteristic norms and constraints, and provide opportunities for recreation, personal growth and service to others.[1]

According to Kaplan, the following conditions are of highest importance: (1) Leisure must be seen as *continuous* or *bulk time,* not chopped up, as in work life. There is instantaneous access to people and places through travel and study, and to the world through mass media. This major new element in leisure experiences requires relatively continuous periods of attention. (2) The *loss of the full-time production role* among many groups—particularly the elderly, disaffected youth, individuals working shortened work cycles or leisure sharing, and the like —requires that our society seek alternative sources of moral strength and value from an eroding work ethic. This condition of the new leisure raises important questions about the usefulness of values from the work life.

Additionally, the evolution of a new concept of leisure is characterized by a convergence of elements, a fusion of life spheres. "Elements of leisure, . . . pleasant expectation or self-growth—become ideals in the work situation; meantime, elements of work—such as the fulfillment of oneself, discipline and craft—find their way into leisure."[2]

EXPLAINING LEISURE FROM A HOLISTIC PERSPECTIVE

A holistic orientation may come closest to accounting for variances not detected or treated in most single-variable studies. Both social-economic-status and personality variables provide some basis for studying leisure activity.[3] According to Ferriss,[4] these factors also suggest a basis for substitutability among activities and help explain what the underlying meanings of various activities are to participants.

Hendee and Burdge suggest that various social groupings may serve as a basis for substitutability, as activities may be interchangeable depending on who participates with whom. The lack of understanding

[1]Max Kaplan, "Implications for Gerontology from a General Theory of Leisure," Paper presented at the Third International Course, "Leisure and the Third Age," Dubrovnik, Yugoslavia, May 15–18, 1972.

[2]*Ibid.*

[3]John C. Hendee and Rabel J. Burdge, "The Substitutability Concept: Implications for Recreation Research and Management," Unpublished research paper, 1974.

[4]Abbot L. Ferriss, "The Social and Personality Correlates of Outdoor Recreation," *The Annals* 389:46–55, 1970.

Factor I: *Cultural Hobbies.* These activities are defined as cultural based on the idea that talent in the forms of skill or education is required. Rewards depend on internal satisfactions for hobbies and "situational" power where the hobbies require the presence of other persons.

Factor II: *Orgnaized Competition.* These are activities characterized by skillful physical action, group competition, and structured social organization with public and peer recognition and apparent underlying goal.

Factor III: *Domestic Maintenance.* These are actitities which include passive activities with low energy requirements derived from present or former domestic necessities. Organizational involvement appears related to service or tradition rather than from the pursuits of status.

Factor IV: *Social Leisure.* These activities are heavily dependent on peer group and family interaction.

Factor V: *Outdoor Activities.* These are predominantly male-oriented, outdoor resource based activities and related facilitating and preparatory activities.

Figure 9–1

Activity Clusters

of leisure preferences—an endemic problem identified by Hendee and Burdge—particularly in resource-based recreation areas, might be overcome through the application of the substitutability concept.

The current concern by recreation managers over excessive crowding, disregard for environmental values, and preference for inappropriate facilities and activities may reflect the selection of outdoor recreation by persons whose leisure interests might reflect other priorities. The popularity and overuse problems in outdoor recreation areas may thus be due in part to the presence of people seeking leisure satisfactions that might be, but are not, met elsewhere.[5]

According to their research, carried out in two independent studies,[6] five activity clusters—cultural hobbies, organized competition, domestic maintenance, social leisure, and outdoor activities—can be identified based on similarity of participation patterns and activity rates of participates (see Figure 9–1). Thus the concept of leisure activity substitutability is defined as the interchangeability of recreation activities in satisfying participants' motives, needs, wishes, and desires.

A major implication is the potential substitutability of activities within and between the five clusters. Since participation is highly correlated, it may be that, at least at a highly generalized level, activities in the same cluster provide similar satisfactions. Thus, for many people some of these activities may be substitutable with little loss in satisfaction.

Cheek, Field, and Burdge point out three policy implications of substitutability.[7]

[5]Hendee and Burdge, "Substitutability Concept," p. 8.

[6]*Ibid.,* pp. 6, 8.

[7]Neil H. Cheek, Donald R. Field, and Rabel J. Burdge. *Leisure and Recreation Places,* (Ann Arbor, Mich.: Ann Arbor Science Publishers, 1976), pp. 158–159.

1. The range of policy and management alternatives is broad. If public responsibility is to satisfy leisure needs, then it may be possible to achieve this goal by utilizing any of several related activities that provide similar satisfactions. If several activities would meet similar leisure needs of the outdoor type, then opportunities are available to economize on public outdoor recreation programs without reducing leisure satisfactions.

2. The substitutability concept is supported by the "opportunity theory" of recreation participation, which specifies that people participate in what is available. It is commonly pointed out by economists that this is particularly true when the opportunity, such as a public park, is provided nearly free of charge. Yet outdoor recreation programs use participation profiles and verbalized preferences as the basis for planning capital investments without probing deeper into the meaning of activities to participants.

3. Outdoor recreation planning procedures are also frequently based on preference for certain types of areas, ignoring the fact that the activities provided in such areas might be the primary source of satisfaction. Limited public money for outdoor recreation and the growing scarcity of some types of areas should encourage the hunt for substitutable activities as an approach to research and planning.

MULTIPLE SATISFACTIONS

The concept of multiple satisfactions[8] refers to the ultimate objectives of leisure experience—human benefits. Researchers have typically used the term "satisfaction" in reference to how satisfied a recreation visitor was after engaging in the overall experience. Hendee[9] has proposed that satisfactions are separate components or dimensions of the experience. He offers a paradigm (Figure 9–2) to explain the multiple-satisfaction concept of recreation resource management.

The paradigm may be explained briefly by stating that recreation resources offer people the opportunity for a range of experiences, which, in turn lead to benefits—the ultimate goal of recreation resource management (by inference it might be suggested that accruing of such benefits for the individual would be characteristic in *any* leisure setting). The nature of recreation experiences, and thus the satisfactions and benefits that follow, can be shaped by management of the surrounding physical, biological, and social conditions.

Hendee[10] offers six tenets in relation to his paradigm, five of which will be outlined here. *First,* the most significant direct products of

[8]*Ibid.,* p. 155.

[9]John C. Hendee, "Multiple-Satisfaction Approach to Game Management," *Wildlife Society Bulletin* 2:104–113, Fall 1974.

[10]*Ibid.,* pp. 106–109.

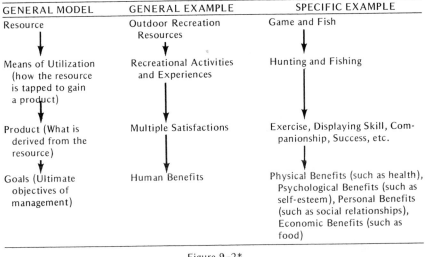

GENERAL MODEL	GENERAL EXAMPLE	SPECIFIC EXAMPLE
Resource ↓	Outdoor Recreation Resources ↓	Game and Fish ↓
Means of Utilization (how the resource is tapped to gain a product) ↓	Recreational Activities and Experiences ↓	Hunting and Fishing ↓
Product (What is derived from the resource) ↓	Multiple Satisfactions ↓	Exercise, Displaying Skill, Companionship, Success, etc. ↓
Goals (Ultimate objectives of management)	Human Benefits	Physical Benefits (such as health), Psychological Benefits (such as self-esteem), Personal Benefits (such as social relationships), Economic Benefits (such as food)

Figure 9–2*
The Multiple-Satisfaction Concept of Recreation
Resource Management

John C. Hendee, "A Multiple-Satisfaction Approach to Game Management," p. 106.

resource management are recreation experiences which produce diverse human satisfactions. *Second,* satisfactions are not the same as benefits but may lead to benefits. Satisfactions are the more specific, immediately gratifying pleasures from certain aspects of the recreation experience. Benefits are the more enduring improved conditions resulting from one or more satisfactions, e.g., improved physical, psychological, and emotional well-being, better personal relationships, a richer quality of life. *Third,* success is an important recreation satisfaction, but only one of many. Recreationists seek a variety of other satisfactions and the human benefits to which those lead. *Fourth,* the quality of the recreation experience is determined by the extent to which the recreationist finds the mix of satisfactions desired. In other words, a "quality recreation experience" means different things to different recreationists. The multiple-satisfactions approach suggests that there is a full range of satisfactions available to each recreationist. A reasonable probability of success plus a full continuum of opportunities for other satisfactions are keys to quality recreation experiences. *Fifth,* recreation satisfactions vary with the conditions under which recreation experiences take place, and these conditions can be managed. Managers of leisure settings can work together to broaden and enhance recreation experiences.

There is a complex of interrelationships between the ecosystem and the social system that regulates human harvest of game. The ecosystem includes a full spectrum of biological factors—all of the flora and fauna making up the habitat. The social system includes such things as land-use

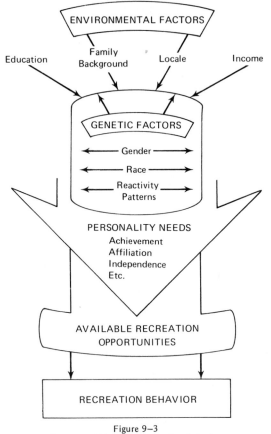

Figure 9–3
Conceptual Model of Recreation Behavior

patterns, laws, regulations, enforcement policy, access, and all other conditions resulting from human activity.[11]

It is suggested by Hendee that under a multiple-satisfactions approach, all these ecosystem and social factors can be coordinated for their total impact. The cooperative, coordinated efforts (e.g., collaboration between land managers and game managers, or public community leisure service managers and private community leisure service managers) can produce high-quality total experiences leading to optimum human benefits.

Howard offers a multivariate model of recreation behavior which is similar to Hendee's paradigm. Howard's model, "A Conceptual Model of Recreation Behavior," depicted in Figure 9–3, stems from his own

[11]*Ibid.*, p. 108.

theoretical work.[12] According to the model, recreation behavior is goal-directed, emanating from the urge to satisfy needs of the individual personality. The initial step in the model is directed toward ameliorating the nature versus nurture controversy through a graphic portrayal of how these factors interact to form one's personality. Personality is seen as a product of the interaction process (generated from genetic factors and learned behavior). Environmental factors (the influence of income, education, family background, etc.) have an influence on leisure behavior. Genetic factors (sex, race, etc.) also influence one's development and response to stimuli. Personality needs are set in motion based on various needs, such as achievement, affiliation, and so on. Recreation participation, then, is essentially a function of personality dynamics affected by available recreation opportunities.

Levy offers an eclectic conceptual paradigm for the study of play (leisure) behavior.[13] His model recognizes the principle of multiple determinants of behavior and thus involves simultaneous statistical analysis of all independent variables. The descriptive model is illustrated in Figure 9–4. Play behavior is determined by the interaction of the person and the environment, and the paradigm provides a perspective for the interdisciplinary and transdisciplinary study of human play behavior.

UNIFIED RESEARCH AND THEORY DEVELOPMENT

Cheek, Field, and Burdge[14] call for a more holistic or broader orientation toward leisure by both research and management. As mentioned earlier, the usefulness of the typical "recreation demand" survey approach in outdoor recreation research is reduced by several procedural shortcomings, including the usual practice of excluding leisure activities other than outdoor recreation from the survey.

The call for more unified research theory development is similarly echoed by Levy. He states:

> The human organism is biologically designed to operate through two complimentary phases—*effort* and *relaxation*. The biological sciences have provided us with some helpful analogies when they tell us that *effort* is to *relaxation* as catabolism is to abolism and systole is to diastole.[15]

[12]Dennis R. Howard, "Multivariate Relationships Between Leisure Activities and Personality," Doctoral Thesis, Oregon State University, Corvallis, Oregon, June 1973.

[13]Joseph Levy, *Play Behavior* (New York: John Wiley & Sons, 1978), p. 58.

[14]Cheek, Field, and Burdge, *Leisure and Recreation Places*, p. 154.

[15]Levy, *Play Behavior*, p. 185.

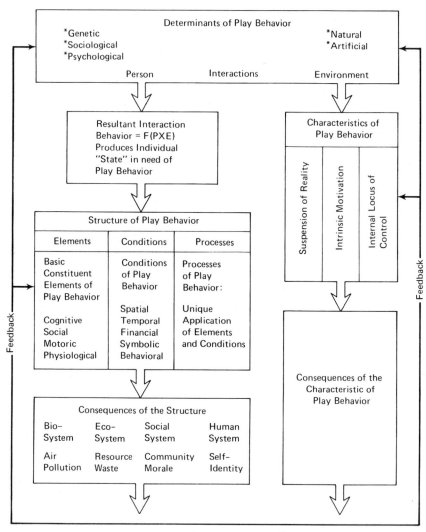

Figure 9–4*
A Conceptual Paradigm for the Study of Play Behavior

*Joseph Levy, Play Behavior, p. 58.

Leisure, according to Levy, is seen as the complementary relation-ship between effort (output) and relaxation (input) at all levels of human biology and psychology. It is suggested by Levy that when work (effort) and leisure (relaxation) take this form, the traditional dichotomy of work and leisure, each of them being subordinate to the other, is removed. Levy discusses the future implications of this integrated work-leisure as play society.

1. By embracing this work-leisure as play society, one would move to smaller scales of producing and organizing. The way in which people would relate to one another and to their work experiences would also be changed to the point where people would welcome more integrated cooperative life-styles.

2. People are forfeiting extrinsic rewards (money, benefits, bonuses, etc.) in favor of meaningful intrinsic rewards (freedom, responsibility, control, etc.).

3. We have been inclined over the past two decades to assume that man's natural state is a form of homeostasis or tranquility. [However] ... people want to stay active and interactive. The stress of effort (work), if optimal, helps to provide a form of biological and psychological "tone" analogous to muscle tone brought about by muscle contraction and relaxation.

4. Effort must be recognized as worthwhile whether manifested during work time or leisure time. The new definition of play (effort-relaxation), which accepts the dictum that effort may be financially rewarding or done solely for the value of the activity, will help to give identity to those who volunteer their efforts without financial reimbursement.

5. The age of leisure will mean that society will have to adopt a playful approach to life where *effort* and *relaxation* are part of a self-fulfilling adaptive life-style. The future will see a tremendous change toward work, since this phase of life will change to effort (autonomous activities), and individuals will graciously consent to undertake unpleasant and even monotonous tasks because they know that they can always assert their full autonomy at any time.[16]

Of particular relevance to the work-leisure unitary society is the idea that play emerges as a forum for societal integration and normalization. Disabled individuals, who by reason of emotional, psychological, physical, mental, or some other characteristic are set apart and isolated from the mainstream and treated differently, no longer can be segregated from the rest of the community. The leisure setting fosters the concept of integration. "Play, through its capacity for fostering *abilities,* has enabled the disabled to achieve self-fulfillment and social recognition, which has heretofore been denied to them in other spheres of life."[17]

THREE SOCIETAL VIEWS OF LEISURE

According to Stanley Parker, the relationship between work and leisure in the individual's life is paralleled by the relationship between these two spheres at the societal level. Parker sees two basic interpretations of the work-leisure spheres in an urban-industrial society. *Segmentalists* see the part of their lives as separate segments,

---

[16]*Ibid.,* pp. 186–187.
[17]*Ibid.,* pp. 189–190.

comparatively unaffected by each other. Segmantalism is likely to have either (1) an opposition (polarized) pattern of work and leisure, or (2) a neutrality pattern of work and leisure, in which work and leisure are fairly self-contained. A person who views the parts of his or her life as integrated is likely to have an extension or *holistic* pattern of work and leisure (paralleled by fusion of work and leisure spheres in the society as a whole, or at least in one's social circle).[18] Integrating the work and leisure spheres of society, a leisure policy maker would attempt to tackle the problems together, while a segmentalist would tackle the problems separately.

A third view, a *pluralistic* perspective, accepts some elements in the two previously indicated approaches, but it finds neither acceptable as an all-embracing theorizing construct. The pluralistic model suggests that leisure is an intrinsic experience that reflects a variety of opportunity and meaning. Its properties are not seen as being determined by any particular institution or even accurately predicted.

Implications of Segmentalism

Pre-industrial societies knew no confrontation between work and leisure, because work included leisure-like attributes. However, during our present phase of industrialization, with a reduced workweek, greater affluency in general, and earlier retirement, leisure has emerged as a significant aspect of life. Each phase of living should be designed to promote maximum fulfillment.

> Those who advocate the differentiation of work and leisure as the solution to at least some of the problems in either sphere do so on the assumption that the segmentation sphere is characteristic and desirable in modern industrial society.[19]

Society should not impose a pattern of social relationship on the individual, but provide him or her with a series of alternatives. Accordingly, the differentiation approach to the problems of work and leisure could be ameliorated in the following manner:

> First, there must be a revaluation of work, which, to be complete, must be carried out simultaneously on three different planes, intellectual, social and moral. Secondly, there must be opportunities for self-realization and self-development for the individual in nonwork activities.[20]

[18]Stanley Parker. *The Future of Work and Leisure* (New York: Praeger Publishers, 1971), p. 99.

[19]*Ibid.,* p. 116.

[20]*Ibid.,* p. 118.

Implications of Holism

The aim of integration is to maximize leisure, but also to fuse it with a uniquely satisfying form of work. Parker notes the implications of the integration of work and leisure.

In this fusion, work may lose its present characteristic feature of constraint and gain the creativity now associated mainly with leisure, while leisure may lose its present characteristic feature of opposition to work and gain the status—now associated mainly with the *product* of work—of a resource worthy of planning to provide the greatest possible human satisfaction.[21]

The goal of leisure service agencies in the future must be the advancement and provision of enriching and satisfying free-time opportunities, particularly because of the increased emphasis in industry on more flexible, shorter working schedules, earlier retirement, the prospect of some form of guaranteed income, and like developments. The central focus on the part of leisure service community catalysts should not be to maximize leisure values and minimize those associated with work. Holists recognize a relationship between work and leisure. Therefore, the central focus of leisure service should be to encourage individual initiative and choice.

Parker suggests a laissez-faire doctrine of leisure as a self-determined, natural, spontaneous experience which cannot be engineered or unnecessarily influenced by various agencies. The individual nature of the leisure experience is diminished if leisure service agencies attempt to direct people's energies into specified channels in advance of participation. "We should aim instead to nourish the individual's potentialities so that each, according to his capacity, could find his own life solution."[22]

Parker notes that our traditional planning approach has considered leisure as a luxury for a few; for the masses, work considerations were of high priority and whatever time remained was to be passed as "wholesomely" and as cheaply to the community as possible. This outmoded leisure policy, which survives widely today,

... concentrates on the requirement of the work environment, giving high priority to efficient physical relationships among factories, offices, schools, shops, houses and transport routes. The residual "open space" that remains is regarded as adequate to meet leisure requirements. Very

[21] *Ibid.,* p. 122.
[22] *Ibid.,* p. 139.

little attention is paid by planners to a positive approach to leisure by understanding and forecasting leisure-time behavior, and by developing resources in line with estimating demand.[23]

Implications of Pluralism

Kelly[24] adds a third approach and suggests a *pluralistic* perspective, which contains elements of the other two. He suggests that there is leisure to be found on the job in conversation, friendships, accomplishments, and even daydreaming. However, the requirements of most employment severely limit any intrinsic satisfaction to be found in the work itself.

People engage in a wide variety of activities and experiences and find multiple satisfactions in those activities. Kelly states, however, it simply is not possible to predict what people will choose and find satisfying simply by knowing their occupation, income, family background, age, gender, or even education level and place in the life cycle. Leisure is still chosen, not determined. Kelly argues that it may be most accurate to understand the relation of leisure to work, family, and community as neither holistic nor dualistic (segmentalist). "Rather, leisure is pluralistic in its varied and combined meaning, its forms, its locales, and to a lesser extent, its associations. Leisure's many forms and orientations are not determined wholly by any other institutional position—in work, education, family or religion."[25]

Pluralism accepts the social, cultural and environmental contexts of leisure that limit and shape participation, but still provides for a diverse amount of outward expression and inner satisfaction. Kelly sees that holism tends to lose sight of what is distinctive about leisure—its freedom and intrinsically nonproductive aims. Pluralism implies a variety of opportunity and meaning that are necessary for leisure to retain its defining dimension of freedom.

Whatever leisure policy—segmentalist, pluralistic, or holistic—is ultimately used by leisure service agencies, it will have broad social planning implications. A segmentalist approach would provide leisure facilities for a certain type of people who need them; a holistic approach would stimulate an awareness of the possibilities of leisure behavior in a variety of situations; a pluralistic approach would allow diverse interpretations and encourage a continuously developing state of perceived freedom by more and more people, an important contribution to the state of being at leisure.

While future work-leisure patterns are uncertain, there is some feel-

---

[23] *Ibid.,* p. 140.
[24] John R. Kelly. *Leisure* (Englewood Cliffs, N.J.: Prentice-Hall, Inc., 1980).
[25] *Ibid.*

ing that work will not be totally enveloped by free time. Whatever pattern emerges, the fundamental focus of leisure planners should be on providing opportunities for individuals to determine leisure choices from a variety of options in a variety of situations and to realize personal fulfillment in leisure that either complements or takes the place of work. "The extent to which the advantage is taken of such opportunities must, of course, remain the choice of the individual."[26]

SUMMARY

A holistic perspective serves as an integrating approach to the understanding of the dynamics of leisure. Some leisure scientists argue that a holistic orientation comes closest to accounting for explained variance not detected or treated in most single-variable studies of leisure behavior. The concepts of substitutability and multiple satisfactions suggest that there is a full range of potential satisfactions available to the recreationists, many of which are interchangeable in certain activities. Managers of leisure settings can make efforts to enhance the recreation experience and potential benefits of the users.

A multivariate or holistic approach to viewing leisure recognizes the interplay of several variables, including social, psychological, genetic, and environmental aspects of the leisure experience. Three societal views, segmental, holistic, and pluralistic, are presented. Each suggests ways of viewing the sociocultural-environmental context of leisure and provides a basis for analysis and interpretation.

[26]Stanley Parker, *The Future of Work and Leisure,* p. 143.

10

Future
Perspectives
of Leisure

Views of the future are presented in this chapter, with particular attention focused on the impact of technology on society and its relationship to leisure. Two scenarios for the future are outlined; each with its particular implication for post-industrial society and leisure behavior. Two approaches to leisure service delivery are further analyzed in relationship to the improvement of community life. Several implications of continued growth and steady-state scenarios for the leisure service field are described.

Any inquiry into the future of work and leisure is at best highly speculative. However, because change has become a permanent fixture in our lives, it is important for social planners, educators, and leisure policy planners to make judgments about the future. Don Fabun states:

We have, in our society at the present, almost no concept of training people for a life of leisure, we do not know even whether people can accept leisure as a way of life.

We are on the threshold of a time when leisure is at last possible for most people in our society, and we are doing almost nothing to prepare them for this new dimension of human life.[1]

The challenge of the future in our post-industrial society seems to be for our economic system to recognize and deal with the consequences of the changed energy flow of production and the resultant

[1]Don Fabun. *The Dynamics of Change* (Englewood Cliffs, N.J.; Prentice-Hall, Inc., 1967), p. 21.

192

need for new ways of perceiving work and leisure. Post-industrialism calls on human beings to develop inner strength and to rely less on conveniences of the material culture. Neighborhood, home-centered, and self-directed leisure behavior patterns may increase as a result of the reduction of nonrenewable natural resources and the limits on government spending.

As we move into an economy of pseudo-abundance (realizing that inflation eats away the increases or profits gained), our needs will change from lower- to higher-level ones. When everyone's needs for food, clothing, and shelter can more easily be met, we will concentrate our energies more on the goal of *self-actualization* through cultural activities, conceived as play on a high level, and a host of experiences which provide stimulation and relief from the daily routine of being confronted every day by a finite world existence. Economic principles have given human beings a one-sided attitude which deprives morality and nonutilitarian striving of their rational basis. According to Walter Weisskopf:

> The "economic man" is the prototype of alienated man. He is confined to conscious, deliberate action. All spontaneous, emotional, nonutilitarian behavior is suppressed. Economic theory has, in spite of its lip-service to economic freedom, eliminated real freedom from its image of man by maintaining that perfect consciousness and knowledge permits only one, unequivocally determined kind of action, that is, action which leads to the maximization of material gain measured in terms of money.... This has led to a disintegration of those aspects of life where this measurement is inapplicable. Friendship, love, charity, creative ability, aesthetic, and religious experiences cannot be calculated according to the economic principle.
>
> In order to balance the economy we have to integrate work with leisure, material need satisfaction with spiritual and intellectual pursuits.... A person will have to be rewarded rather on the basis of what he is than of what he does in the market place.[2]

Work is no longer the central life interest for many people in post-industrial society. Historically, life styles have been defined by economic class and occupational status. Rationality, efficiency, and notion of time as money were pervasive concepts and attitudes in a nation oriented to a scarce economy.

> By and large, modern life styles have lost this mandatory component and inflexibility. Work and occupational role no longer determine so directly the life styling of individuals in a nonwork-oriented culture. The detach-

[2]Walter Weisskopf, "Existence and Values," in *New Knowledge in Human Vales,* ed. Abraham H. Maslow (Chicago: Henry Regnery Co., 1959), pp. 116–117.

ment of the way of life from the way of earning life, or living, does not replace work with leisure, but alters the meaning of both terms; it is not nonwork or leisure, but the decline of exclusively economic measures for human activities.[3]

John McHale has predicted that in the future the factors which have traditionally determined role and life style will no longer be relevant —ways of earning a living, occupational status, economic and geographic location will not be important constraints. Human beings' social and physical milieu will be seen increasingly as interdependent and coexistent. Therefore, it will no longer be meaningful to conceive of various societal components as separate, compartmentalized sequences. "The overlapping of work/vacation/weekend living is also accompanied by the flexible adoption of appropriate styling for the many different social roles that the individual now occupies."[4]

TWO SCENARIOS FOR POST-INDUSTRIAL SOCIETY

With the onset of the 1980's several future scenarios for North American society seem plausible. At least two deserve discussion.

First, a *continued-growth state,* which would be represented by the basic goals that have dominated the industrial era (e.g., material progress, individualism, freedom of enterprise, few restraints on capital accumulation, social responsibility being mainly the concern of government rather than other institutions). These larger goals have been approached through a set of fundamental subgoals (e.g., efficiency, productivity, material wealth, continual growth of production, of consumption, and of technological and manipulative power). They have resulted in processes and states characterized by division of labor, specialization, cybernation, stimulated consumption, planned obsolescence, private exploitation of resources held in common. Some people will argue that this scenario will continue to counteract human ends, represented by enriching work roles, resource conservation, environmental enchancement, equitable sharing of the world's resources. Industrializing the production of goods and services has resulted in the creation of an insatiable consumer demand.

Second, a *steady-state society,* which would result in a movement toward "voluntary simplicity" characterized by lowered consumption, increased emphasis on community, inner exploration, relationship to nature, and meaningful work or effort. This appears to be one of the most viable alternative scenarios to the future. This scenario suggests

[3]John McHale. *The Future of the Future* (New York: Ballantine Books, 1969), p. 320.
[4]*Ibid.*

the eventual reconciliation of growth in human terms with a high quality of life, appropriate technology, and human social institutions. A steady-state scenario fosters several possible ethics, including:

1. An *ecological ethic,* which recognizes the limited nature of resources, sees Homo sapiens as an integral part of the natural world, hence insepa-rable from its governing processes and laws. The ecological ethic fosters a sense of the total community and responsibility for the fate of the planet, and relates self-interest to the interests of fellow human beings and future generations.

2. A *self-realization ethic,* which asserts the proper end of all individual experiences is the further development of the emergent self. The appro-priate function of *all* social institutions is to create an environment which will foster that process. The self-realization ethic would push society toward a restructuring of social institutions to satisfy the indi-vidual's need to full participation in society. As corollaries to this ethic, self-determination of individuals and minority groups should be fos-tered, and social decision-making should be highly decentralized.

3. A *holistic ethic,* which sees meaning and satisfaction in both work and leisure. The freedom, relationships, and satisfactions that express our humanity cannot be allocated to either work or leisure. Rather, each may be designed and developed to maximize the realization of the full-est human values.

These three ethics—one emphasizing the total community of Homo sapiens-in-nature and oneness of the human race, another the placing of the highest value on the development of selfhood, and the third expressive of an integration of life through the human ordering of both work and leisure in a unified human life space—together encourage both cooperation and individual achievement and opportunity for a fusion of life roles.

It might be argued that the steady-state scenario might be most plausible within the context of a world society. We are approaching the time when the "good life" can no longer be defined solely in terms of increasing material wealth and of consumption of leisure activities which deplete energy and nonrenewable resources. Considering the extent to which the increasing material affluence permeates our per-sonal and social values, life styles, and institutions, the transition from a status quo continued-growth state to a steady-state society could cause serious problems as well as create unprecedented opportunities.

It would seem that an important role for recreation and leisure service personnel in the near future would be to recognize the personal and societal conditions that would encourage self-generated, noncon-sumptive, spontaneous leisure and make this a viable alternative to leisure activities dependent upon material goods and energy. This potential role involves the consideration of two separate but complementary issues: (1) how to develop an individual's capabilities for self-generated leisure, and (2) how to design the relevant environments, facilities, and resources to be compatible with these leisure activities.

The leisure "problem" in a steady-state society would seem to revolve around the combination of potential increases in nonwork time and the relatively decreased opportunities to utilize this time in the ways in which we have been accustomed. While some of this time could be taken up by such relatively low-resource-consuming activities as education, athletics, and cultural pursuits, these activities may not be enough to compensate for the decreased availability of leisure-related goods.

However, alternatives to leisure activities that require the consumption of goods and energy do exist. Self-generated activities that are relatively independent of consumer goods, and that require little more than an individual's own imagination and spontaneity and the stimulation of other people and of the environment, are excellent steady-state economic forms.

Some self-generated forms of leisure, such as daydreams, fantasy, reflection, meditation, reverie, problem-solving, self-analysis, awareness, and exploration, require little more than time, peace and quiet, and one's own imagination. Interaction with friends, lovers, casual acquaintances, and total strangers can also be entertaining, increasing the diversity of the activities in which we engage, can provide additional sources of stimulation and knowledge, and can offer valuable social feedback that can be used to increase self-awareness and satisfaction in interpersonal relations. Outdoor recreation activities such as hiking and camping in the natural environment would provide another leisure form of expression that is essentially self-generated.

> Leisure activities of this sort would not deplete natural resources as much as would those activites that are largely dependent upon energy resources and material goods. In addition, they would rely less upon the ability of private enterprise to continually provide new products to meet the changing leisure needs of the consuming public. The spontaneous ability to generate novel and absorbing activities, perspectives, and experiences suggests a leisure resource of almost limitless variation. In effect, the whole world, internal and external, can be a potential resource for the person with the flexibility and imagination to take advantage of it."[5]

There are increasing demands being placed upon both U.S. and Canadian institutions to participate more actively in social, cultural, and

[5]Don Mankin, "Leisure in the Steady-State Society," *Society and Leisure*, 8:99, 1976.

political programs designed to improve the quality of life but at reduced expenditure levels. Leisure service administrators and managers must continually strike a balance in achieving practical accomplishment from theoretical analysis. This delicate combination of management demands that the administrator who is bombarded from the local service area constituents—government regulatory agencies, consumer rights forces, various civil and human rights groups, and the exploding research and information environment of the university setting—must develop a "workable" theoretical framework from which to operate on a daily basis. The leisure service administrator must seek to blend all of the management responsibilities of planning, coordinating, staffing, directing, and controlling within the context of the continually changing framework of human values and relationships in community life. *All* leisure service practitioners must have meaningful guidelines to direct their own lives and to facilitate opportunities for others. By endorsing a philosophy of leisure, the administrator is better able to appraise existing knowledge, beliefs, and human relations; he or she is more likely to evolve a systematic and coherent plan of life in general and provide more astute professional focus in order to determine what is important and significant.

Much of the knowledge base, values, and beliefs which guided the Recreation and Park Movement in general, and the development of agency approaches to serving people specifically, have essentially been characterized by a *continued-growth*-oriented society. The view which separates time into segments of work and leisure no longer may be a useful guide in a world which might be defined as a *steady-state* economy in the future. Such a concept of leisure, which is based upon quantitative growth and a materialistic value system to sustain it, views life in a highly fragmented manner with its leisure moments to be compulsively consumed.

Industrializing goods and services has resulted in the creation of an insatiable consumer demand for all kinds of things. Some economists, sociologists, political scientists, and leisure scholars have argued that the continuation of this type of society will counteract human ends, represented by the demand for enriching work roles, resource conservation, environmental enhancement, and equitable sharing of resources. The steady-state scenario, while projecting seemingly worthwhile images of human relationships and community life, nonetheless serves as a threat to most current social institutions and is deemed untenable by many recreation and leisure service organizations.

Leisure service personnel would be challenged to adopt a delivery system strategy comparable to the type Mankin suggests, with changes in educational goals, content, and structure.

1. Paying more attention to individually defined goals and the satisfactions inherent to the learning process [play process] to balance the present emphasis on education as a means to the extrinsic ends of eventual vocational productivity [alter emphasis on competition and extrinsic rewards of consumer-collector life-style];

2. Developing in each student recreationist such characteristics as personal responsibility, autonomy, flexibility, spontaneity, creativity, and the ability for self-initiation and direction utilizing a catalyst-enabler leadership style to facilitate self-reliance in leisure; and

3. Placing more emphasis on "learning to learn" play and relatively less emphasis on the learning of facts, principles, and theories which are relatively unending and can be easily modified or rendered obsolete by societal change and the development of new knowledge.[6]

Extension of the continued-growth ethic and a lack of adherence to a steady-state scenario in the 1980's could result in the following developments:

1. Increased pervasiveness of narcissistic behavior resulting in "consciousness raising" excesses which might result in the proliferation of various exaggerated forms of self-expression. The devotion to self-oriented products, values, and life styles could erode efforts to build community sentiment, neighborhood unity, and partner involvement.
Self-interests carried to an extreme could lead to conflict between competing leisure interest recreationists, such as ORV (off-road motor vehicle) enthusiasts and conservation-oriented individuals.

2. A further development of "leisure ghettos" in which enclaves of individuals of similar life styles emerge as the dominant basis for segregation in society (e.g., personal expression in which leisure opportunities differentiate a person's choices, behavior, and social grouping more than do one's age, gender, occupation, ethnic background, etc.). These segregated settlement patterns are likely to be the result of influences stemming principally from the mass media's portrayal of the "good life" as exemplified by posh Club Mediterranean type resorts, but on a year-round basis.

3. The potential for leisure riots could become manifest. The lack of sufficient diverse, accessible, consumption-oriented leisure opportunities and the growing availability of larger blocks of free time could result in the clamoring for the dismantling and destruction of facilities which do not respond to increased demands for personal fulfillment. People who feel that a capitalist economy which guarantees the pursuit of happiness for everyone but seemingly is unable to keep up with the insatiable demand for a consumption-convenience life style could become more

[6]*Ibid.,* p. 100.

and more impatient. Such impatience might lead to destructive behavior against leisure resources and the disruption of programs and services.

4. The inability to adapt to new energy sources (other than fossil fuels) could result in a crisis of Limited Leisure Options. Customary leisure forms of expression generated from electrical, fossil fuel, and mechanized means of leisure are expected to be limited and even prohibited. Customary nonrenewable and specialized resource-dependent forms of leisure expression could be subject to great reductions in use. This may result in people's having to alter their extrinsic-oriented leisure behavior patterns to self-generated, intrinsic-oriented forms of leisure expression.

5. Conspicuous leisure, a life style representative of a consumption-convenience ethic, is likely to become more predominant. Its continued manifestation seemingly would seriously threaten all remaining nonrenewable resources, pull the United States into a possible war with Third World and nonaligned nations, and increase confrontation with steady-state oriented groups in America and Canada.

6. The prospect of total computerization (cataloging, programming, and forecasting of all possible leisure experiences, facilities, resources, and options) will most likely be developed and readily made available in the homes of all individuals who subscribe to such a Leisure Information Network of Knowledge (LINK). A LINK prototype could conceivably be available on a regular home screen terminal or in a portable compact viewer form. Unfortunately, the element of human interaction, guidance, and support would be almost totally eliminated from such an electronics-oriented leisure world.

7. Leisure might paradoxically serve as a disintegrator of social life, resulting in the fragmentation of community and family life. This could turn people's moral and ethical principles askew because of its tantalizing effects tied to status. While leisure contributes significantly to the Gross National Product (a conservative estimate was $180 billion in 1978, 12 percent more than in 1977), the various forms of leisure expression which proliferate spending, buying, consuming, displaying, and competing for greater personal recognition may result in reduced intrinsic and developmental benefits and a focus on limited, extrinsic rewards.

8. Certainly, many positive things would continue to occur under the present ethic. There appears, however, to be a question of how long such an ethic can sustain itself. There is a likelihood of greater numbers of skiers, racquetball and tennis players, joggers, motorcyclists, motorized sport participants, and the like. While these sports are recognized as exciting and most often conducive to fitness and well-being, their continued development and exploitation may bring about two deterrents: (1) the equation of profit, prestige, and status with leisure expression will serve to undermine its intrinsic qualities and (2) to the degree certain leisure activities utilize limited energy resources, they may eventually

give way to electronic and simulation activities. The advantages of being able to incorporate the gains of personal freedom and greater discretionary powers over the entirety of one's life span could be weakened by the overcommercialization of leisure and a widening gap between those who can afford leisure at *any* cost (for the sake of status rather than its intrinsic value) and individuals who desire to become more fully human and complement their lives through leisure.

A continued-growth society, while leading to runaway inflation, high unemployment, environmental imbalances, and a consumption-convenience way of life representative of a growing number of people, has made leisure resources and experiences available to a great number of people and led to an accepted profession of leisure services. However, with a constantly changing society, the social fabric of community life in a continued-growth state has become depersonalized and fragmented for many people, and various forms of human association, rituals, and ceremony have broken down altogether. As indicated earlier, community life, representative of work, family, and leisure, are inseparable components of living and essential ingredients of human life. Leisure involves social interaction, celebration, relaxation, mastery, and self-expression. These are *not* segmented aspects of living: they are a part of life.

However, the influences of industrialization and technology have severed family ties by freeing individuals to express their life styles independently of others and have divided and weaned craftsmanship from work. Therefore, there is an increasing need for recreation and leisure service administrators to work toward improving the quality of life by fusing the shredded and disjointed parts of community life into a whole, as represented in Figure 10–1.

In the *direct provider* delivery service approach, leisure service personnel select, plan, and organize recreation activities for community patrons. This is a "cafeteria style" approach to the delivery of program services: the agency organizes a broad array of "ready-made" leisure opportunities and then allows people to choose from the possibilities offered. This is an essentially centralized, agency-determined approach to the delivery of program services. Minimal input from service recipients is required.

Administrators will increasingly be challenged to incorporate an *enabling process,* extending the leisure service delivery continuum to include a spectrum of programming encompassing a wider diversity of human expression and encouraging individual responsibility for leisure choices. This approach is related to a new philosophy which promotes the capacity of individuals to grow, to explore new possibilities, and to realize their full potential.

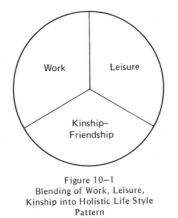

Figure 10–1
Blending of Work, Leisure,
Kinship into Holistic Life Style
Pattern

There is an increasing recognition that a more flexible and transcending leisure perspective is needed to fit the needs of a qualitatively oriented civilization, one which emphasizes relationships and experiences rather than things and possessions. We have tended to attribute our private concerns regarding our relationships, work, and leisure to personal deficiencies and not societal problems. We tend to remain isolated and attempt to solve these problems on our own. These efforts may include growth-centered therapy programs to enable us to be better equipped to "cope" with life. Certainly there are benefits from such courses but there is a need to relate personal problems to larger institutional structures and work with other people to overcome root causes for alienation, anxiety, depression, boredom, and dissatisfaction that are endemic within institutions. It has been suggested that the traditional approach to most program models has involved personal (often isolated) experiences. Perhaps there is a growing desire by people to create a more meaningful sense of community, where self-generated skills can be practiced and shared with others.

In viewing the near future, and incorporating a perspective which embraces the steady-state scenario, some of the following considerations for education, leisure service delivery, and management of agencies seem appropriate:

1. There is a need to adopt an enabling concept within recreation and leisure service organizations. The enabling concept of program delivery serves both as a process and political strategy. The typical facility management which has dominated the Recreation and Park Movement in America for over fifty years, characterized by an activity-oriented and centralized agency service delivery approach, makes assumptions of client groups' recreation needs and provides leisure opportunities within a limited-knowledge framework. This approach was the basis

of preparation for careers in recreation and leisure service and the basis of in-service training for leadership and supervision personnel, but it is no longer seen as the only professional preparatory approach for several reasons. The dominant detracting views include a program mentality which results in recreation and leisure service personnel being responsible not with the development of people, but with the management of a center or referral service or activity dissemination operation; not with service to the community or encouragement of independence and self-reliance, but with supervision of grounds or computer print-out sheets. Such an approach, if used exclusively, is ecologically unsound, results in participant dependency, fragments the recreation experience from the rest of a person's total development, and results in the agencies "fitting people in" to predetermined behavior patterns based on archaic roles no longer functional or acceptable. Additionally, it became apparent at the close of the decade of the 1970's that citizens were not pleased with the delivery of local government services as characterized by a direct leadership model. The apparent waste of taxpayers' money symbolized by inept and inappropriate bureaucratic service delivery methods, resulted in greater scrutiny of municipal recreation and park operations. One marked change was the movement of leisure service departments toward fee-based programs. This development seemed to underscore the need by professional re-creators to:

1. Redefine leadership advocating more risk-taking and innovation;
2. Transform recreation and park activities into human development experiences;
3. Better define the needs of communities through social planning;
4. Take a leadership role in liveability and life style issues;
5. Develop multi-service projects through interagency cooperation and integration; and
6. Organize people to develop more self-help programs and organize clients to support recreation and human service programs.[7]

2. Since the first Earth Day held on April 22, 1970, there has been a greater *environmental impact* on decisions relating to our growth patterns in the areas of housing, production and manufacturing, waste disposal, transportation, nuclear energy, and recreation. We have all learned about the interrelated life support system that exists on earth and the dangers of unrestricted growth. The recreation professional in the years ahead will need to become a more viable part of the community in participating as a team member to facilitate life enhancement for everyone. Recreators (like other members of local government, state government, and all human service professionals) cannot continue to arbitrarily encourage some forms of human expression while denying others without understanding the environmental and human impact of such decisions.

[7]Jack Foley and Frank Benest. "Proposition 13 Aftermath—A Crisis in Recreation and Park Leadership?" *Parks and Recreation* 15: 87, 98, January 1980.

3. *Leisure symmetry* is replacing arbitrary forms of individual distinction; each person must be granted the opportunity to participate in any phase of life and treated impartially without regard to former discriminatory social class divisions, sex-role segregation, or other forms of arbitrary social or physical restrictions. It is the leisure milieu which emerges as an important vehicle for the realization of human rights for various nonaligned groups, where stigma and repression have often prevented the extension of these rights into work and civic life.

   A general shift in people's values, life styles, and personal rhythms is resulting in the change in laws, such as those regarding decriminalization of pot; constitutional guarantees for gay people; extension of mandatory retirement age to 70; the rights of women to terminate the life of an unborn child; the guarantee of civil rights to disabled people; shifting work time and careers to accommodate individual preferences for work/leisure/education/family patterns; and legislation of adult "recreation" sex (acceptance of the right for consenting adults to engage in sexual activity in the privacy of their home). There is increased public tolerance of diverse (even deviant) forms of expression and an increased recognition of the need for widened avenues of leisure behavior to fulfill the human rights of individuals lacking identity and support from the dominant society. The old bases of individual distinction, including age, gender, religion, family status, and occupation no longer serve as a determinant for grouping and delineating work, leisure, education, and family patterns.

   The leisure professional should take on a responsibility to see that the legal and human rights of all individuals are not unjustly restricted in leisure expression, that all people may realize their leisure needs and maintain a full relationship with community life as a partner in the process of exercising their rights as well as responsibilities for their actions as free people.

4. It is anticipated that in the near future the philosophical justification for leisure service programs will be expanded to include a full spectrum of instrumental and expressive components, which sees recreation activity serving as an end in itself, for a multiplicity of human benefits.

   The primary goal of leisure services will be *human development.* There will be a shift from a segmentalist activity-oriented approach to an integrative, multidisciplinary and human-oriented approach to the domain of recreation professional preparation. The new professional will have to perform in different manners from the past. It seems the fundamental role of a recreation professional will be that of helping relation vis-a-vis the client, as counselor, guide, advisor.

5. There is increasing recognition of the need to provide an opportunity for disabled individuals to participate fully in community life. *Mainstreaming* (this concept also refers to normalization and integration) involves the right of disabled people to become active participants in programs serving able-bodied people. As a philosophy, mainstreaming promotes the premise that all people have the ability to learn, grow, and

become more independent, and have the right to choice, dignity, and self-determination. As a process, it provides the support services to maximize individual ability and to minimize the effects of disability and of psychosocial, cultural, and physical barriers. As a goal, mainstreaming enables people, regardless of ability or disability, to interact with each other in settings of individual choice.

6. A holistic approach suggests that leisure service personnel *function in advocacy roles,* at appropriate times. In this sense, advocacy is a staff member's acting on behalf of potential users to get decision makers to act favorably in the community interest. Because municipal recreation and leisure service personnel are the closest units of government to the people, they will increasingly advocate the "rights" and responsibilities of individuals as related to leisure services.

7. Because of the shrinkage of open space in and near urban areas, leisure service personnel will need to become more astute regarding *land management* in general, and more actively aware in particular of how open space, green belts, and land amenities support a more life-enhancing community.

8. Americans cherish the right of *freedom.* We have taken for granted the right to move around as we please. Previously unexplored or low-use environments, including the desert, the mountains, the depths of water-based recreation areas, and certain parts of the countryside, will serve as future play spaces with more intense use (if people juggle their gas allotments). Recreators will need to understand how technical mobility has created a desire for intense, short-term pleasure experiences. An emerging society of risk-taking, nomadic individuals in pursuit of instant opportunities may require that facilities become more versatile in meeting the varying needs of people less dependent on specific types of activities or of facilities necessary to engage in them.

9. While more people are seeking momentary leisure experiences, others are demanding that education, work, and leisure be viewed as an unending *process of continued personal growth.* Leisure personnel who view leisure as an opportunity complex occurring at fixed time periods of nonwork will need to become more aware of how the human organism develops throughout the life span and will need to understand how the interrelationship of all human experience contributes to our development as human beings.

10. Finally, there appears to be a need for a *multiservice approach to combat isolation and loneliness.* Loneliness may be one of the most important causes of human misery in our society today. The isolation and withdrawal of people from each other has resulted from the fragmentation of the family, neighborhood, and community. The community has been rendered more fragile and left with fewer responsibilities. Leisure personnel need to involve more individuals in the planning and decision-making at the neighborhood level. This will require them to ex-

tend service delivery into people's homes in order to combat the total mechanization of society and encourage as many individual, self-determined choices as possible to be made by people. While it is possible to envision an era of personal freedom, withdrawal and disinterest in collective human growth could result in a near collapse of the community. The prospect of community disorientation suggests the need for a multiservice approach in which all community agencies collaborate to serve the *whole* person through a community services exchange. This approach would help to conserve the shrinking public tax dollar, fight the rising inflation rate, and facilitate the development of the community.

Existing bases for examining the recreation and leisure service career potential provide only a limited understanding of the future possibilities of professional service. Our evolving society is unfolding new institutional forms and opportunities for human expression. The career aspirant may find a field not based on existing knowledge or belief system and one that does not conform to current professional guidelines or even resembling the historical roots of the development of organized recreation as documented in textbooks and professional journals.

Certainly a challenge to our society and the Recreation and Park Movement—if it is to be oriented toward human development and the fulfillment of human needs rather than just toward the provision of activities to fill up free time—will be to embrace a leisure philosophy which views the need to be more responsive to the total community needs and problems and more multidisciplined in leisure service delivery approach. The focus of the Recreation and Park Movement in the future may well be centered on the need for understanding all aspects of our social and physical environments, the delicate balance of living in a steady-state world, the necessity of becoming more ecologically oriented, and the Movement's ability to merge with other human services to create an opportunity system serving the paramount goal of human development.

SUMMARY

To determine the future of post-industrial society is a highly speculative task. It does appear that traditional roles, approaches to viewing human behavior, and ways of living will be considerably altered in the near future.

Two scenarios for the future—a continued growth state (characterized by individuality, material progress, wealth, efficiency, and technological manipulative power) and steady-state society (characterized by controlled growth, lowered consumption, emphasis on community, and meaningful work)—are identified in their relationship to leisure. The steady-state perspective is seen as the most plausible approach for the near future and characteristic of three types of ethos: ecological, self-realization, and holistic. This philosophical and systematic operational way of viewing human/nonhuman relationships sees leisure as a pivotal construct for the future. Leisure expression will be a potential battleground for those with conflicting interpretations of the use of play areas. Such differences (preservationist, limited-use oriented groups versus consumption, user-oriented groups) can be potentially resolved if leisure service administrators can find ways of improving the quality of life but at reduced expenditure levels and with a holistic frame of reference.

Subject Index

A

Affluence, 7–8
Americans, attitude changes in, 5

B

Bimodal consciousness, 89–91

C

Continued-growth scenario, 194, 197,
  198–200
  self-generated leisure, 196
  steady-state, 194–196, 197, 201–5
Culture, transportation of, 56 (table)

D

Disabled, 11

E

Education, 6–7
Energy, 5, 14
Environmental management, 174–75

F

Family life cycle, leisure and, 111–13
Family relationships, leisure and, 119–24
Flow, concept of, 163–65
Free time, 6
  frustration of, 157

H

Human development, leisure and, 125–26
Human life span, stages of development,
  111
Human nature, views of 52–54
Human services, 10

L

Leisure, concepts of historical roots,
  23–26
  behavioral context of, 29–30
  discretionary time, 26–29, 42–43
  environmental perspective of, 33
  functional perspective, 29–33
  holistic view of, 33–35
  psychological function of, 30–32
  socioeconomic characteristics of, 30–32
Leisure, conceptualization of, 22–23
  conceptual typology of, 23 (figure)
  conspicuous, 134–35
  decrease in, 103–4
  environmental perspectives of, 167–75
  future perspectives of, 192–206
  growth of, 6–11
  holistic perspectives of, 179–91
    explanation of, 180–82
    holistic research, 185-87
    multiple satisfaction, 182–85
    multivariate model, 184–85
  increase in, 102–3
Leisure activities, 7–8
  patterns of, 120–22
  years spent on, 70 (figure)
Leisure and family, 119–24
Leisure and lifestyle, 109–33
  definition of, 110
  patterns of, 110
Leisure and race, 145–51
Leisure locales, 168–69
  philosophical dimensions of, 13–35
  problems of, 41, 57–59
  psychological perspectives of, 153–66
  social groupings and, 114, 115–18
  social worlds of, 118–19
  socioeconomic-status perspectives of:
    age, 140–42
    education, 139–40
    gender, 142–44
    income, 144–45

Author Index